HOME PLANNERS'

MOST POPULAR HOME DESIGNS

360 of America's Favorite Houses

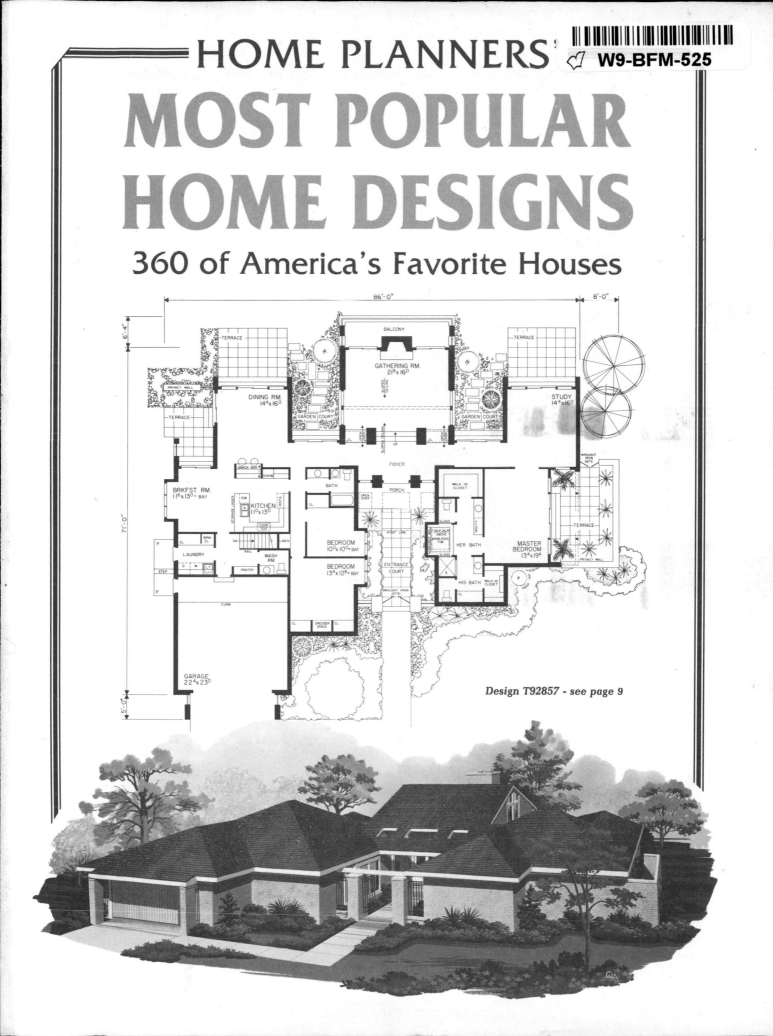

Design T92857 - see page 9

Contents

                                                       Page

- Index to Designs 3
- How to Read Floor Plans and Blueprints 4
- How to Choose a Contractor 5
- How to Shop for Mortgage Money 6
- One-Story Homes Over 2000 Sq. Ft. 7
  Favorite Plans With Extra Amenities
- 1½ Story Homes 23
  Popular Houses With Charm Galore
- Two-Story Homes 39
  Outstanding Livability For Growing Families
- One-Story Home Under 2000 Sq. Ft. 63
  Selected Designs For Modest Budgets
- Multi-Level Homes 83
  Preferred Living Patterns For Sloping Sites
- Home Planners' Services 251
- The Complete Blueprint Package 252
- The Plan Books 255
- More Products From Home Planners 256
- Before You Order 259

Chairman: Charles W. Talcott
President & Publisher: Rickard D. Bailey

HOME PLANNERS, INC.
23761 RESEARCH DRIVE, FARMINGTON HILLS, MICHIGAN 48024

Index to Designs

DESIGN NO.	PAGE NO.	DESIGN NO.	PAGE NO.	DESIGN NO.	PAGE NO.	DESIGN NO.	PAGE NO.	DESIGN NO.	PAGE NO.	DESIGN NO.	PAGE NO.
T91054	121	T91929	124	T92281	178	T92612	234	T92798	184		
T91060	153	T91933	52	T92283	177	T92615	138	T92800	193		
T91075	217	T91935	264	T92294	100	T92617	57	T92802	222		
T91091	221	T91939	216	T92309	158	T92618	57	T92803	222		
T91094	220	T91956	50	T92317	10	T92619	57	T92804	222		
T91142	53	T91957	49	T92318	116	T92622	166	T92805	223		
T91191	216	T91974	96	T92320	41	T92624	271	T92806	223		
T91208	54	T91986	165	T92330	74	T92626	150	T92807	223		
T91220	268	T91987	32	T92335	130	T92628	245	T92809	225		
T91223	101	T91988	191	T92343	20	T92637	188	T92810	218		
T91228	152	T91989	128	T92351	220	T92650	142	T92811	218		
T91241	146	T91991	147	T92354	272	T92655	27	T92812	219		
T91269	54	T91993	155	T92356	186	T92657	26	T92813	219		
T91285	45	T91996	45	T92374	76	T92661	23	T92814	218		
T91300	80	T92107	174	T92377	262	T92662	171	T92815	218		
T91301	81	T92123	200	T92378	115	T92668	176	T92816	219		
T91305	211	T92124	34	T92379	198	T92670	11	T92817	219		
T91308	272	T92127	146	T92386	231	T92671	215	T92818	74		
T91310	269	T92128	62	T92390	201	T92678	69	T92820	131		
T91311	217	T92129	114	T92391	190	T92680	140	T92821	78		
T91323	229	T92131	44	T92392	94	T92682	24	T92822	78		
T91325	214	T92132	136	T92393	262	T92683	173	T92823	208		
T91345	120	T92133	104	T92395	36	T92686	145	T92824	63		
T91346	226	T92134	120	T92488	209	T92687	180	T92826	183		
T91354	50	T92135	113	T92500	136	T92688	144	T92829	194		
T91357	226	T92136	196	T92502	86	T92693	111	T92832	109		
T91358	266	T92137	261	T92504	87	T92694	60	T92842	258		
T91361	50	T92140	175	T92505	67	T92701	203	T92843	241		
T91365	36	T92141	188	T92508	195	T92704	235	T92846	242		
T91372	38	T92142	116	T92510	133	T92705	235	T92847	89		
T91380	228	T92143	264	T92511	84	T92706	235	T92848	243		
T91381	228	T92145	29	T92520	164	T92707	232	T92850	240		
T91382	211	T92146	28	T92524	174	T92708	156	T92851	114		
T91383	211	T92148	187	T92527	7	T92711	202	T92854	148		
T91387	82	T92150	210	T92528	221	T92713	58	T92855	195		
T91388	82	T92151	210	T92534	17	T92716	238	T92856	250		
T91389	82	T92162	38	T92536	246	T92718	152	T92857	9		
T91394	133	T92170	76	T92538	42	T92728	68	T92858	8		
T91701	134	T92171	260	T92539	42	T92729	204	T92859	236		
T91711	105	T92174	136	T92540	166	T92731	52	T92864	224		
T91715	48	T92176	181	T92543	185	T92733	54	T92867	132		
T91718	134	T92181	127	T92544	15	T92737	70	T92877	99		
T91719	165	T92183	126	T92549	178	T92740	12	T92883	207		
T91726	230	T92189	44	T92552	263	T92741	71	T92886	65		
T91748	233	T92192	170	T92557	74	T92746	128	T92887	163		
T91754	132	T92200	230	T92558	166	T92748	202	T92888	22		
T91761	126	T92206	77	T92559	30	T92756	106	T92889	178		
T91767	168	T92209	122	T92560	237	T92758	270	T92890	141		
T91770	266	T92211	47	T92563	30	T92761	90	T92892	162		
T91778	268	T92212	110	T92565	66	T92765	107	T92901	248		
T91783	199	T92214	197	T92568	192	T92766	118	T92902	64		
T91787	139	T92218	97	T92569	30	T92767	14	T92905	206		
T91788	124	T92220	122	T92570	214	T92768	103	T92906	159		
T91791	32	T92221	46	T92571	34	T92769	239	T92908	61		
T91793	134	T92223	42	T92573	129	T92771	161	T92909	182		
T91827	58	T92224	58	T92583	91	T92772	160	T92915	112		
T91829	227	T92230	172	T92585	56	T92774	39	T92918	73		
T91835	124	T92236	130	T92586	56	T92776	142	T92920	19		
T91850	269	T92242	93	T92587	56	T92778	118	T92921	18		
T91856	62	T92243	261	T92596	34	T92779	12	T92925	198		
T91858	169	T92245	154	T92597	227	T92780	160	T92927	149		
T91868	46	T92248	243	T92599	178	T92781	205	T92929	72		
T91882	266	T92251	108	T92603	70	T92782	157	T92932	249		
T91887	40	T92254	88	T92604	232	T92784	119	T92934	83		
T91890	212	T92256	16	T92606	213	T92785	116	T92936	247		
T91892	123	T92272	98	T92607	213	T92786	92	T92937	85		
T91911	102	T92276	189	T92608	244	T92787	93	T93126	32		
T91920	212	T92277	69	T92610	168	T92788	270	T93189	37		
T91927	264	T92278	151	T92611	234	T92789	21	T93221	80		
								T93223	81		

On the Cover: Front Cover design can be found on page 149. Back cover designs can be found on pages 13 & 186.

How To Read Floor Plans and Blueprints

Selecting the most suitable house plan for your family is a matter of matching your needs, tastes, and life-style against the many designs we offer. When you study the floor plans in this issue, and the blueprints that you may subsequently order, remember that they are simply a two-dimensional representation of what will eventually be a three-dimensional reality.

Floor plans are easy to read. Rooms are clearly labeled, with dimensions given in feet and inches. Most symbols are logical and self-explanatory: The location of bathroom fixtures, planters, fireplaces, tile floors, cabinets and counters, sinks, appliances, closets, sloped or beamed ceilings will be obvious.

A blueprint, although much more detailed, is also easy to read; all it demands is concentration. The blueprints that we offer come in many large sheets, each one of which contains a different kind of information. One sheet contains foundation and excavation drawings, another has a precise plot plan. An elevations sheet deals with the exterior walls of the house; section drawings show precise dimensions, fittings, doors, windows, and roof structures. Our detailed floor plans give the construction information needed by your contractor. And each set of blueprints contains a lengthy materials list with size and quantities of all necessary components. Using this list, a contractor and suppliers can make a start at calculating costs for you.

When you first study a floor plan or blueprint, imagine that you are walking through the house. By mentally visualizing each room in three dimensions, you can transform the technical data and symbols into something more real.

Start at the front door. It's preferable to have a foyer or entrance hall in which to receive guests. A closet here is desirable; a powder room is a plus.

Look for good traffic circulation as you study the floor plan. You should not have to pass all the way through one main room to reach another. From the entrance area you should have direct access to the three principal areas of a house—the living, work, and sleeping zones. For example, a foyer might provide separate entrances to the living room, kitchen, patio, and a hallway or staircase leading to the bedrooms.

Study the layout of each zone. Most people expect the living room to be protected from cross traffic. The kitchen, on the other hand, should connect with the dining room—and perhaps also the utility room, basement, garage, patio or deck, or a secondary entrance. A homemaker whose workday centers in the kitchen may have special requirements: a window that faces the backyard; a clear view of the family room where children play; a garage or driveway entrance that allows for a short trip with groceries; laundry facilities close at hand. Check for efficient placement of kitchen cabinets, counters, and appliances. Is there enough room in the kitchen for additional appliances, for eating in? Is there a dining nook?

Perhaps this part of the house contains a family room or a den/bedroom/office. It's advantageous to have a bathroom or powder room in this section.

As you study the plan, you may encounter a staircase, indicated by a group of parallel lines, the number of lines equaling the number of steps. Arrows labeled "up" mean that the staircase leads to a higher level, and those pointing down mean it leads to a lower one. Staircases in a split-level will have both up and down arrows on one staircase because two levels are depicted in one drawing and an extra level in another.

Notice the location of the stairways. Is too much floor space lost to them? Will you find yourself making too many trips?

Study the sleeping quarters. Are the bedrooms situated as you like? You may want the master bedroom near the kids, or you may want it as far away as possible. Is there at least one closet per person in each bedroom or a double one for a couple? Bathrooms should be convenient to each bedroom—if not adjoining, then with hallway access and on the same floor.

Once you are familiar with the relative positions of the rooms, look for such structural details as:

• Sufficient uninterrupted wall space for furniture arrangement.

• Adequate room dimensions.

• Potential heating or cooling problems—i.e., a room over a garage or next to the laundry.

• Window and door placement for good ventilation and natural light.

• Location of doorways—avoid having a basement staircase or a bathroom in view of the dining room.

• Adequate auxiliary space—closets, storage, bathrooms, countertops.

• Separation of activity areas. (Will noise from the recreation room disturb sleeping children or a parent at work?)

As you complete your mental walk through the house, bear in mind your family's long-range needs. A good house plan will allow for some adjustments now and additions in the future.

Each member of your family may find the listing of his, or her, favorite features a most helpful exercise. Why not try it?

How To Choose a Contractor

A contractor is part craftsman, part businessman, and part magician. As the person who will transform your dreams and drawings into a finished house, he will be responsible for the final cost of the structure, for the quality of the workmanship, and for the solving of all problems that occur quite naturally in the course of construction. Choose him as carefully as you would a business partner, because for the next several months that will be his role in your life.

As soon as you have a building site and house plans, start looking for a contractor, even if you do not plan to break ground for several months. Finding one suitable to build your house can take time, and once you have found him, you will have to be worked into his schedule. Those who are good are in demand and, where the season is short, they are often scheduling work up to a year in advance.

There are two types of residential contractors: the construction company and the carpenter-builder, often called a general contractor. Each of these has its advantages and disadvantages.

The carpenter-builder works directly on the job as the field foreman. Because his background is that of a craftsman, his workmanship is probably good—but his paperwork may be slow or sloppy. His overhead—which you pay for—is less than that of a large construction company. However, if the job drags on for any reason, his interest may flag because your project is overlapping his next job and eroding his profits.

Construction companies handle several projects concurrently. They have an office staff to keep the paperwork moving and an army of subcontractors they know they can count on. Though you can be confident that they will meet deadlines, they may sacrifice workmanship in order to do so. Because they emphasize efficiency, they are less personal to work with than a general contractor. Many will not work with an individual unless he is represented by an architect. The company and the architect speak the same language; it requires far more time to deal directly with a homeowner.

To find a reliable contractor, start by asking friends who have built homes for recommendations. Check with local lumber yards and building supply outlets for names of possible candidates.

Once you have several names in hand, ask the Chamber of Commerce, Better Business Bureau, or local department of consumer affairs for any information they might have on each of them. Keep in mind that these watchdog organizations can give only the number of complaints filed; they cannot tell you what percent of those claims were valid. Remember, too, that a large-volume operation is logically going to have more complaints against it than will an independent contractor.

Set up an interview with each of the potential candidates. Find out what his specialty is—custom houses, development houses, remodeling, or office buildings. Ask each to take you into—not just to the site of—houses he has built. Ask to see projects that are complete as well as work in progress, emphasizing that you are interested in projects comparable to yours. A $300,000 dentist's office will give you little insight into a contractor's craftsmanship.

Ask each contractor for bank references from both his commercial bank and any other lender he has worked with. If he is in good financial standing, he should have no qualms about giving you this information. Also ask if he offers a warranty on his work. Most will give you a one-year warranty on the structure; some offer as much as a ten-year warranty.

Ask for references, even though no contractor will give you the name of a dissatisfied customer. While previous clients may be pleased with a contractor's work overall, they may, for example, have had to wait three months after they moved in before they had any closet doors. Ask about his follow-through. Did he clean up the building site, or did the owner have to dispose of the refuse? Ask about his business organization. Did the paperwork go smoothly, or was there a delay in hooking up the sewer because he forgot to apply for a permit?

Talk to each of the candidates about fees. Most work on a "cost plus" basis; that is, the basic cost of the project—materials, subcontractors' services, wages of those working directly on the project, but not office help—plus his fee. Some have a fixed fee; others work on a percentage of the basic cost. A fixed fee is usually better for you if you can get one. If a contractor works on a percentage, ask for a cost breakdown of his best estimate and keep very careful track as the work progresses. A crafty contractor can always use a cost overrun to his advantage when working on a percentage.

Do not be overly suspicious of a contractor who won't work on a fixed fee. One who is very good and in great demand may not be willing to do so. He may also refuse to submit a competitive bid.

If the top two or three candidates are willing to submit competitive bids, give each a copy of the plans and your specifications for materials. If they are not each working from the same guidelines, the competitive bids will be of little value. Give each the same deadline for turning in a bid; two or three weeks is a reasonable period of time. If you are willing to go with the lowest bid, make an appointment with all of them and open the envelopes in front of them.

If one bid is remarkably low, the contractor may have made an honest error in his estimate. Do not try to hold him to it if he wants to withdraw his bid. Forcing him to build at too low a price could be disastrous for both you and him.

Though the above method sounds very fair and orderly, it is not always the best approach, especially if you are inexperienced. You may want to review the bids with your architect, if you have one, or with your lender to discuss which to accept. They may not recommend the lowest. A low bid does not necessarily mean that you will get quality with economy.

If the bids are relatively close, the most important consideration may not be money at all. How easily you can talk with a contractor and whether or not he inspires confidence are very important considerations. Any sign of a personality conflict between you and a contractor should be weighed when making a decision.

Once you have financing, you can sign a contract with the builder. Most have their own contract forms, but it is advisable to have a lawyer draw one up or, at the very least, review the standard contract. This usually costs a small flat fee.

A good contract should include the following:

• Plans and sketches of the work to be done, subject to your approval.

• A list of materials, including quantity, brand names, style or serial numbers. (Do not permit any "or equal" clause that will allow the contractor to make substitutions.)

• The terms—who (you or the lender) pays whom and when.

• A production schedule.

• The contractor's certification of insurance for workmen's compensation, damage, and liability.

• A rider stating that all changes, whether or not they increase the cost, must be submitted and approved in writing.

Of course, this list represents the least a contract should include. Once you have signed it, your plans are on the way to becoming a home.

A frequently asked question is: "Should I become my own general contractor?" Unless you have knowledge of construction, material purchasing, and experience supervising subcontractors, we do not recommend this route.

How To Shop For Mortgage Money

Most people who are in the market for a new home spend months searching for the right house plan and building site. Ironically, these same people often invest very little time shopping for the money to finance their new home, though the majority will have to live with the terms of their mortgage for as long as they live in the house.

The fact is that all banks are not alike, nor are the loans that they offer—and banks are not the only financial institutions that lend money for housing. The amount of down payment, interest rate, and period of the mortgage are all, to some extent, negotiable.

• Lending practices vary from one city and state to another. If you are a first-time builder or are new to an area, it is wise to hire a real estate (not divorce or general practice) attorney to help you unravel the maze of your specific area's laws, ordinances, and customs.

• Before talking with lenders, write down all your questions. Take notes during the conversation so you can make accurate comparisons.

• Do not be intimidated by financial officers. Keep in mind that *you are not begging for money*, you are buying it. Do not hesitate to reveal what other institutions are offering; they may be challenged to meet or better the terms.

• Use whatever clout you have. If you or your family have been banking with the same firm for years, let them know that they could lose your business if you can get a better deal elsewhere.

• Know your credit rights. The law prohibits lenders from considering only the husband's income when determining eligibility, a practice that previously kept many people out of the housing market. If you are turned down for a loan, you have a right to see a summary of the credit report and change any errors in it.

A GUIDE TO LENDERS

Where can you turn for home financing? Here is a list of sources for you to approach:

Savings and loan associations are the best place to start because they write well over half the mortgages in the United States on dwellings that house from one to four families. They generally offer favorable interest rates, require lower down payments, and allow more time to pay off loans than do other banks.

Savings banks, sometimes called mutual savings banks, are your next best bet. Like savings and loan associations, much of their business is concentrated in home mortgages.

Commercial banks write mortgages as a sideline, and when money is tight many will not write mortgages at all. They do hold about 15 percent of the mortgages in the country, however, and when the market is right, they can be very competitive.

Mortgage banking companies use the money of private investors to write home loans. They do a brisk business in government-backed loans, which other banks are reluctant to handle because of the time and paperwork required.

Some credit unions are now allowed to grant mortgages. A few insurance companies, pension funds, unions, and fraternal organizations also offer mortgage money to their membership, often at terms more favorable than those available in the commercial marketplace.

A GUIDE TO MORTGAGES

The types of mortgages available are far more various than most potential home buyers realize.

Traditional Loans

Conventional home loans have a fixed interest rate and fixed monthly payments. About 80 percent of the mortgage money in the United States is lent in this manner. Made by private lending institutions, these fixed rate loans are available to anyone whom the bank officials consider a good credit risk. The interest rate depends on the prevailing market for money and is slightly negotiable if you are willing to put down a large down payment. Most down payments range from 15 to 33 percent.

You can borrow as much money as the lender believes you can afford to pay off over the negotiated period of time—usually 20 to 30 years. However, a 15 year mortgage can save you considerably and enable you to own your home in half the time. For example, a 30 year, $60,800 mortgage at 12% interest will have a monthly payment of $625.40 per month vs $729.72 per month for a 15 year loan at the same interest rate. At the end of 30 years you have paid $164,344 in interest vs $70,550 for the 15 year. Remember - this is only $104.32 more per month. Along with saving with a 15 year mortgage, additional savings

can be realized with a biweekly payment plan. So be sure to consult your borrowing institution for all of your options.

The FHA does not write loans; it insures them against default in order to encourage lenders to write loans for first-time buyers and people with limited incomes. The terms of these loans make them very attractive, and you may be allowed to take as long as 25 to 30 years to pay it off.

The down payment also is substantially lower with an FHA-backed loan. At present it is set at 3 percent of the first $25,000 and 5 percent of the remainder, up to the $75,300 limit. This means that a loan on a $75,300 house would require a $750 down payment on the first $25,000 plus $2,515 on the remainder, for a total down payment of $3,265. In contrast, the down payment for the same house financed with a conventional loan could run as high as $20,000.

Anyone may apply for an FHA-insured loan, but both the borrower and the house must qualify.

The VA guarantees loans for eligible veterans, and the husbands and wives of those who died while in the service or from a service-related disability. The VA guarantees up to 60 percent of the loan or $27,500, whichever is less. Like the FHA, the VA determines the appraised value of the house, though with a VA loan, you can borrow any amount up to the appraised value.

The Farmers Home Administration offers the only loans made directly by the government. Families with limited incomes in rural areas can qualify if the house is in a community of less than 10,000 people and is outside of a large metropolitan area; if their income is less than $18,000; and if they can prove that they do not qualify for a conventional loan.

For more information, write Farmers Home Administration, Department of Agriculture, Washington, D.C. 20250, or your local office.

New loan instruments

If you think that the escalating cost of housing has squeezed you out of the market, take a look at the following new types of mortgages.

The graduated payment mortgage features a monthly obligation that gradually increases over a negotiated period of time—usually five to ten years. Though the payments begin lower, they stabilize at a higher monthly rate than a standard fixed rate mortgage. Little or no equity is built in the first years, a disadvantage if you decide to sell early in the mortgage period.

These loans are aimed at young people who can anticipate income increases that will enable them to meet the escalating payments. The size of the down payment is about the same or slightly higher than for a conventional loan, but you can qualify with a lower income. As of last year, savings and loan associations can write these loans, and the FHA now insures five different types.

The flexible loan insurance program (FLIP) requires that part of the down payment, which is about the same as a conventional loan, be placed in a pledged savings account. During the first five years of the mortgage, funds are drawn from this account to supplement the lower monthly payments.

The deferred interest mortgage, another graduated program, allows you to pay a lower rate of interest during the first few years and a higher rate in the later years of the mortgage. If the house is sold, the borrower must pay back all the interest, often with a prepayment penalty. Both the FLIP and deferred interest loans are very new and not yet widely available.

The variable rate mortgage is most widely available in California, but its popularity is growing. This instrument features a fluctuating interest rate that is linked to an economic indicator—usually the lender's cost of obtaining funds for lending. To protect the consumer against a sudden and disastrous increase, regulations limit the amount that the interest rate can increase over a given period of time.

To make these loans attractive, lenders offer them without prepayment penalties and with "assumption" clauses that allow another buyer to assume your mortgage should you sell.

Flexible payment mortgages allow young people who can anticipate rising incomes to enter the housing market sooner. They pay only the interest during the first few years; then the mortgage is amortized and the payments go up. This is a valuable option only for those people who intend to keep their home for several years because no equity is built in the lower payment period.

The reverse annuity mortgage is targeted for older people who have fixed incomes. This new loan allows those who qualify to tap into the equity on their houses. The lender pays them each month and collects the loan when the house is sold or the owner dies.

ONE-STORY HOMES over 2000 Sq. Ft.
Favorite Plans With Extra Amenities

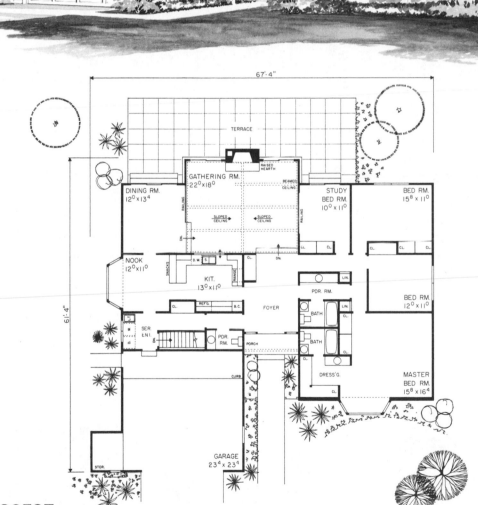

Design T92527 2,392 Sq. Ft.; 42,579 Cu. Ft.

● Vertical boards and battens, field-stone, bay window, a dovecote, a gas lamp, and a recessed front entrance are among the appealing exterior features of this U-shaped design. Through the double front doors flanked by glass side lites one enters the spacious foyer. Straight ahead is the cozy sunken gathering room with its sloping, beamed ceiling, raised hearth fireplace, and two sets of sliding doors to the rear terrace. To the right of the foyer is the sleeping wing with its three bedrooms, study (make it the fourth bedroom if you wish), and two baths. To the left is the strategically located powder room and large kitchen with its delightful nook space and bay window.

Design T92858
2,231 Sq. Ft.; 28,150 Cu. Ft.

● This sun oriented design was created to face the south. By doing so, it has minimal northern exposure. It has been designed primarily for the more temperate U.S. latitudes using 2 x 6 wall construction. The morning sun will brighten the living and dining rooms, along with the adjacent terrace. Sun enters the garden room by way of the glass roof and walls. In the winter, the solar heat gain from the garden room should provide relief from high energy bills. Solar shades allow you to adjust the amount of light that you want to enter in the warmer months. Interior planning deserves mention, too. The work center is efficient. The kitchen has a snack bar on the garden room side and a serving counter to the dining room. The breakfast room with laundry area is also convenient to the kitchen. Three bedrooms are on the northern wall. The master bedroom has a large tub and a separate shower with a four foot square skylight above. When this design is oriented toward the sun, it should prove to be energy efficient and a joy to live in.

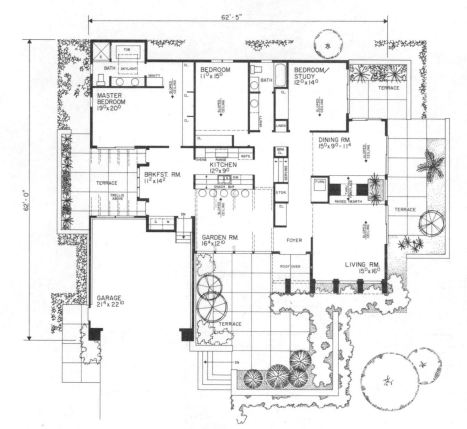

Design T92857
2,982 Sq. Ft.; 60,930 Cu. Ft.

● Imagine yourself occupying this home! Study the outstanding master bedroom. You will be forever pleased by its many features. It has "his" and "her" baths each with a large walk-in closet, sliding glass doors to a private, side terrace (a great place to enjoy a morning cup of coffee) and an adjacent study. Notice that the two family bedrooms are separated from the master bedroom. This allows for total privacy both for the parents and the children. Continue to observe this plan. You will have no problem at all entertaining in the gathering room. Your party can flow to the adjacent balcony on a warm summer evening. The work center has been designed in an orderly fashion. The U-shaped kitchen utilizes the triangular work pattern, said to be the most efficient. Only a few steps away, you will be in the breakfast room, formal dining room, laundry or washroom. Take your time and study every last detail in this home plan.

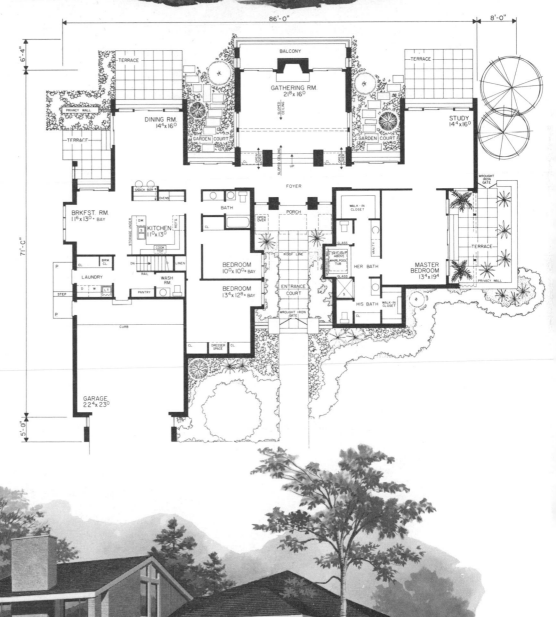

Design T92317 3,161 Sq. Ft.; 57,900 Cu. Ft.

● Here's a rambling English manor with its full measure of individuality. Its fine proportions and irregular shape offer even the most casual of passersby delightful views of fine architecture. The exterior boasts an interesting use of varying materials. In addition to the brick work, there is vertical siding, wavy-edged horizontal siding and stucco. Three massive chimneys provide each of the three major wings with a fireplace. The overhanging roof provides the cover for the long front porch. Note the access to both the foyer as well as the service hall. The formal living room, with its sloping beamed ceiling, and fireplace flanked by book shelves and cabinets, will be cozy, indeed. Study rest of plan. It's outstanding. Don't miss the three fireplaces and three full baths.

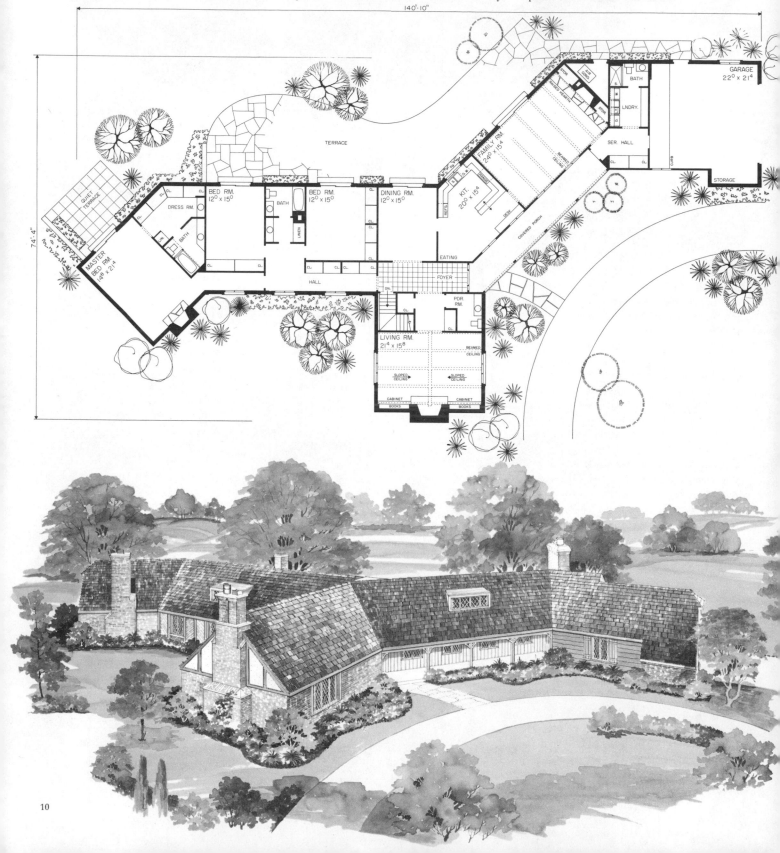

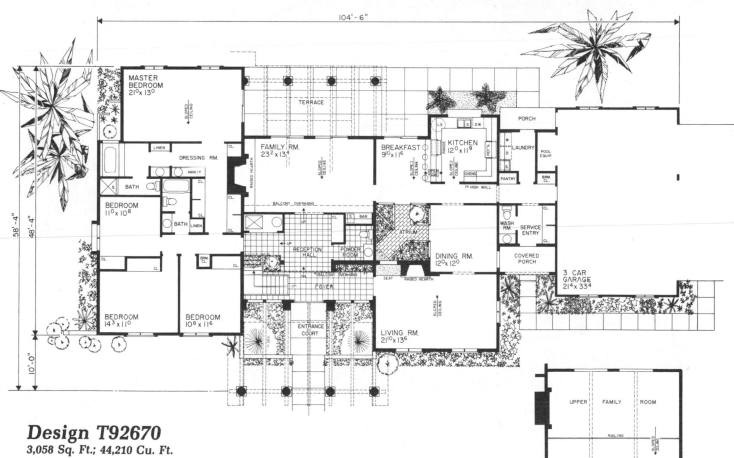

Design T92670
3,058 Sq. Ft.; 44,210 Cu. Ft.

● A centrally located interior atrium is one of the most interesting features of this Spanish design. The atrium has a built-in seat and will bring light to its adjacent rooms; living, dining and breakfast. Beyond the foyer, sunken one step, is a tiled reception hall that includes a powder room. This area leads to the sleeping wing and up one step to the family room. Overlooking the family room is a railed lounge, 279 square feet, which can be used for various activities. The work center area will be convenient to work in.

● You'll want life's biggest investment — the purchase of a home — to be a source of everlasting enjoyment. To assure such a rewarding dividend, make every effort to match your family's desired living patterns with a workable plan. Of course, you'll want your plan enveloped by a stunning exterior. Consider both the interior and exterior of this design. Each is impressive. The sleeping zone comprises a separate wing and is accessible from both living and kitchen areas. There are four bedrooms, two full baths and plenty of closets. The 32 foot wide living and dining area will be just great fun to decorate. Then, there is the large family room with its raised hearth fireplace and sliding glass doors to the terrace. Note the fine laundry with wash room nearby. The extra curb area in the garage is great for storing small garden equipment.

● This French design is surely impressive. The exterior appearance will brighten any area with its French roof, paned-glass windows, masonry brick privacy wall and double front doors. The inside is just as appealing. Note the unique placement of rooms and features. The entry hall is large and leads to each of the areas in this plan. The formal dining room is outstanding and guests can enter through the entry hall. While serving one can enter by way of the butler's pantry (notice it's size and that it has a sink). To the right of the entry is a sizable parlor. Then there is the gathering room with fireplace, sliding glass doors and adjacent study. The work center is also outstanding. There is the U-shaped kitchen, island range, snack bar, breakfast nook, pantry plus wash room and large laundry near service entrance. Basement stairs are also nearby.

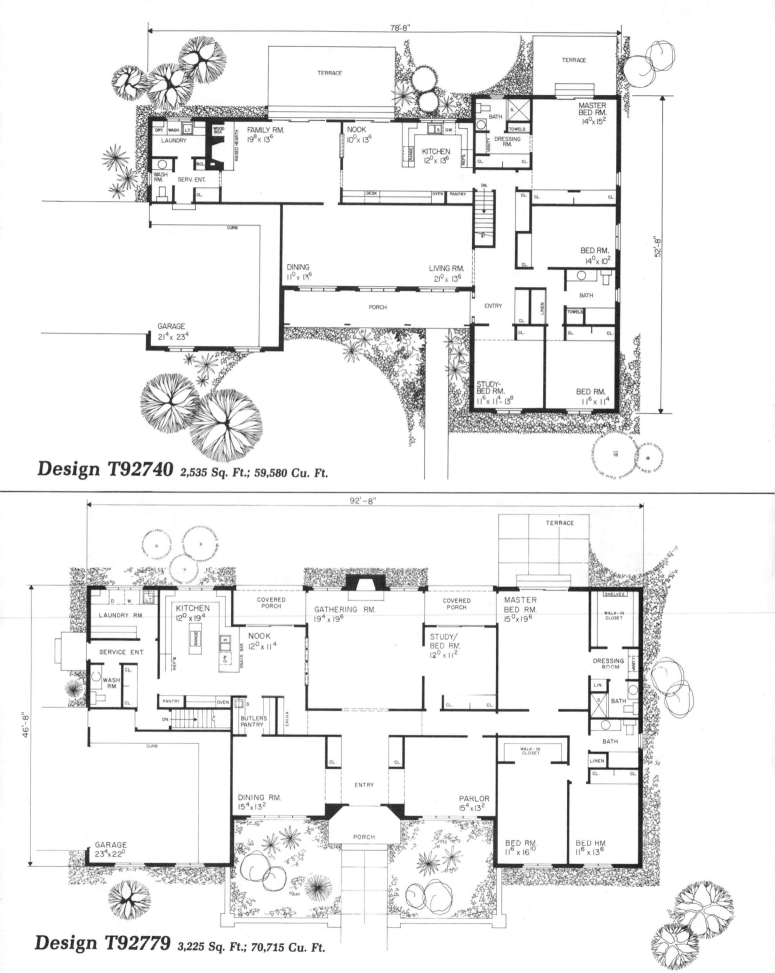

Design T92740 2,535 Sq. Ft.; 59,580 Cu. Ft.

Design T92779 3,225 Sq. Ft.; 70,715 Cu. Ft.

13

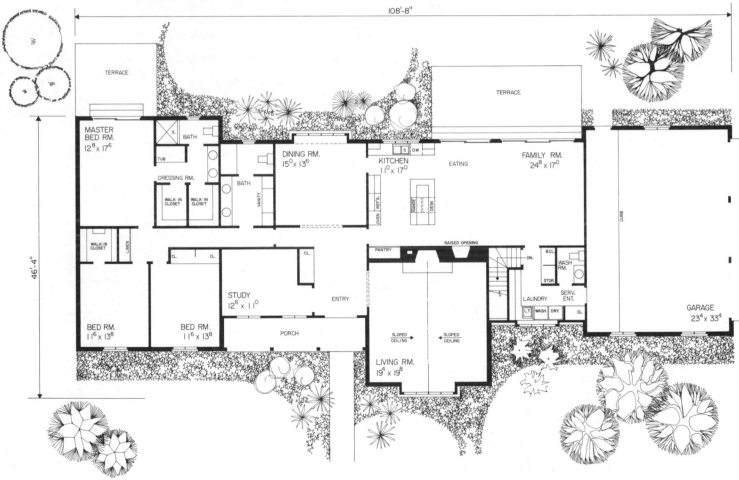

Design T92767 *3,000 Sq. Ft.; 58,460 Cu. Ft.*

● What a sound investment this impressive home will be. And while its value withstands the inflationary pressures of ensuing years, it will serve your family well. It has all the amenities to assure truly pleasurable living. The charming exterior will lend itself to treatment other than the appealing fieldstone, brick and frame shown. Inside, the plan will impress you with large, spacious living areas, formal and informal dining areas, three large bedrooms, two full baths with twin lavatories, walk-in closets and a fine study. The kitchen features an island work center with range and desk. The two fireplaces will warm their surroundings in both areas. Two separate terraces for a variety of uses. Note laundry, wash room and three-car garage with extra curb area.

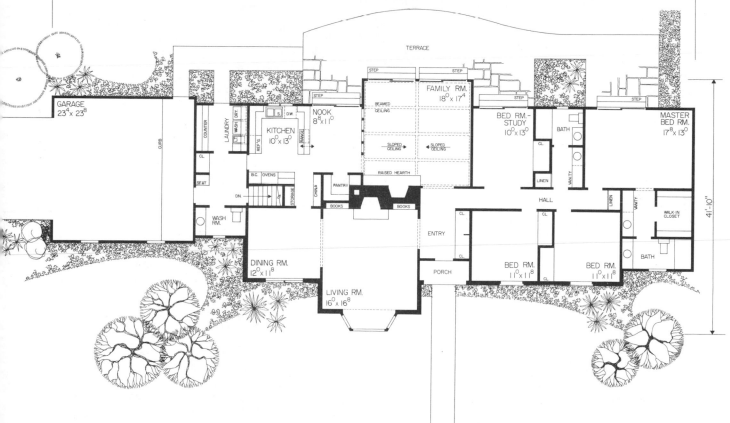

GARAGE
23⁴ x 23⁸

LAUNDRY

KITCHEN
10⁰ x 13⁰

NOOK
8⁸ x 11⁰

FAMILY RM.
18⁰ x 17⁴

BEAMED CEILING

SLOPED CEILING

SLOPED CEILING

RAISED HEARTH

TERRACE

STEP

BED RM.-
STUDY
10⁰ x 13⁰

BATH

LINEN

MASTER
BED RM.
17⁸ x 13⁰

LINEN

VANITY

WALK IN
CLOSET

HALL

BATH

B.C. OVENS

CHINA

PANTRY

BOOKS

BOOKS

WASH
RM.

DINING RM.
12⁰ x 11⁸

LIVING RM.
16⁰ x 16⁸

ENTRY

PORCH

BED RM.
11⁰ x 11⁸

BED RM.
11⁰ x 11⁸

106'-8"

41'-10"

Design T92544 2,527 Sq. Ft.; 61,943 Cu. Ft.

● A fine blend of exterior materials enhance the beauty of this fine home. Here, the masonry material used is fieldstone to contrast effectively with the horizontal siding. You may substitute brick or quarried stone if you wish. Adding to the appeal are the various projections and their roof planes, the window treatment and the recessed front entrance. Two large living areas highlight the interior. Each has a fireplace. The homemaking effort will be easily and enjoyably dispatched with such features as the efficient kitchen, the walk-in pantry, the handy storage areas, the first floor laundry and extra washroom. The sleeping zone has four bedrooms, two baths with vanities and good closet accommodations. There's a basement for additional storage and recreation.

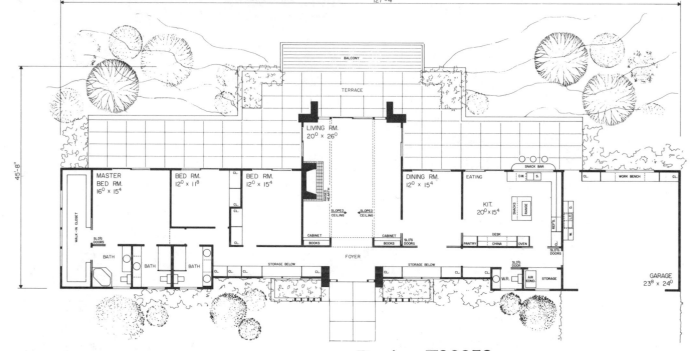

127'-4"

45'-8"

BALCONY

TERRACE

LIVING RM.
20⁰ x 26⁰

MASTER
BED RM.
16⁰ x 15⁴

BED RM.
12⁰ x 11⁸

BED RM.
12⁰ x 15⁴

DINING RM.
12⁰ x 15⁴

EATING

SNACK BAR

D.W.   S.

CL.   WORK BENCH   CL.

WALK-IN CLOSET

CL.

CL.

SLO'G
DOORS

RAISED HEARTH

SLOPED CEILING

SLOPED CEILING

KIT.
20⁰ x 15⁴

SNACKS

RANGE

REF'G.

CABINET
BOOKS

CABINET
BOOKS

SLO'G
DOORS

PANTRY   CHINA   OVEN

DESK

SLO'G
DOORS

BATH

BATH

BATH

CL.

STORAGE BELOW

FOYER

STORAGE BELOW

CL.

CL.

CL.

W.R.

AIR
KOND.

STORAGE

GARAGE
23⁸ x 24⁰

Design T92256 2,632 Sq. Ft.; 35,023 Cu. Ft.

● A dream home for those with young ideas. A refreshing, contemporary exterior with an unique, highly individualized interior. What are your favorite features?

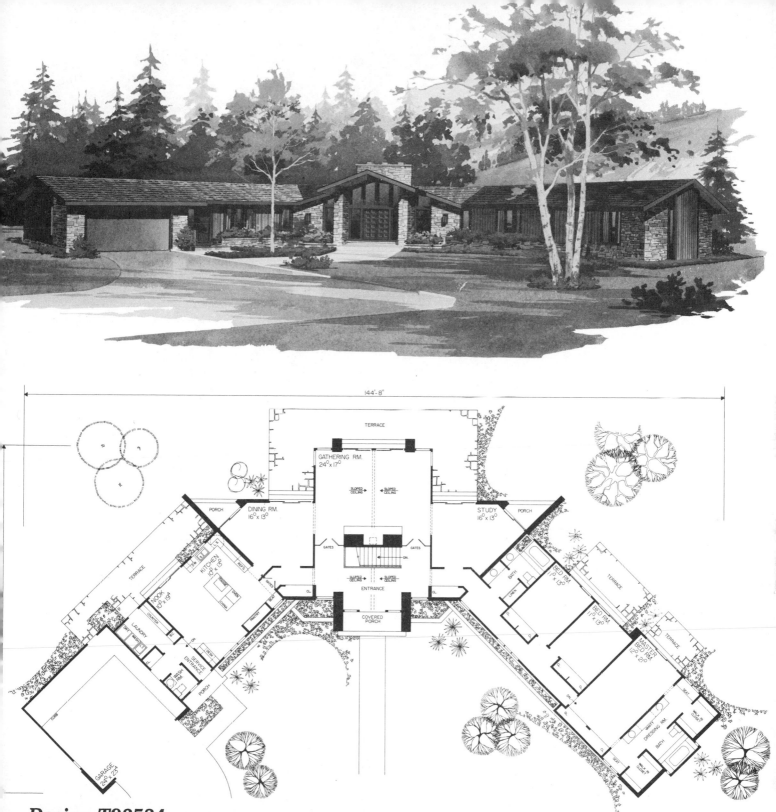

Design T92534 *3,262 Sq. Ft.; 58,640 Cu. Ft.*

● The angular wings of this ranch home surely contribute to the unique character of the exterior. These wings effectively balance what is truly a dramatic and inviting front entrance. Massive masonry walls support the wide overhanging roof with its exposed wood beams. The patterned double front doors are surrounded by delightful expanses of glass. The raised planters and masses of quarried stone (make it brick if you prefer) enhance the exterior appeal. Inside, a distinctive and practical floor plan stands ready to shape and serve the living patterns of the active family. The spacious entrance hall highlights a sloped ceiling and an attractive open stairway to the lower level recreation area. An impressive fireplace and an abundance of glass are features of the big gathering room. Interestingly shaped dining room and study flank this main living area. The large kitchen offers many of the charming aspects of the family-kitchen of yesteryear. The bedroom wing offers a sunken master bedroom suite.

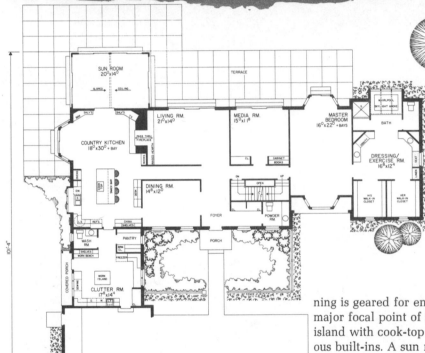

Design T92921
3,215 Sq. Ft - First Floor
711 Sq. Ft - Second Floor; 69,991 Cu. Ft.

● This popular traditionally styled house features bay windows, shutters, a fanlight and a cupola on the roof. Interior planning was designed for the empty-nester; those whose children are grown and moved out on their own. Open planning is geared for entertaining and relaxing rather than child-rearing. The major focal point of the interior will be the country kitchen. It has a work island with cook-top and snack bar and a spacious dining area with numerous built-ins. A sun room, 296 sq. ft. and 3,789 cu. ft. not included in the totals above, is in the rear corner of the house, adjacent to the kitchen. Its sloped ceiling and glass walls open this room to the outdoors. Also adjacent to the kitchen, there is a "clutter room". It includes a workshop, laundry, pantry and washroom.

| BEDROOM 13⁸x14⁰ | BEDROOM 13⁸x14⁰ |
(floor plan labels: ROOF, BATH, CL, CL, CL, LINEN, BALCONY, RAILING, DN, OPEN, UPPER FOYER, ROOF, ROOF)

● Utilizing the same floor plan as Design T92921, this contemporary design also has a great deal to offer. Study the living areas. A fireplace opens up to both the living room and country kitchen. Privacy is the key word when describing the sleeping areas. The first floor master bedroom is away from the traffic of the house and features a dressing/exercise room, whirlpool tub and shower and a spacious walk-in closet. Two more bedrooms and a full bath are on the second floor. The three-car garage is arranged so that the owners have use of a double-garage with an attached single on reserve for guests.

Design T92920
3,067 Sq. Ft. - First Floor
648 Sq. Ft. - Second Floor; 67,881 Cu. Ft.

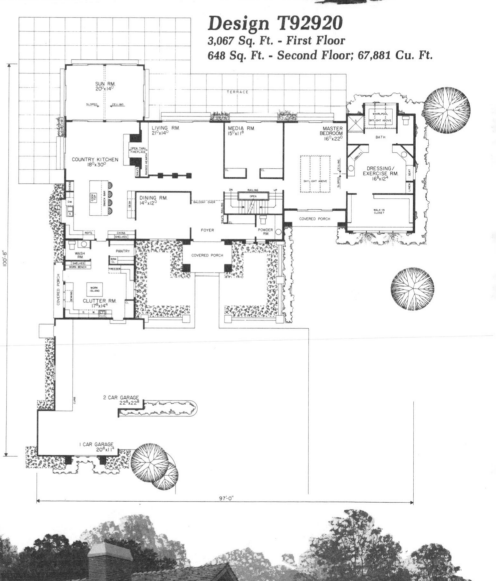

(floor plan labels: SUN RM. 20⁰x14⁰, TERRACE, SLOPED CEILING, LIVING RM. 21⁰x14⁰, MEDIA RM. 15⁰x11⁸, MASTER BEDROOM 16⁰x22⁰, WHIRLPOOL, SKYLIGHT ABOVE, BATH, COUNTRY KITCHEN 18⁰x30⁰, OPEN THRU FIREPLACE, RAISED HEARTH, DRESSING/EXERCISE RM. 16⁸x12⁴, DINING RM. 14⁰x12⁰, SNACK BAR, BALCONY OVER, DN, UP, RAILING, OPEN, SKYLIGHT ABOVE, SLOPED CEILING, SEAT, WALK-IN CLOSET, REF'S., CHINA SHELVES, FOYER, POWDER RM., COVERED PORCH, COVERED PORCH, WASH RM., PANTRY, SHELVES, WORK BENCH, FREEZER, WORK ISLAND, CLUTTER RM. 17⁸x14⁴, COVERED PORCH, 100'-8", 2 CAR GARAGE 22⁸x22⁸, 1 CAR GARAGE 20⁸x11⁴, 97'-0")

19

Design T92343 3,110 Sq. Ft.; 51,758 Cu. Ft.

● If yours is a growing active family the chances are good that they will want their new home to relate to the outdoors. This distinctive design puts a premium on private outdoor living. And you don't have to install a swimming pool to get the most enjoyment from this home. Developing this area as a garden court will provide the indoor living areas with a breathtaking awareness of nature's beauty. Notice the fine zoning of the plan and how each area has its sliding glass doors to provide an unrestricted view. Three bedrooms plus study are serviced by three baths. The family and gathering rooms provide two great living areas. The kitchen is most efficient.

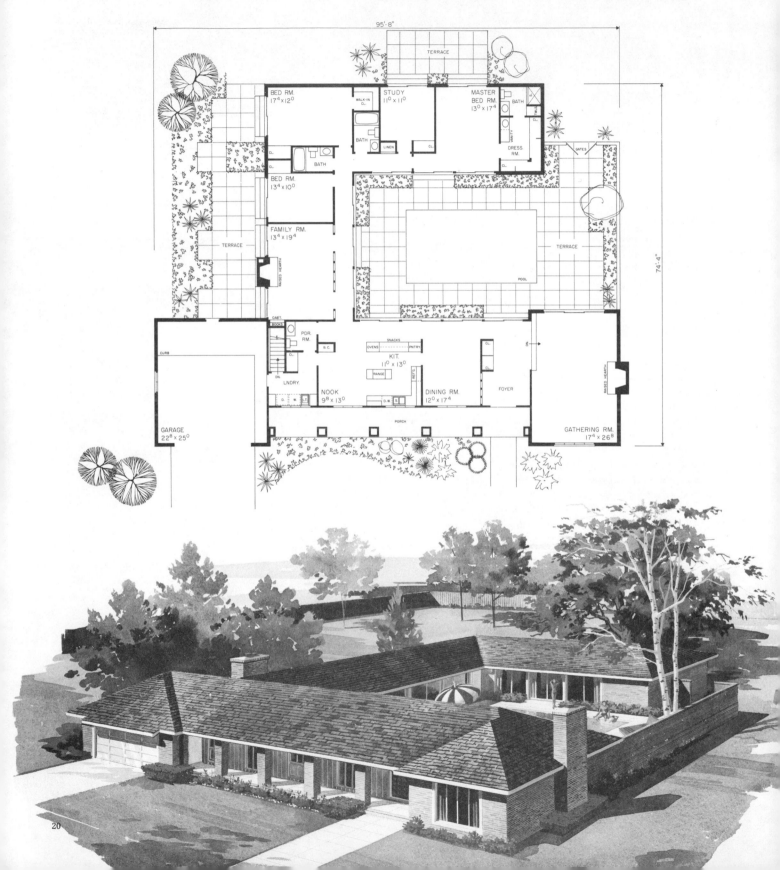

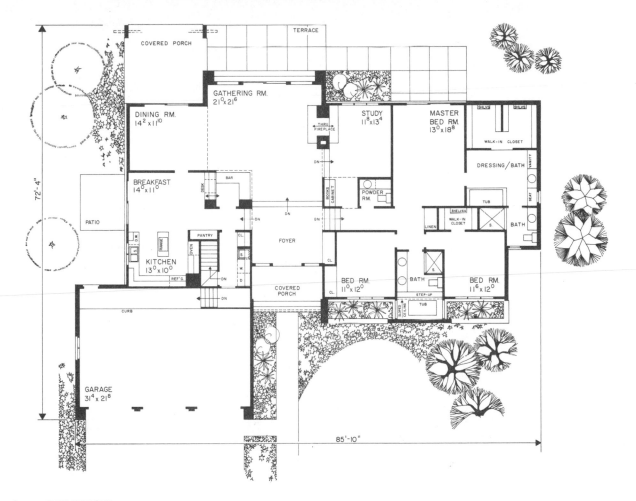

Design T92789 *2,732 Sq. Ft.; 54,935 Cu. Ft.*

● An attached three car garage! What a fantastic feature of this three bedroom contemporary design. And there's more. As one walks up the steps to the covered porch and through the double front doors the charm of this design will be overwhelming. Inside, a large foyer greets all visitors and leads them to each of the three areas, each down a few steps. The living area has a large gathering room with fireplace and a study adjacent on one side and the formal dining room on the other. The work center has an efficient kitchen with island range, breakfast room, laundry and built-in desk and bar. Then there is the sleeping area. Note the raised tub with sloped ceiling.

Design T92888
3,018 Sq. Ft.; 59,769 Cu. Ft.

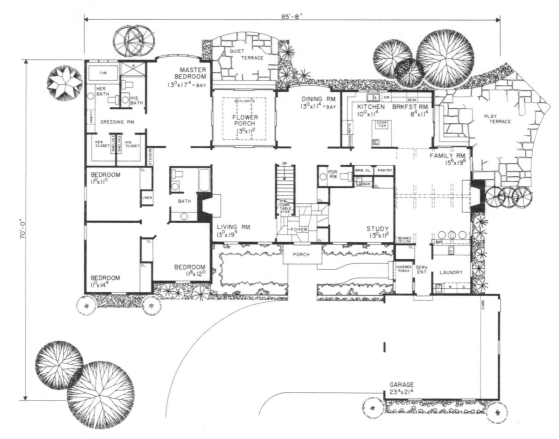

(One-Story Homes over 2000 Sq. Ft. continued on pg. 99)

● This is an outstanding Early American design for the 20th-Century. The exterior detailing with narrow clapboards, multi-paned windows and cupola are the features of yesteryear. Interior planning, though, is for today's active family. Formal living room, informal family room plus a study are present. Every activity will have its place in this home. Picture yourself working in the kitchen. There's enough counter space for two or three helpers. Four bedrooms are in the private area. Stop and imagine your daily routine if you occupied the master bedroom. Both you and your spouse would have plenty of space and privacy. The flower porch, accessible from the master bedroom, living and dining rooms, is a very delightful "plus" feature. Study this design's every detail.

1½-STORY HOMES
Popular Houses With Charm Galore

Design T92661
1,020 Sq. Ft. - First Floor
777 Sq. Ft. - Second Floor; 30,745 Cu. Ft.

● Any other starter house or retirement home couldn't have more charm than this design. Its compact frame houses a very livable plan. An outstanding feature of the first floor is the large country kitchen. Its fine attractions include a beamed ceiling, raised hearth fireplace, built-in window seat and a door leading to the outdoors. A living room is in the front of the plan and has another fireplace which shares the single chimney. The rear dormered second floor houses the sleeping and bath facilities.

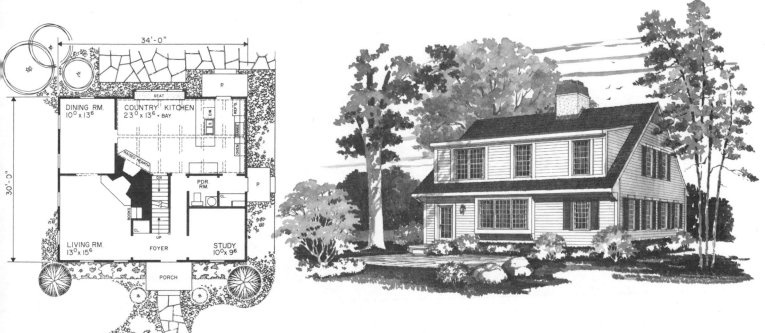

Expanding the Half-House

Design T92682 976 Sq. Ft. - First Floor (Basic Plan)
1,230 Sq. Ft. - First Floor (Expanded Plan); 744 Sq. Ft. - Second Floor (Both Plans)
29,355 Cu. Ft. Basic Plan; 35,084 Cu. Ft. Expanded Plan

● Here is an expandable Colonial with a full measure of Cape Cod Charm. For those who wish to build the basic house, there is an abundance of low-budget livability. Twin fireplaces serve the formal living room and the informal country kitchen. Note the spaciousness of both areas. A dining room and powder room are also on the first floor of this basic plan. Upstairs three bedrooms and two full baths.

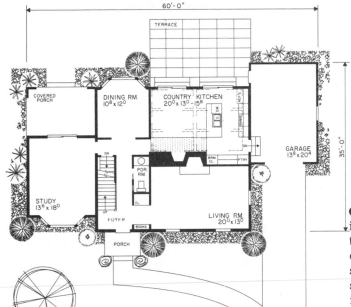

60'-0"

TERRACE

COVERED PORCH

DINING RM.
10⁸ x 12⁰

COUNTRY KITCHEN
20⁰ x 13⁰ - 15⁸

GARAGE
13⁸ x 20⁴

35'-0"

PDR. RM.

BRM. CL.

P'TRY

DN

CL.

STUDY
13⁶ x 18⁰

UP

FOYER

BOOKS

LIVING RM.
20⁰ x 13⁰

PORCH

ROOF

BEDROOM
12¹⁰ x 9⁸

BEDROOM
12¹⁰ x 9⁸

ATTIC STORAGE
(FUTURE ROOM)

CL.

CL.

ROOF

DN

LINEN

BATH

CL.

BATH

CL.

MASTER BEDROOM
11¹⁰ x 14⁰

ROOF

ROOF

● This expanded version of the basic house on the opposite page is equally as reminiscent of Cape Cod. Common in the 17th-Century was the addition of appendages to the main structure. This occurred as family size increased or finances improved. This version provides for the addition of wings to accommodate a large study and a garage. Utilizing the alcove behind the study results in a big, covered porch. Certainly a charming design whichever version you decide to build for your family.

Design T92657 1,217 Sq. Ft. - First Floor
868 Sq. Ft. - Second Floor; 33,260 Cu. Ft.

● Deriving its design from the traditional Cape Cod style, this facade features clapboard siding, small-paned windows and a transom-lit entrance flanked by carriage lamps. A central chimney services two fireplaces, one in the country-kitchen and the other in the formal living room which is removed from the disturbing flow of traffic. The master suite is located to the left of the upstairs landing. A full bathroom services two additional bedrooms.

Design T92655
893 Sq. Ft. - First Floor
652 Sq. Ft. - Second Floor; 22,555 Cu. Ft.

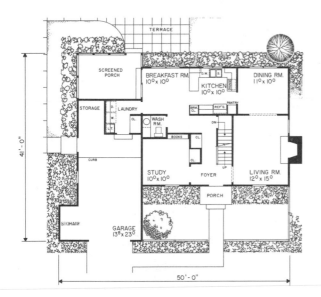

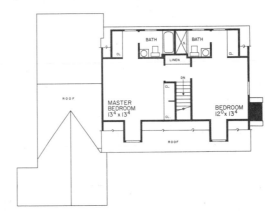

● Wonderful things can be enclosed in small packages. This is the case for this two-story design. The total square footage is a mere 1,545 square feet yet its features are many, indeed. Its exterior appeal is very eye-pleasing with horizontal lines and two second story dormers. Livability will be enjoyed in this plan. The front study is ideal for a quiet escape. Nearby is a powder room also convenient to the kitchen and breakfast room. Two bedrooms and two full baths are located on the second floor.

Design T92145

1,182 Sq. Ft. - First Floor
708 Sq. Ft. - Second Floor
28,303 Cu. Ft.

● Historically referred to as a "half house", this authentic adaptation has its roots in the heritage of New England. With completion of the second floor, the growing family doubles their sleeping capacity. Notice that the overall width of the house is only 44 feet. Take note of the covered porch leading to the garage and the flower court.

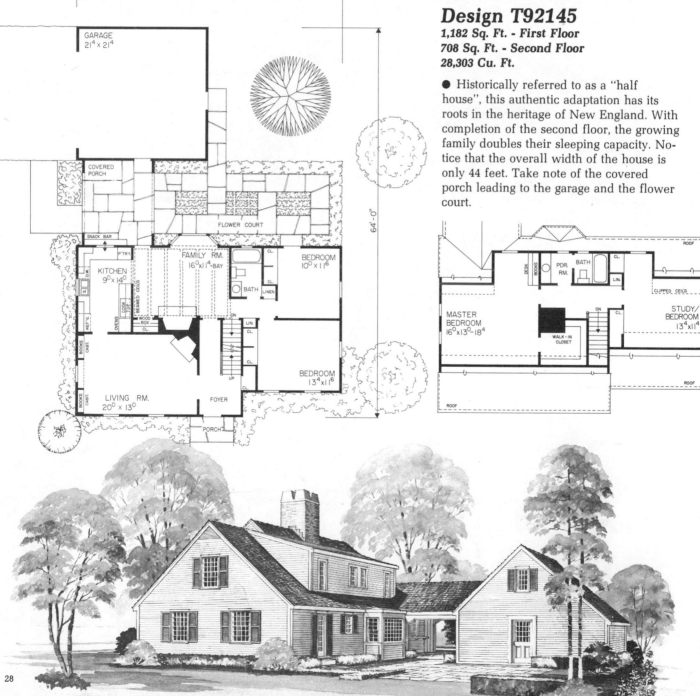

GARAGE
21⁴ x 21⁴

44'-0"

64'-0"

COVERED PORCH

FLOWER COURT

SNACK BAR

P'TRY

KITCHEN
9⁰ x 14⁰

FAMILY RM.
16⁰ x 11⁴ BAY

BEAMED CEIL'G

OVENS

COOK TOP

WOOD BOX

CL.

BATH

LINEN

CL.

BEDROOM
10⁰ x 11⁶

REF'G.

D.W.

BOOKS CABT.

LIVING RM.
20⁰ x 13⁰

FOYER

UP

LIN.

CL.

DN

CL.

BEDROOM
13⁴ x 11⁶

PORCH

MASTER BEDROOM
16⁰ x 13⁰ - 18⁴

DESK

BOOKS

PDR. RM.

BATH

LIN.

CL.

ROOF

CLIPPED CEIL'G

WALK-IN CLOSET

DN

CL.

STUDY/ BEDROOM
13⁴ x 11⁴

ROOF

ROOF

Design T92146

1,182 Sq. Ft. - First Floor
708 Sq. Ft. - Second Floor
28,303 Cu. Ft.

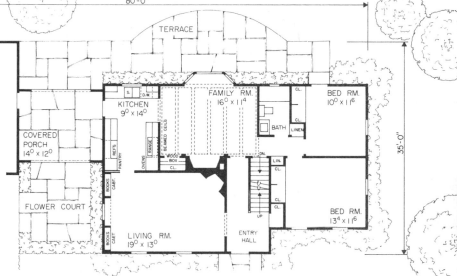

GARAGE
21⁴ x 21⁴

COVERED
PORCH
14⁰ x 12⁰

FLOWER COURT

TERRACE

KITCHEN
9⁰ x 14⁰

FAMILY RM.
16⁰ x 11⁴

BED RM.
10⁰ x 11⁶

BATH

LINEN

OVENS

RANGE

WOOD BOX

PANTRY

LIVING RM.
19⁰ x 13⁰

ENTRY HALL

UP

DN.

BED RM.
13⁴ x 11⁶

80'-0"

35'-0"

MASTER
BED RM.
16⁰ x 13⁰

DESK

BOOKS

PDR. RM.

BATH

LIN.

CL.

CLIPPED CEIL.

STUDY
BED RM.
13⁴ x 11⁴

WALK-IN CLOSET

DN.

ROOF

● Like its corner lot version on the opposing page, this "half house" has a center entry which routes traffic efficiently to all areas. The beamed ceilinged family room effectively serves as the dining and informal living area. Don't miss the two fireplaces, the built-in units in the living room and the well-planned kitchen.

Design T92569

1,102 Sq. Ft. - First Floor
764 Sq. Ft. - Second Floor; 29,600 Cu. Ft.

● What an enchanting updated version of the popular Cape Cod cottage. There are facilities for both formal and informal living pursuits. Note first floor laundry.

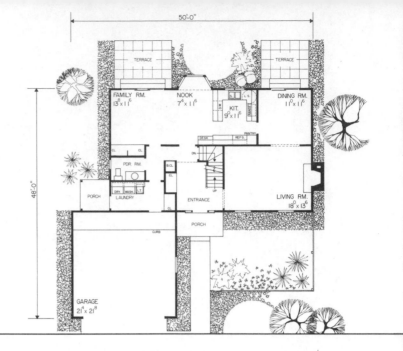

Design T92559

1,388 Sq. Ft. - First Floor
809 Sq. Ft. - Second Floor; 36,400 Cu. Ft.

● Imagine, a 26 foot living room with fireplace, a quiet study with built-in bookshelves and excellent dining facilities. Within such an appealing exterior, too.

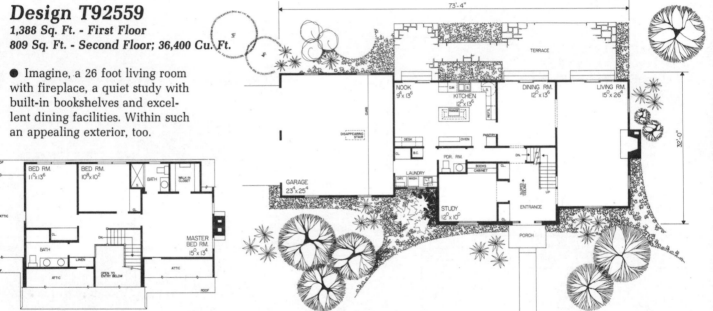

Design T92563

1,500 Sq. Ft. - First Floor
690 Sq. Ft. - Second Floor; 38,243 Cu. Ft.

● You'll have all kinds of fun deciding just how your family will function in this dramatically expanded half-house. There is lots of attic storage, too. Observe three-car garage.

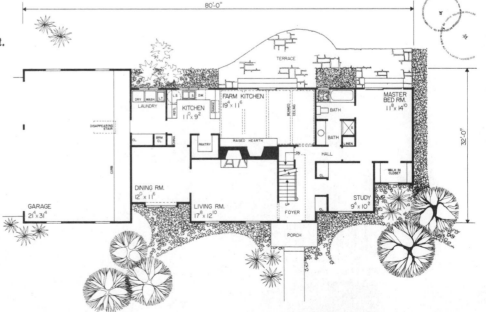

31

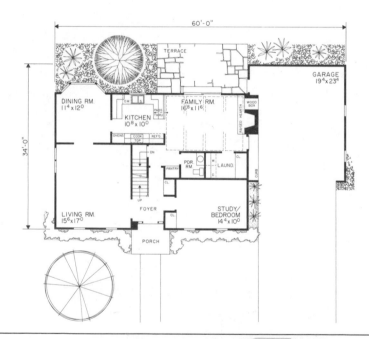

Design T91791
1,157 Sq. Ft. - First Floor
875 Sq. Ft. - Second Floor
27,790 Cu. Ft.

● Wherever you build this little house an aura of Cape Cod is sure to unfold. The symmetry is pleasing, indeed. The authentic center entrance projects a beckoning call.

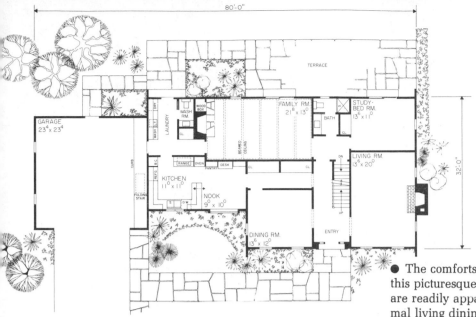

Design T91987
1,632 Sq. Ft. - First Floor
980 Sq. Ft. - Second Floor
35,712 Cu. Ft.

● The comforts of home will be endless when enjoyed in this picturesque Colonial adaptation. And the reasons why are readily apparent. Note cozy family room, study, formal living dining room, etc.

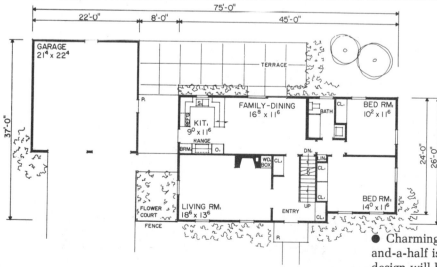

Design T93126
1,141 Sq. Ft. - First Floor
630 Sq. Ft. - Second Floor
25,533 Cu. Ft.

● Charming, indeed! The traditional flavor of this story-and-a-half is most inviting. As an expandable house this design will be hard to beat. There is a full basement for extra recreational space.

33

Design T92571

1,137 Sq. Ft. - First Floor
795 Sq. Ft. - Second Floor; 28,097 Cu. Ft.

● Cost-efficient space! That's the bonus with this attractive Cape Cod. An efficient kitchen! With a pass-through to the family room and a large storage pantry. Three bedrooms on second floor.

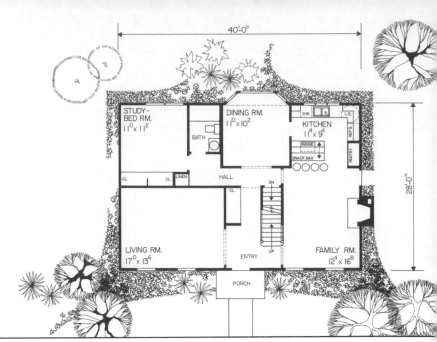

Design T92596

1,489 Sq. Ft. - First Floor
982 Sq. Ft. - Second Floor; 38,800 Cu. Ft.

● Captivating as a New England village! From the weathervane atop the garage to the roofed side entry and paned windows, this home is perfectly detailed.

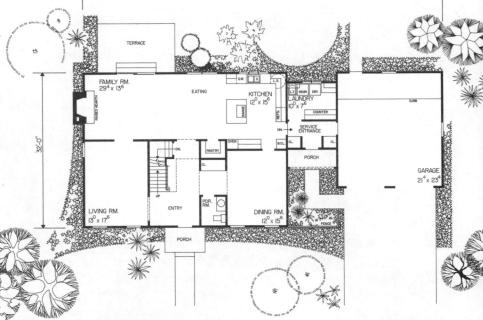

Design T92124

1,176 Sq. Ft. - First Floor;
922 Sq. Ft. - Second Floor; 29,854 Cu. Ft.

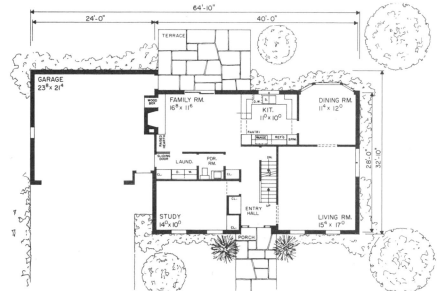

● Surely your list of favorite features will be fun to compile. It certainly will be a long one. The center entry hall helps establish excellent traffic patterns and good zoning. The formal living and dining rooms function well together, as do the kitchen and family room. Note laundry and study.

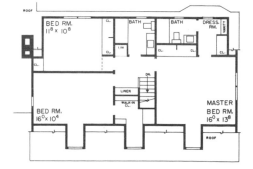

Design T91365

975 Sq. Ft. - First Floor
583 Sq. Ft. - Second Floor
20,922 Cu. Ft.

● Here are three wonderfully livable houses. Each provides facilities to function as either three or four bedroom, two bath homes. Compare each of the three designs. Consider them in light of your building budget and your family's living requirements. Whichever design you choose it will be a credit to your family's design taste.

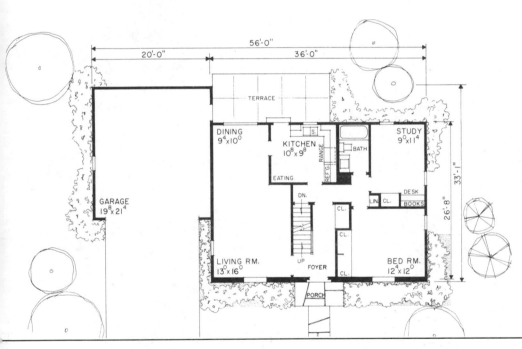

Design T92395

1,481 Sq. Ft. - First Floor
861 Sq. Ft. - Second Floor
34,487 Cu. Ft.

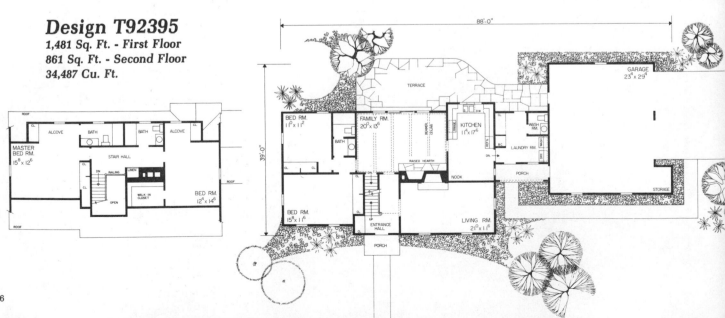

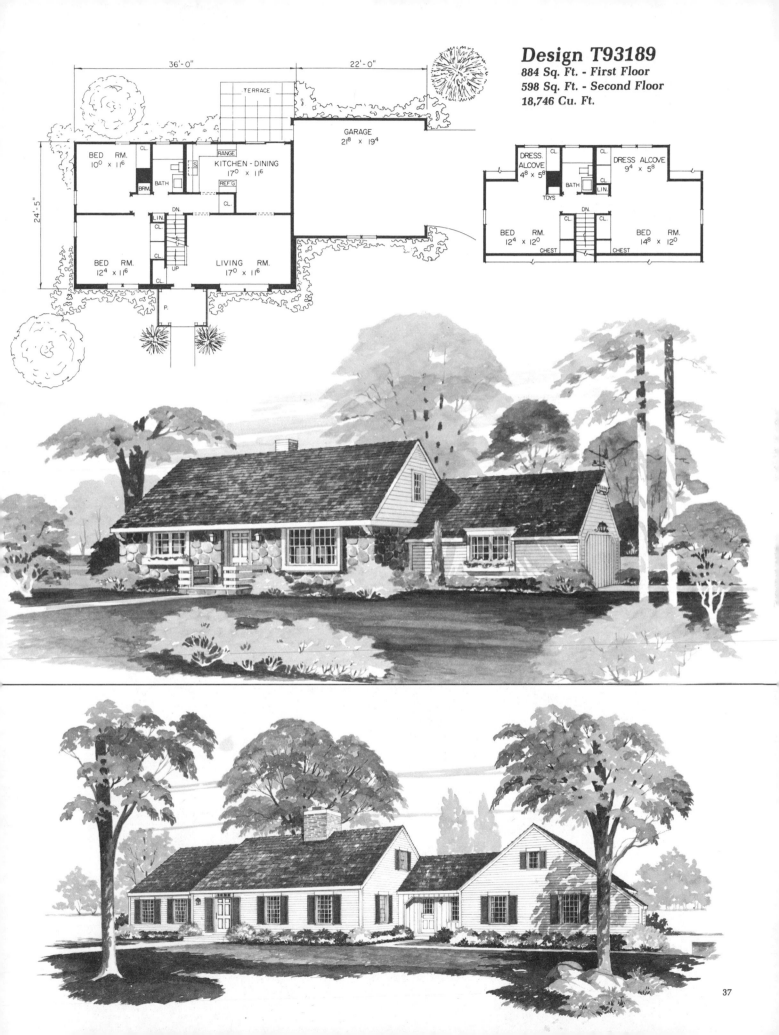

Design T93189
884 Sq. Ft. - First Floor
598 Sq. Ft. - Second Floor
18,746 Cu. Ft.

36'-0"

22'-0"

TERRACE

GARAGE
21⁸ x 19⁴

24'-5"

BED RM.
10⁰ x 11⁶

CL.

BATH

BRM.

RANGE

KITCHEN - DINING
17⁰ x 11⁶

REF'G

CL.

DN.

LIN.

CL.

CL.

UP

BED RM.
12⁴ x 11⁶

CL.

LIVING RM.
17⁰ x 11⁶

P.

DRESS. ALCOVE
4⁸ x 5⁸

CL.

BATH

CL.

LIN.

TOYS

DRESS ALCOVE
9⁴ x 5⁸

BED RM.
12⁴ x 12⁰

CL.

DN.

CL.

CHEST

CHEST

BED RM.
14⁸ x 12⁰

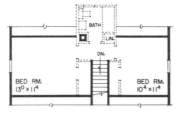

Design T91372

768 Sq. Ft. - First Floor
432 Sq. Ft. - Second Floor
17,280 Cu. Ft.

● Low cost livability could hardly ask for more. Here, is an enchanting exterior and a four bedroom floor plan. Note stairs to basement.

Design T92162

741 Sq. Ft. - First Floor
504 Sq. Ft. - Second Floor
17,895 Cu. Ft.

● This economical design delivers great exterior appeal and fine livability. In addition to kitchen eating space there is a separate dining room.

(1½-Story Homes continued on pg. 133)

TWO-STORY HOMES
Outstanding Livability For Growing Families

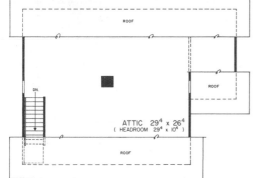

ROOF

DN.

ATTIC 29⁴ x 26⁴
(HEADROOM 29⁴ x 10⁴)

ROOF

ROOF

BEDROOM / STUDY 11⁰ x 13²

BATH DRESS. RM.

VANITY

MASTER BEDROOM 13⁰ x 13²

CL.

BATH

CL.

DN.

CL.

UP TO ATTIC

CL.

BEDROOM 10⁰ x 10⁶

BEDROOM 13⁰ x 10⁶

CL.

CL.

LIN.

Design T92774
1,370 Sq. Ft. - First Floor
969 Sq. Ft. - Second Floor
38,305 Cu. Ft.

● Another Farmhouse adaptation with all the most up-to-date features expected in a new home. Beginning with the formal areas, this design offers pleasures for the entire family. There is the quiet corner living room which has an opening to the sizable dining room. This room will enjoy plenty of natural light from the delightful bay window overlooking the rear yard. It is also conveniently located with the efficient U-shaped kitchen just a step away. The kitchen features many built-ins with pass-thru to the beamed ceiling breakfast room. Sliding glass doors to the terrace are fine attractions in both the sunken family room and breakfast room. The service entrance to the garage is flanked by a clothes closet and a large, walk-in pantry. There is a secondary entrance thru the laundry room. Recreational activities and hobbies can be pursued in the basement area. Four bedrooms, two baths upstairs.

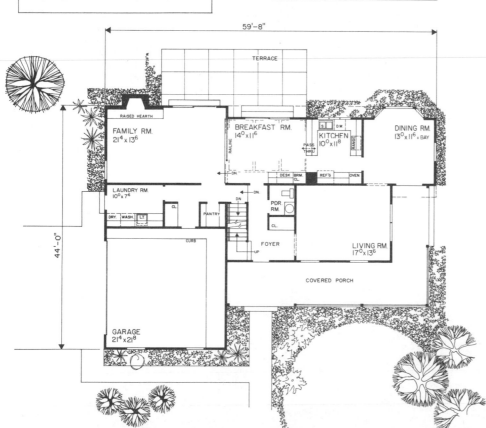

59'-8"

TERRACE

RAISED HEARTH

FAMILY RM. 21⁴ x 13⁶

BREAKFAST RM. 14⁰ x 11⁶

KITCHEN 10⁰ x 11⁸

DINING RM. 13⁰ x 11⁶ + BAY

RAILING

PASS THRU

LAUNDRY RM. 10⁰ x 7⁶

DN.

DESK

BRM. CL.

REF'G

OVEN

DRY. WASH.

CL.

PANTRY

DN.

PDR. RM.

CL.

UP

FOYER

LIVING RM. 17⁰ x 13⁶

44'-0"

CURB

COVERED PORCH

GARAGE 21⁴ x 21⁸

Design T91887

1,518 Sq. Ft. - First Floor
1,144 Sq. Ft. - Second Floor
40,108 Cu. Ft.

● This Gambrel roof Colonial is steeped in history. And well it should be, for its pleasing proportions are a delight to the eye. The various roof planes, the window treatment, and the rambling nature of the entire house revive a picture of rural New England.

The covered porch protects the front door which opens into a spacious entrance hall. Traffic then flows in an orderly fashion to the end living room, the separate dining room, the cozy family room, and to the spacious country-kitchen. There is a first floor

laundry, plenty of coat closets, and a handy powder room. Two fireplaces enliven the decor of the living areas. Upstairs there is an exceptional master bedroom layout and abundant storage. Note walk-in closets. Garage is over-sized and features storage cabinets.

Design T92320

1,856 Sq. Ft. - First Floor
1,171 Sq. Ft. - Second Floor
46,699 Cu. Ft.

● A charming Colonial adaptation with a Gambrel roof front exterior and a Salt Box rear. The focal point of family activities will be the spacious family kitchen with its beamed ceiling and fireplace. Blueprints include details for both three and four bedroom options.

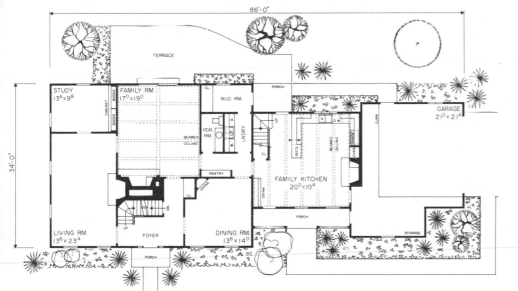

OPTIONAL SECOND FLOOR PLAN

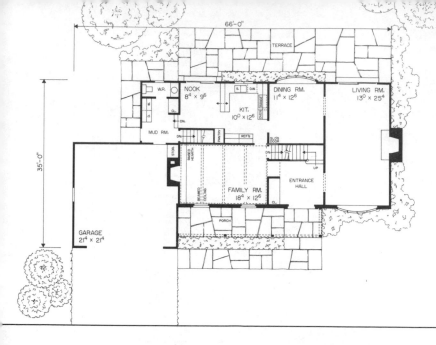

Design T92223 1,266 Sq. Ft. - First Floor
1,232 Sq. Ft. - Second Floor; 34,286 Cu. Ft.

● The appealing double front doors of this home
open wide to fine livability. Entertaining can be
enjoyed in the formal, end living room and the
all-purpose, beamed ceiling family room, both
having a fireplace. Five bedrooms, two full baths
and plenty of closets complete the second floor.

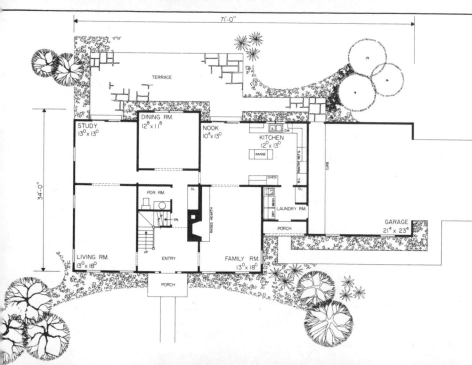

Design T92538
1,503 Sq. Ft. - First Floor
1,095 Sq. Ft. - Second Floor; 44,321 Cu. Ft.

● This Salt Box is charming, indeed. The
livability it has to offer to the large and
growing family is great. The entry is spacious and is open to the second floor balcony. For living areas, there is the study in
addition to the living and family rooms.

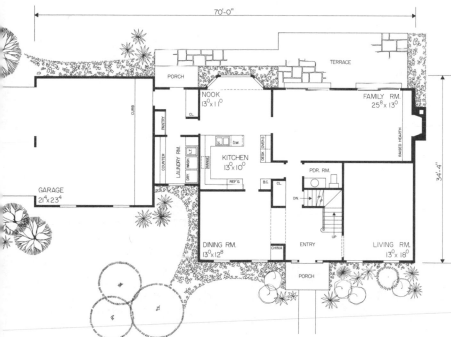

Design T92539
1,450 Sq. Ft. - First Floor
1,167 Sq. Ft. - Second Floor; 46,738 Cu. Ft.

● This appealingly proportioned four bedroom Gambrel exudes an aura of coziness. The beauty of the main part of the house is delightfully symmetrical and is enhanced by the attached garage and laundry room.

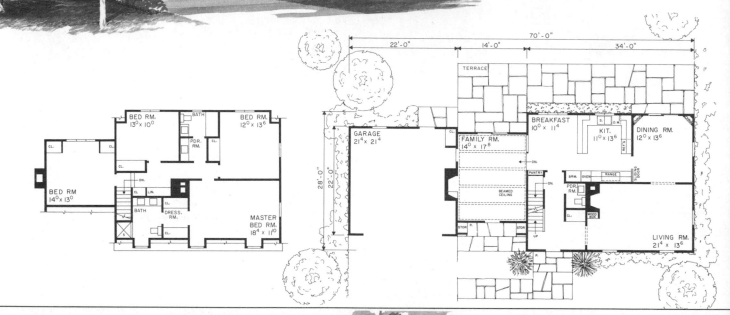

Design T92131

1,214 Sq. Ft. - First Floor
1,097 Sq. Ft. - Second Floor
30,743 Cu. Ft.

● A Gambrel roof design from our Colonial past. The growing family will have plenty of space in this modest house.

Design T92189

1,134 Sq. Ft. - First Floor
1,063 Sq. Ft. - Second Floor
31,734 Cu. Ft.

● Imagine this Colonial adaptation on your new building site! The symmetry and the pleasing proportion make it a wonderful addition to the local scene.

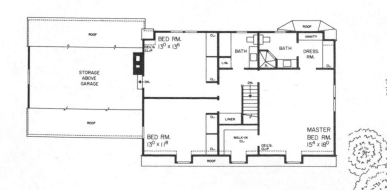

Design T91285

1,202 Sq. Ft. - First Floor
896 Sq. Ft. - Second Floor
27,385 Cu. Ft.

● Designed for years of livability. And what great livability this two-story traditional has to offer. The spacious center entry hall routes traffic conveniently to all areas. The formal living room is big and features two windows overlooking the front yard. The separate dining room is but a step from its own terrace. A convenient spot to enjoy dessert, or a second cup of coffee. The breakfast room, the kitchen, and the family room all look out upon the rear yard. A pantry/china storage wall will be a popular feature.

Design T91996

1,056 Sq. Ft. - First Floor
1,040 Sq. Ft. - Second Floor
29,071 Cu. Ft.

● Here is a Farmhouse adaptation with a delightful mixture of natural stone and narrow, horizontal siding. The covered front porch extends across the entire front affording protection for the large windows and the double front doors. The center entry hall dispatches traffic most effectively. The room relationships are outstanding. The fine work center is strategically located between the formal dining and informal breakfast rooms. While there is a basement, there is also a separate first floor laundry with adjacent washroom. Upstairs, four bedrooms, two full baths with twin lavatories and plenty of closets.

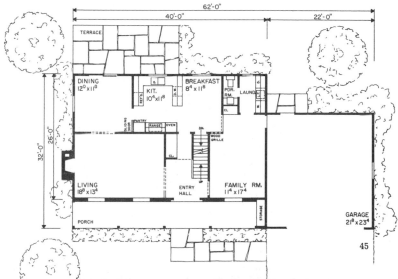

45

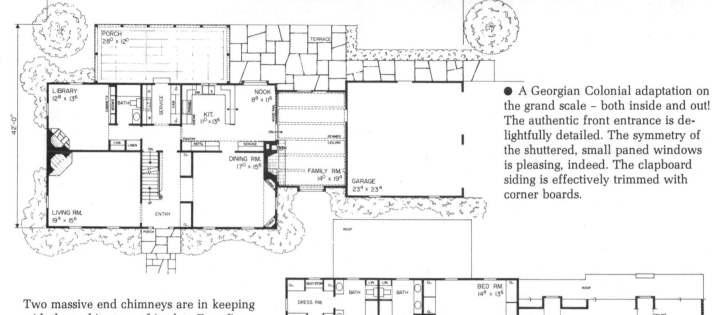

Design T92221

1,726 Sq. Ft. - First Floor
1,440 Sq. Ft. - Second Floor
50,204 Cu. Ft.

● A Georgian Colonial adaptation on the grand scale – both inside and out! The authentic front entrance is delightfully detailed. The symmetry of the shuttered, small paned windows is pleasing, indeed. The clapboard siding is effectively trimmed with corner boards.

Two massive end chimneys are in keeping with the architecture of its day. Four fireplaces provide the proper atmosphere for the family room, living room, library, and master bedroom. The spacious center entrance hall leads straight back to the practical, rear service area.

Design T91868

1,190 Sq. Ft. - First Floor
1,300 Sq. Ft. - Second Floor
32,327 Cu. Ft.

Design T92211

1,214 Sq. Ft. - First Floor
1,146 Sq. Ft. - Second Floor
32,752 Cu. Ft.

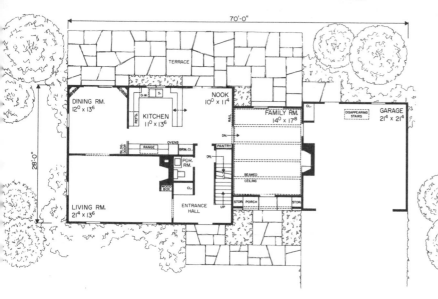

● The appeal of this Colonial home will be virtually everlasting. It will improve with age and service the growing family well. The architectural detailing is exquisite, indeed. The window treatment, the narrow siding, the massive chimneys, the service porch and the garage are attractive features.

Imagine your family living here. There are four bedrooms, 2½ baths, a formal and an informal living area, two fireplaces, a separate dining room, a breakfast nook, an efficient work center, and a basement. Sliding glass doors lead from dining and family rooms to rear terraces.

● For the large family – a second floor featuring five bedrooms, three full baths, and plenty of closet space! Downstairs, there are two big living areas, two sizeable dining areas, two sets of sliding glass doors, an outstanding kitchen and handy powder room. Note fireplace.

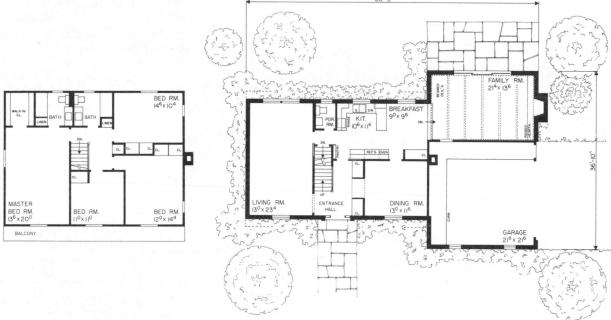

WALK-IN CL. | LINEN | BATH | BATH | LINEN

BED RM.
14⁶ x 10⁴

DN.

CL. CL. CL. CL.

CL.

UP

MASTER BED RM.
13⁶ x 20⁰

BED RM.
11⁰ x 11⁰

BED RM.
12⁰ x 14⁴

BALCONY

60'-5"

FAMILY RM.
21⁴ x 13⁶

BEAMED CEIL'G

RAISED HEARTH

DN.

PDR. RM.

KIT.
10⁶ x 11⁶

RANGE

BREAKFAST
9⁰ x 9⁶

REF'G OVEN

DN.

CL.

36'-10"

LIVING RM.
13⁰ x 23⁴

ENTRANCE HALL

CL.

DINING RM.
13⁰ x 11⁶

CURB

GARAGE
21⁹ x 21⁶

Design T91715 1,276 Sq. Ft. - First Floor; 1,064 Sq. Ft. - Second Floor; 31,295 Cu. Ft.

● The blueprints you order for this design show details for building each of these three appealing exteriors. Which do you like best? Whatever your choice, the interior will provide the growing family with all the facilities for fine living.

Design T91957 1,042 Sq. Ft. - First Floor; 780 Sq. Ft. - Second Floor; 24,982 Cu. Ft.

● Here is another floor plan which can also be built with three optional exteriors. Being a relatively low-budget home it will be hard to beat. Four bedrooms, 2½ baths, two eating area, formal living room, family room, efficient kitchen and more.

Design T91361

965 Sq. Ft. - First Floor
740 Sq. Ft. - Second Floor
23,346 Cu. Ft.

● An abundance of livability in a charming traditional adaptation which will be most economical to build. Count the features, they are numerous. Study the layout. It is outstanding. All the elements are present in this design for fine family living. Three bedrooms, 2½ baths, family room, dining room, and first floor laundry.

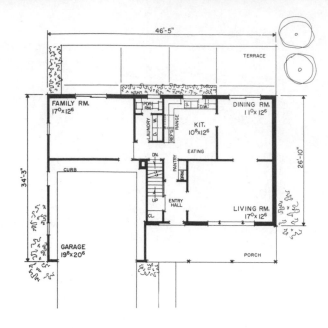

Design T91956

990 Sq. Ft. - First Floor
728 Sq. Ft. - Second Floor
23,703 Cu. Ft.

● Even a modest house can function like a mansion. The large family will spend much time in the beamed ceiling family room. When doing so, there are still the living, dining, and four bedrooms ready to serve. Note three bedroom plan.

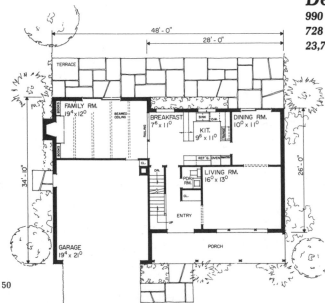

OPTIONAL 3 BEDROOM PLAN

Design T91354

644 Sq. Ft. - First Floor
572 Sq. Ft. - Second Floor
11,490 Cu. Ft.

● Livability galore for the 50 foot building site. The homemaker will enjoy her U-shaped work center with the extra washroom, laundry equipment nearby. There is a separate dining room, plus an informal family room with sliding doors to rear terrace. Note basement option.

OPTIONAL BASEMENT

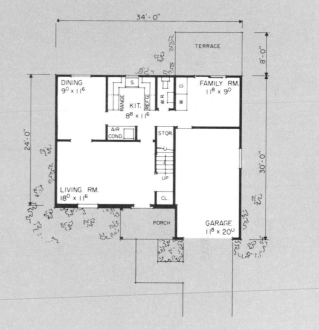

Design T92731
1,039 Sq. Ft. - First Floor
973 Sq. Ft. - Second Floor; 29,740 Cu. Ft.

● The multi-paned windows with shutters of this two-story highlight the exterior delightfully. Inside the livability is ideal. Formal and informal areas are sure to serve your family with ease. Note efficient U-shaped kitchen with handy first-floor laundry. Sleeping facilities on second floor.

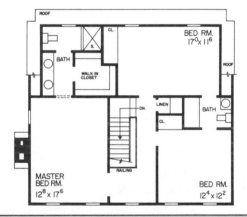

Design T91142 1,525 Sq. Ft. - First Floor
952 Sq. Ft. - Second Floor (1,053 Sq. Ft. - Four Bedroom Option); 32,980 Cu. Ft.

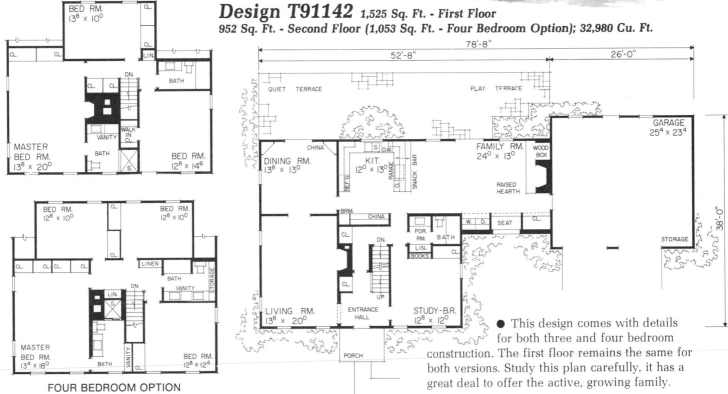

BED RM.
13⁸ x 10⁰

CL.

CL.

CL. CL.

LIN.

BATH

DN.

CL. CL.

MASTER
BED RM.
13⁸ x 20⁰

VANITY

WALK
IN
CL.

BATH

S

BED RM.
12⁸ x 14⁶

BED RM.
12⁸ x 10⁰

CL.

BED RM.
12⁸ x 10⁰

CL.

CL.

CL. CL. CL.

LINEN

CL.

BATH

STORAGE

DN.

LIN.
CL.

VANITY

MASTER
BED RM.
13⁴ x 18⁰

BATH

VANITY

CL.

BED RM.
12⁸ x 12⁴

FOUR BEDROOM OPTION

78'-8"

52'-8"

26'-0"

QUIET TERRACE

PLAY TERRACE

GARAGE
25⁴ x 23⁴

DINING RM.
13⁸ x 13⁰

CHINA

KIT.
12⁰ x 13⁰

S

D.W.

RANGE

SNACK BAR

FAMILY RM.
24⁰ x 13⁰

WOOD
BOX

RAISED
HEARTH

38'-0"

REF'G.

BRM.

CHINA

CL.

DN.

PDR.
RM.

BATH

W. D.

SEAT

CL.

STORAGE

LIN.

BOOKS

CL.

LIVING RM.
13⁸ x 20⁰

ENTRANCE
HALL

UP

STUDY-B.R.
12⁸ x 12⁰

PORCH

● This design comes with details for both three and four bedroom construction. The first floor remains the same for both versions. Study this plan carefully, it has a great deal to offer the active, growing family.

Design T91933 1,184 Sq. Ft. - First Floor
884 Sq. Ft. - Second Floor; 27,976 Cu. Ft.

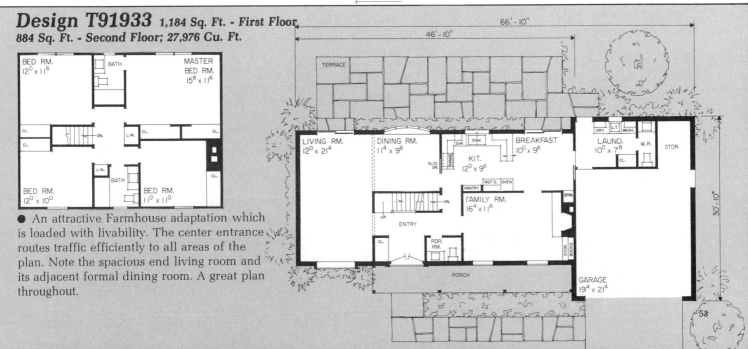

BED RM.
12⁰ x 11⁶

BATH

MASTER
BED RM.
15⁸ x 11⁶

CL.

DN.

LIN.

CL.

CL.

BED RM.
12⁰ x 10⁰

LIN.

BATH

BED RM.
11⁰ x 11⁰

CL.

66'-10"

46'-10"

TERRACE

LIVING RM.
12⁰ x 21⁴

DINING RM.
11⁴ x 9⁶

D.W.

SINK

BREAKFAST
10⁰ x 9⁶

LAUND.
10⁰ x 7⁸

DRY.

L.T.

WASH.

W.R.

STOR.

SLID.
DR.

RANGE

KIT.
12⁰ x 9⁶

CL.

30'-10"

PANTRY

REF'G.

OVEN

UP

UN.

FAMILY RM.
16⁴ x 11⁶

BRM.

ENTRY

CL.

STOR.

STOR.

BOOKS

PDR.
RM.

PORCH

GARAGE
19⁴ x 21⁴

● An attractive Farmhouse adaptation which is loaded with livability. The center entrance routes traffic efficiently to all areas of the plan. Note the spacious end living room and its adjacent formal dining room. A great plan throughout.

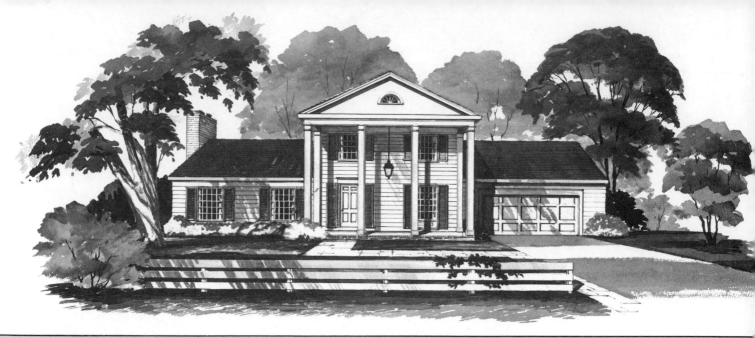

Design T91269

1,232 Sq. Ft. - First Floor
1,232 Sq. Ft. - Second Floor
33,344 Cu. Ft.

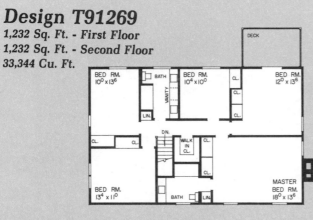

● Here are three homes of modest size each one completely capable of catering most successfully to the living requirements of the large family. There is no lack of sleeping space. Bath facilities are excellent. Eating potential is outstanding. Formal and informal living space is exceptional.

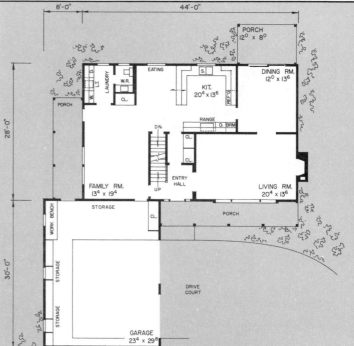

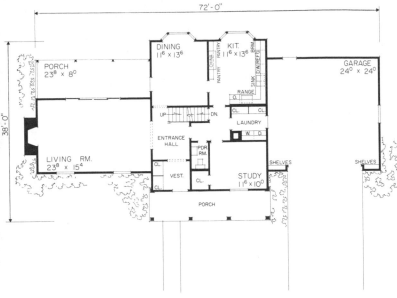

Design T91208

**1,170 Sq. Ft. - First Floor
768 Sq. Ft. - Second Floor
26,451 Cu. Ft.**

● Reminiscent of the stately grandeur of Mount Vernon, this two-story with its living room and garage wings, is yet another example of an earlier era recaptured. Up-to-date floor planning retains a feeling of gracious formality in a most convienient and efficent manner.

Design T92733

**1,177 Sq. Ft. - First Floor
1,003 Sq. Ft. - Second Floor; 32,040 Cu. Ft.**

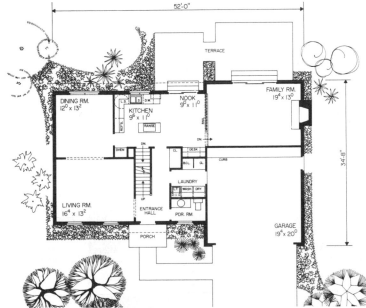

This is definitely a four bedroom Colonial with charm galore. The kitchen features an island range and other built-ins. All will enjoy the sunken family room with fireplace, which has sliding glass doors leading to the terrace. Also a basement for recreational activities with laundry remaining on first floor for extra convenience.

Design T92585

990 Sq. Ft. - First Floor
1,011 Sq. Ft. - Second Floor; 30,230 Cu. Ft.

● A traditional Colonial, a stately Tudor and an elegant French facade house this two-story floor plan. The exteriors are highlighted with large paned-glass windows. Note that the second floor overhangs in the front to extend the size of the master bedroom. After entering through the front door one can either go directly to the formal area or to the informal area.

Design T92586

984 Sq. Ft. - First Floor
1,003 Sq. Ft. - Second Floor; 30,080 Cu. Ft.

● The formal area consists of the living and dining rooms. These two areas stretch from the front to the rear of the house. Together they offer the correct setting for the most formal occasion. The informal area is the front family room. A fireplace will warm this casual, family living area. The work center is easily accessible from all areas, including the garage and terrace.

Design T92587

984 Sq. Ft. - First Floor
993 Sq. Ft. - Second Floor; 30,090 Cu. Ft.

● The second floor has been designed to please all of the family. Four good-sized bedrooms, plenty of closet space and two baths are available. Not a bit of wasted space will be found in these sleeping facilities. Choose your favorite facade to go with this floor plan. Order Design T92585 for the Colonial; Design T92586 for the Tudor and for the French, order Design T92587.

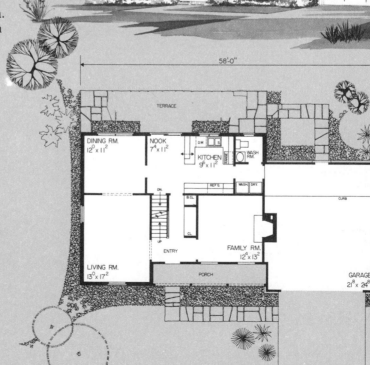

Design T92617

1,223 Sq. Ft. - First Floor
1,018 Sq. Ft. - Second Floor; 30,784 Cu. Ft.

● This Gambrel roof version shares the two-story floor plan below with the Tudor and the hip-roofed design from the Southwest. Each of these exterior facades, housing the same practical plan, will be an outstanding investment for a lifetime of proud ownership. Don't miss the delightful symmetry of the window treatment and the front opening garage of Design T92617.

Design T92618

1,269 Sq. Ft. - First Floor
1,064 Sq. Ft. - Second Floor; 33,079 Cu. Ft.

● Tudor design has become very popular in recent years; if this is your choice, order Design T92618. Inside, the large family will enjoy all of the features that will aide a family to easy living. Note the large 13 x 23 foot formal end-living room. It is assured excellent privacy. A separate dining room, too. It has easy access to the kitchen for ease in serving.

Design T92619

1,269 Sq. Ft. - First Floor
1,064 Sq. Ft. - Second Floor; 29,195 Cu. Ft.

● The Southwest is captured ideally in this hip-roofed house. To receive this elevation, order Design T92619. Along with the other two designs, the informal area is a sunken family room. It features a raised hearth fireplace and access to the terrace, as does the nook. Four bedrooms and two bathrooms with economical back-to-back plumbing are on the second floor.

57

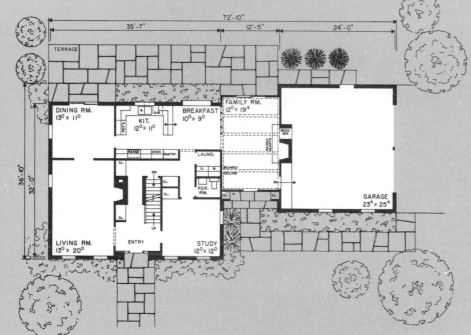

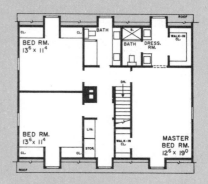

Design T91827

1,442 Sq. Ft. - First Floor
1,098 Sq. Ft. - Second Floor; 35,275 Cu. Ft.

● There is great livability in this two-story design. Three bedrooms are on the second floor while the first floor houses the outstanding living and work areas.

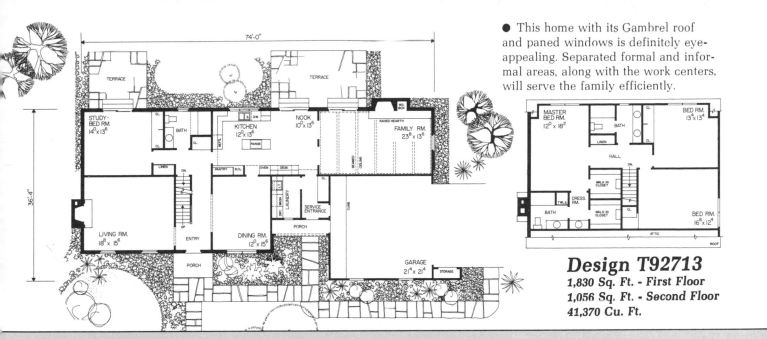

● This home with its Gambrel roof and paned windows is definitely eye-appealing. Separated formal and informal areas, along with the work centers, will serve the family efficiently.

Design T92713

1,830 Sq. Ft. - First Floor
1,056 Sq. Ft. - Second Floor
41,370 Cu. Ft.

Design T92224

1,567 Sq. Ft. - First Floor
1,070 Sq. Ft. - Second Floor; 37,970 Cu. Ft.

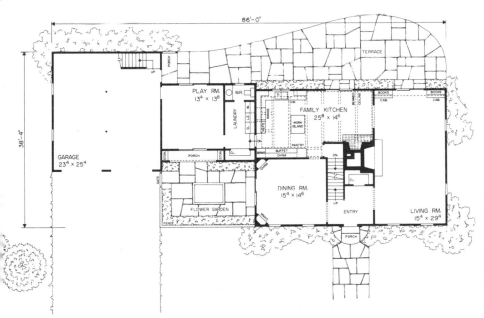

● Certainly reminiscent of the charm of rural New England. The focal point of the first floor is easily the spacious family-kitchen. Formerly referred to as the country-kitchen, this area with its beamed ceiling and fireplace will have a warm and cozy atmosphere, indeed.

59

Design T92694
2,026 Sq. Ft. - First Floor
1,386 Sq. Ft. - Second Floor
69,445 Cu. Ft.

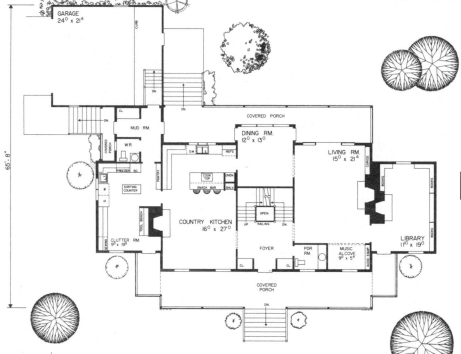

● This two-story design recalls the 18th-Century homestead of Sec. of Foreign Affairs John Jay in Katonah, N.Y. Downstairs features include a large country kitchen, clutter room, music alcove, and library wing. Upstairs are three sizable bedrooms, including a master suite with whirlpool.

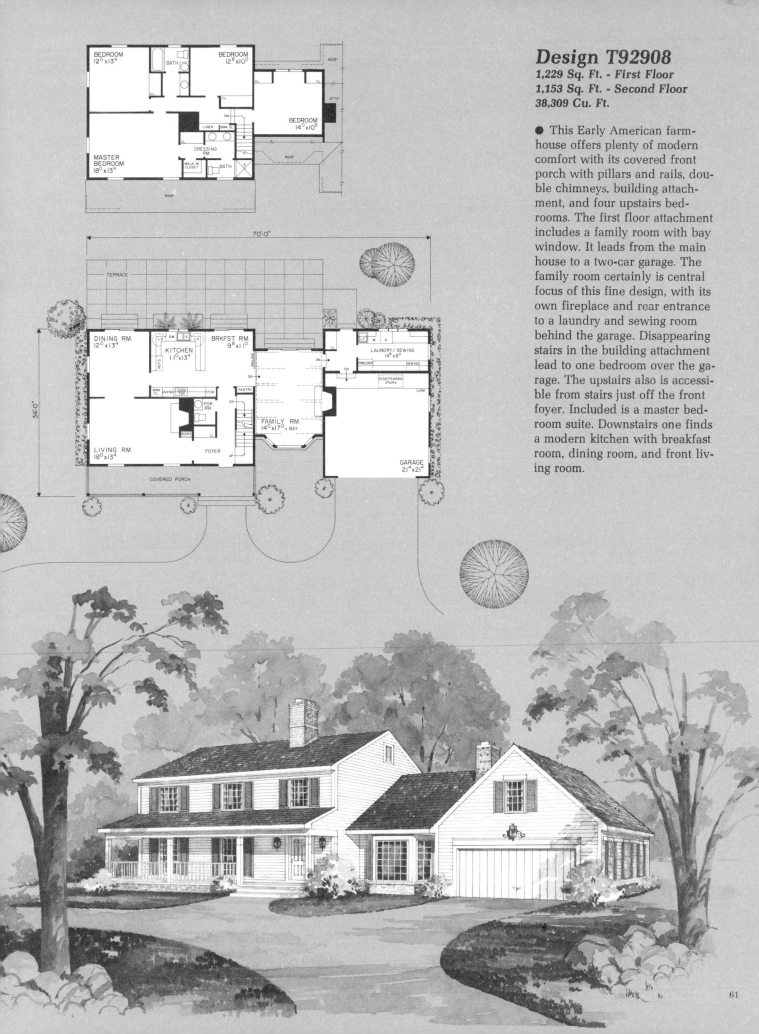

Design T92908

1,229 Sq. Ft. - First Floor
1,153 Sq. Ft. - Second Floor
38,309 Cu. Ft.

● This Early American farm-house offers plenty of modern comfort with its covered front porch with pillars and rails, double chimneys, building attachment, and four upstairs bedrooms. The first floor attachment includes a family room with bay window. It leads from the main house to a two-car garage. The family room certainly is central focus of this fine design, with its own fireplace and rear entrance to a laundry and sewing room behind the garage. Disappearing stairs in the building attachment lead to one bedroom over the garage. The upstairs also is accessible from stairs just off the front foyer. Included is a master bedroom suite. Downstairs one finds a modern kitchen with breakfast room, dining room, and front living room.

Design T92128
1,152 Sq. Ft. - First Floor
896 Sq. Ft. - Second Floor; 30,707 Cu. Ft.

● Here is proof that your restricted building budget can return to you wonderfully pleasing design and loads of livability. This is an English Tudor adaptation that will surely become your subdivision's favorite facade. Its mark of individuality is obvious to all.

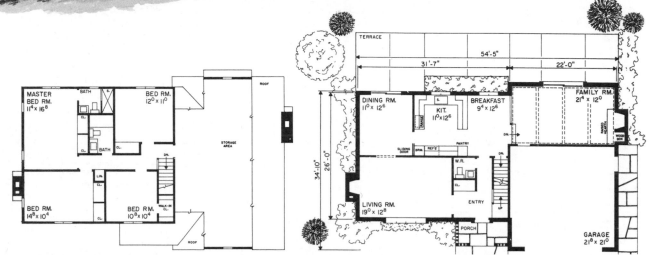

Design T91856
1,023 Sq. Ft. - First Floor
784 Sq. Ft. - Second Floor; 25,570 Cu. Ft.

● Small house with big house features and livability. Some of the features are two full baths and extra storage upstairs; laundry, wash room and two fireplaces downstairs. The pantry is above the wood box and accessible from the kitchen which has eating space.

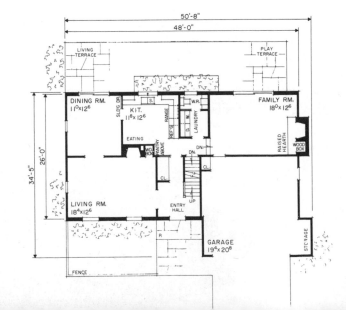

(Two-Story Homes continued on pg. 165)

ONE-STORY HOMES under 2000 Sq. Ft.
Selected Designs For Modest Budgets

Design T92824
1,550 Sq. Ft.; 34,560 Cu. Ft.

● Low-maintenance and economy in building are the outstanding exterior features of this sharp one-story design. It is sheathed in long-lasting cedar siding and trimmed with stone for an eye-appealing facade. Entrance to this home takes you through a charming garden courtyard then a covered walk to the front porch. The garage extending from the front of the house serves two purposes; to reduce lot size and to buffer the interior of the house from street noise. Sliding glass doors are featured in each of the main rooms for easy access to the outdoors. A sun porch is tucked between the study and gathering rooms. Optional non-basement details are included with the purchase of this design.

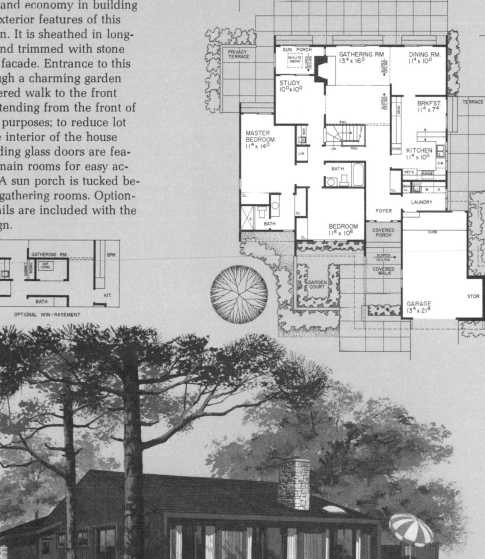

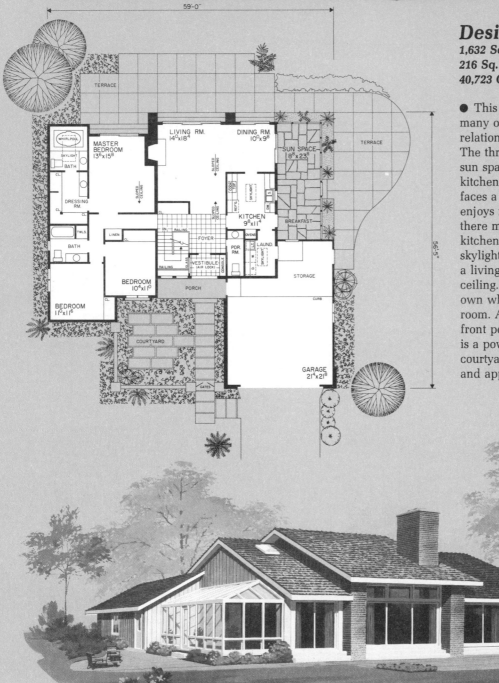

Design T92902
1,632 Sq. Ft. - Living Area
216 Sq. Ft. - Sun Space
40,723 Cu. Ft.

● This modern trend home captures many of the comforts and indoor-outdoor relationships sought by families today. The three-bedroom home incorporates a sun space just off the breakfast room, kitchen, and dining room. The sun space faces a side terrace. The modern kitchen enjoys its own skylight to make work there more cheerful. Adjacent to the kitchen is a handy laundry with its own skylight. The formal dining room opens to a living room with fireplace and sloped ceiling. A master bedroom suite enjoys its own whirlpool, skylight, and dressing room. An air-locked vestibule buffers the front porch from foyer. Just off the foyer is a powder room for guests. A front courtyard further enhances the comfort and appearance of this sunlit, cozy home.

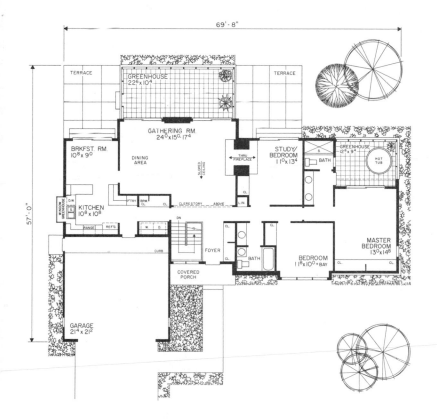

Design T92886

1,733 Sq. Ft.; 34,986 Cu. Ft.

● This one-story house is attractive with its contemporary exterior. It has many excellent features to keep you and your family happy for many years. For example, notice the spacious gathering room with sliding glass doors that allow easy access to the greenhouse. Another exciting feature of this room is that you will receive an abundance of sunshine through the clerestory windows. Also, this plan offers you two nice-sized bedrooms. The master suite is not only roomy but also unique because through both the bedroom and the bath you can enter a greenhouse with a hot tub. The hot tub will be greatly appreciated after a long, hard day at work. Don't forget to note the breakfast room with access to the terrace. You will enjoy the efficient kitchen that will make preparing meals a breeze. A greenhouse window here is charming. An appealing, open staircase leads to the basement. The square and cubic footages of the greenhouses are 394 and 4,070 respectively and are not included in the above figures.

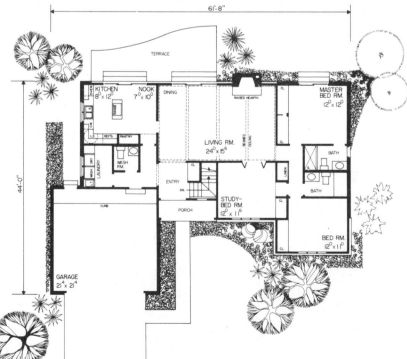

Design T92565
1,540 Sq. Ft.; 33,300 Cu. Ft.

● This modest sized floor plan has much to offer in the way of livability. It may function as either a two or three bedroom home. The living room is huge and features a fine, raised hearth fireplace. The open stairway to the basement is handy and will lead to what may be developed as the recreation area. In addition to the two full baths, there is an extra washroom. Adjacent is the laundry room and the service entrance from the garage. The blueprints you order for this design will show details for each of the three delightful elevations above. Which is your favorite? The Tudor, the Colonial, or the Contemporary?

Design T92505
1,366 Sq. Ft.; 29,329 Cu. Ft.

● This design offers you a choice of three distinctively different exteriors. Which is your favorite? Blueprints show details for all three optional elevations. A study of the floor plan reveals a fine measure of livability. In less than 1,400 square feet there are features galore. An excellent return on your construction dollar. In addition to the two eating areas and the open planning of the gathering room, the indoor-outdoor relationships are of great interest. The basement may be developed for recreational activities. Be sure to note the storage potential, particularly the linen closet, the pantry, the china cabinet and the broom closet.

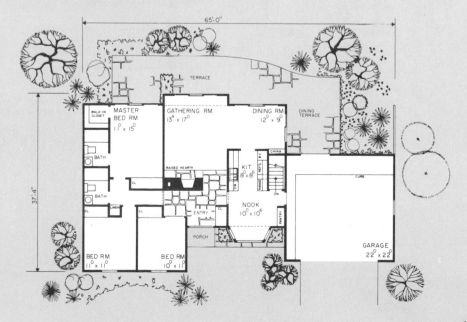

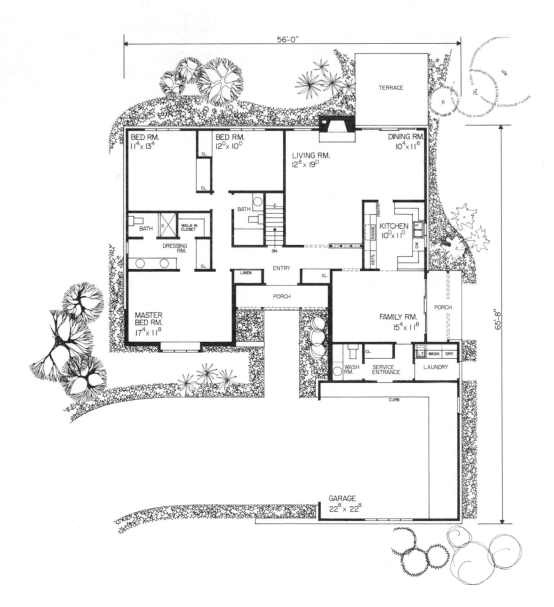

Design T92728
1,825 Sq. Ft.; 38,770 Cu. Ft.

● Your family's new life-style will surely flourish in this charming, L-shaped English adaptation. The curving front driveway produces an impressive approach. A covered front porch shelters the centered entry hall which effectively routes traffic to all areas. The fireplace is the focal point of the spacious, formal living and dining area. The kitchen is strategically placed to service the dining room and any informal eating space developed in the family room. In addition to the two full baths of the sleeping area, there is a handy washroom at the entrance from the garage. A complete, first floor laundry is nearby and has direct access to the yard. Sliding glass doors permit easy movement to the outdoor terrace and side porch. Don't overlook the basement and its potential for the development of additional livability and/or storage.

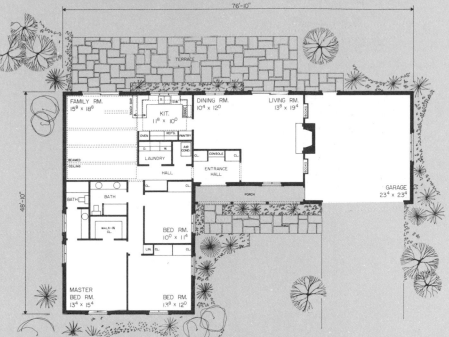

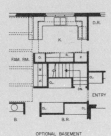

OPTIONAL BASEMENT

Design T92277
1,903 Sq. Ft.; 25,087 Cu. Ft.

● Tudor design front and center! And what an impact this beautifully proportioned L-shaped home does deliver. Observe the two different floor plans.

● The similarities in these two floor plans are many. Each provides excellent traffic patterns to well-defined zones. The sleeping wing is off by itself and features two full baths. The kitchen area functions well with the formal and informal living and dining areas. It overlooks the rear yard and is but a few steps from the terrace. One design features an open planned, formal living and dining area with a separate family room. The other, features a spacious country-kitchen with a separate dining room. Which arrangement do you prefer?

Design T92678
1,971 Sq. Ft.; 42,896 Cu. Ft.

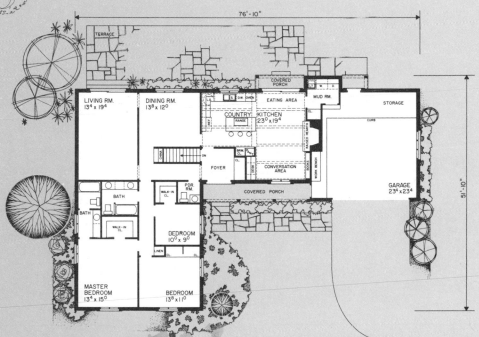

Design T92737

1,796 Sq. Ft.; 43,240 Cu. Ft.

● You will be able to build this distinctive, modified U-shaped one-story home on a relatively narrow site. But, then, if you so wished, with the help of your architect and builder you may want to locate the garage to the side of the house. Inside, the living potential is just great. The interior U-shaped kitchen handily services the dining and family rooms and nook. A rear covered porch functions ideally with the family room while the formal living room has its own terrace. Three bedrooms and two baths highlight the sleeping zone (or make it two bedrooms and a study). Notice the strategic location of the washroom, laundry, two storage closets and the basement stairs.

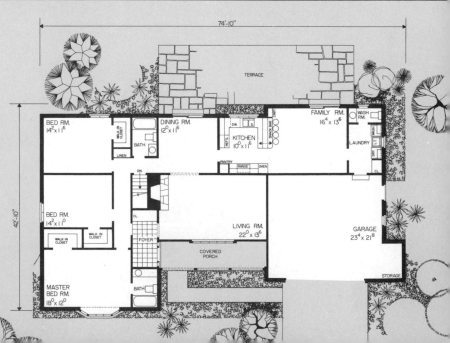

Design T92603

1,949 Sq. Ft.; 41,128 Cu. Ft.

● Surely it would be difficult to beat the appeal of this traditional one-story home. Its slightly modified U-shape with the two front facing gables, the bay window, the covered front porch and the interesting use of exterior materials all add to the exterior charm. Besides, there are three large bedrooms serviced by two full baths and three walk-in closets. The excellent kitchen is flanked by the formal dining room and the informal family room. Don't miss the pantry, the built-in oven and the pass-thru to the snack bar. The handy first floor laundry is strategically located to act as a mud room. The extra washroom is but a few steps away. The sizable living room highlights a fireplace and a picture window. Note the location of the basement stairs.

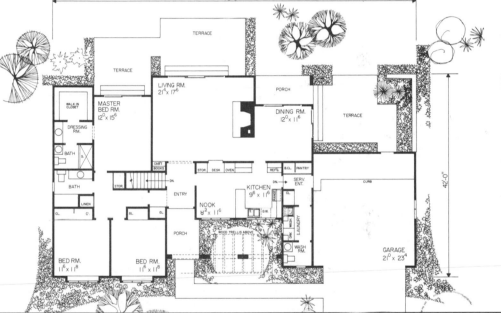

Design T92741
1,842 Sq. Ft.; 37,045 Cu. Ft.

● Here is another example of what 1,800 square feet can deliver in comfort and convenience. The setting reminds one of the sun country of Arizona. However, this design would surely be an attractive and refreshing addition to any region. The covered front porch with its adjacent open trellis area shelters the center entry. From here traffic flows efficiently to the sleeping, living and kitchen zones. There is much to recommend each area. The sleeping with its fine bath and closet facilities; the living with its spaciousness, fireplace and adjacent dining room; the kitchen with its handy nook, excellent storage, nearby laundry and extra washroom.

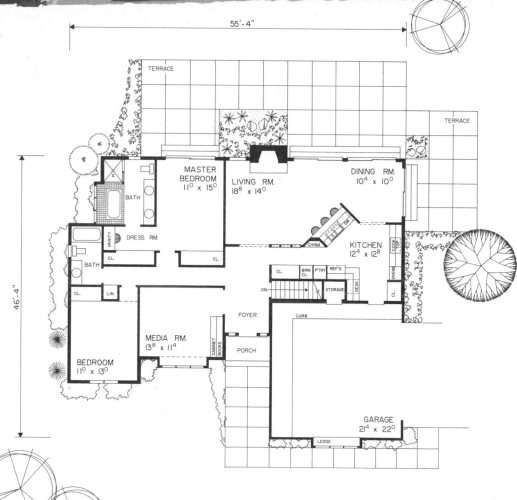

55'-4"

46'-4"

TERRACE

TERRACE

MASTER BEDROOM
11⁰ x 15⁰

BATH

DRESS. RM.

VANITY

BATH

CL.

LIN.

CL.

LIVING RM.
18⁸ x 14⁰

DINING RM.
10⁴ x 10⁰

CL.

CHINA

KITCHEN
12⁴ x 12⁸

COOK

OVENS

CL.

CL.

BRM. CL.

P'TRY

REF'G

DESK

DN.

STORAGE

FOYER

CURB

MEDIA RM.
13⁸ x 11⁴

CABINET BOOKS

PORCH

BEDROOM
11⁰ x 13⁰

GARAGE
21⁴ x 22⁰

LEDGE

Design T92929 1,608 Sq. Ft.; 38,150 Cu. Ft.

● Here is a cozy Tudor exterior with a contemporary interior for those who prefer the charm of yesteryear combined with the convenience and practicality of today. This efficient floor plan will cater nicely to the living patterns of the small family; be it a retired couple or newlyweds. The efficient kitch- en is strategically located handy to the garage, dining room, dining terrace and the front door. The spacious living area has a dramatic fireplace that functions with the rear terrace. A favorite spot will be the media room. Just the place for the TV, VCR and stereo systems. The master bedroom is large and has plenty of wardrobe storage along with a master bath featuring twin lavatories and a tub plus stall shower. Don't miss the extra guest room (or nursery). This affordable home has a basement for the development of additional recreational facilities.

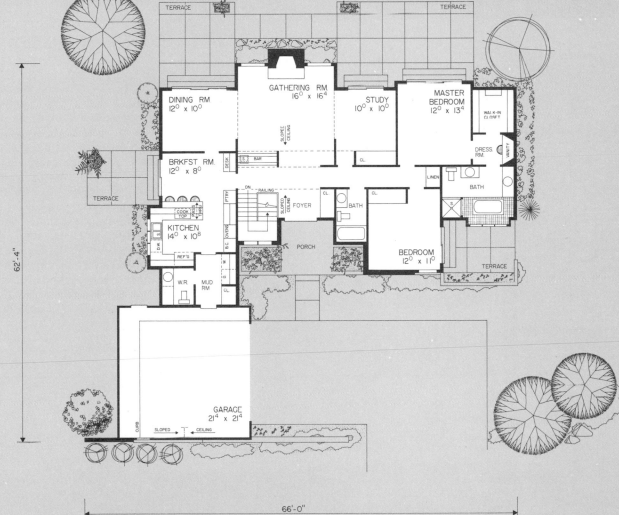

Design T92918 1,693 Sq. Ft.; 41,325 Cu. Ft.

● An exciting contemporary facade with fieldstone, vertical siding and interesting roof lines. The projecting garage creates a pleasing drive court as the impressive approach to this moderately-sized home. Double front doors open into a spacious foyer. Traffic is efficiently routed to all areas of the interior. Of particular interest is the open staircase to the lower level basement. Sloped ceilings in this area and the gathering room, along with the open planning reinforce the delightful feeling of spaciousness. The U-shaped kitchen is handy to the utility area and works well with the formal and informal dining areas. Like the dining room, the study flanks the gathering room. Open planning makes this 38 foot wide area a cheerful one, indeed. The master bedroom suite features a big walk-in closet, a dressing area with vanity and an outstanding bath. Note the terraces.

Design T92557
1,955 Sq. Ft.; 43,509 Cu. Ft.

● This eye-catching design with a flavor of the Spanish Southwest will be as interesting to live in as it will be to look at. The character of the exterior is set by the wide overhanging roof with its exposed beams; the massive arched pillars; the arching of the brick over the windows; the panelled door and the horizontal siding that contrasts with the brick. The master bedroom/study suite is one of the focal points of the interior. However, if necessary, the study could become the fourth bedroom.

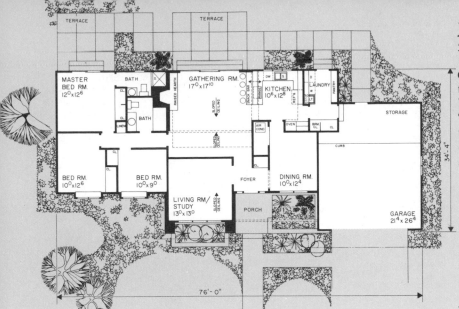

Design T92818
1,566 Sq. Ft.; 20,030 Cu. Ft.

● This is most certainly an outstanding contemporary design. Study the exterior carefully before your journey to inspect the floor plan. The vertical lines are carried from the siding to the paned windows to the garage door. A overhanging hip-roof. The front entry is recessed so the overhanging roof creates a covered porch. Note the planter court with privacy wall. The floor plan is just as outstanding. The rear gathering room has a sloped ceiling, raised hearth fireplace, sliding glass doors to the terrace and a snack bar with pass-thru to the kitchen.

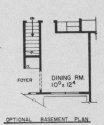

OPTIONAL BASEMENT PLAN

Design T92330
1,854 Sq. Ft.; 30,001 Cu. Ft.

● Your family will never tire of the living patterns offered by this appealing home with its low-pitched, wide overhanging roof. The masonry masses of the exterior are pleasing. While the blueprints call for the use of stone, you may wish to substitute brick veneer. Sloping ceiling and plenty of glass will assure the living area of a fine feeling of spaciousness. Two covered porches enhance the enjoyment of outdoor living. Two baths serve the three bedroom sleeping area.

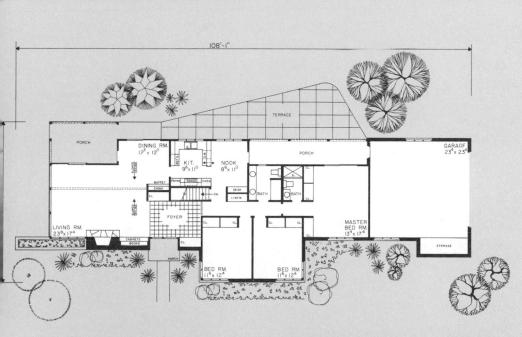

Design T92374
1,919 Sq. Ft.; 39,542 Cu. Ft.

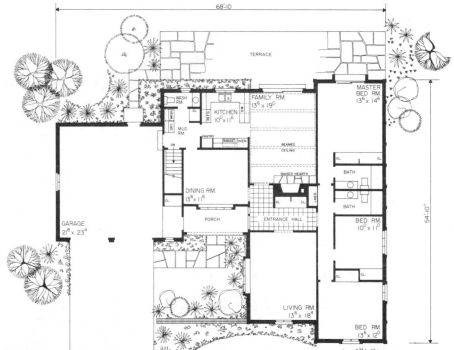

● This English adaptation will never grow old. There is, indeed, much here to please the eye. The wavy-edged siding contrasts pleasingly with the diagonal pattern of brick below. The diamond lites of the window create their own special effect. The projecting brick wall creates a pleasant court outside the covered front porch. The floor plan is well-zoned with the three bedrooms and two baths comprising a distinct sleeping wing. Flanking the entrance hall are the formal living room and the informal, multi-purpose family room with raised hearth fireplace. Note the number of closets for varying uses.

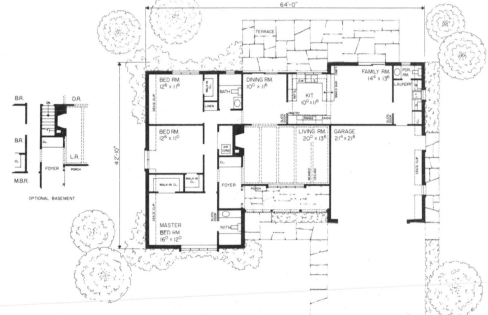

Design T92206
1,769 Sq. Ft.; 25,363 Cu. Ft.

● The charm of Tudor adaptations is becoming increasingly popular. And little wonder. Its freshness of character adds a unique touch to any neighborhood. This interesting one-story home will be a standout wherever built. The covered front porch leads to the formal front entry — the foyer. From this point traffic flows freely to the living and sleeping areas. The outstanding plan features three bedrooms, with two full baths, walk-in closets, a separate dining room, a beamed ceiling living room and efficient kitchen, and an informal family room.

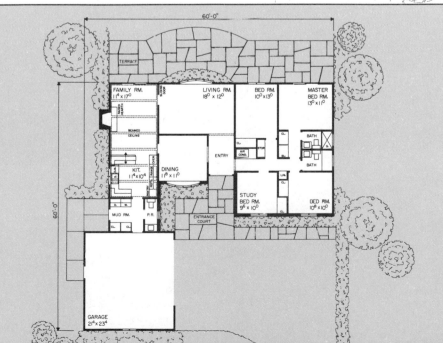

Design T92170
1,646 Sq. Ft.; 22,034 Cu. Ft.

● An L-shape home with an enchanting Olde English styling. The wavy-edged siding, the simulated beams, the diamond lite windows, the unusual brick pattern, and the interesting lines all are elements which set the character of authenticity. The center entry routes traffic directly to the formal living and sleeping zones of the house. Between the kitchen-family room area and the attached two-car garage is the mud room. Here is the washer and dryer with extra powder room nearby.

Design T92821
1,363 Sq. Ft. - First Floor
357 Sq. Ft. - Second Floor
37,145 Cu. Ft.

**Mansard Roof
Adaptation**

A Trend House . . .

● Here is a truly unique house whose interior was designed with the current decade's economies, lifestyles and demographics in mind. While functioning as a one-story home, the second floor provides an extra measure of livability when required. In addition, this two-story section adds to the dramatic appeal of both the exterior and the interior. Within only 1,363 square feet, this contemporary delivers refreshing and outstanding living patterns for those who are buying their first home, those who have raised their family and are looking for a smaller home and those in search of a retirement home. The center entrance routes traffic effectively to each area. The great room with its raised hearth fireplace, two-story arching and delightful glass areas is most distinctive. The kitchen is efficient and but a step from the dining room. The covered porch will provide an ideal spot for warm-weather, outdoor dining. The separate laundry room is strategically located. The sleeping area may consist of one bedroom and a study, or two bedrooms. Each room functions with the sheltered wood deck - a perfect location for a hot tub.

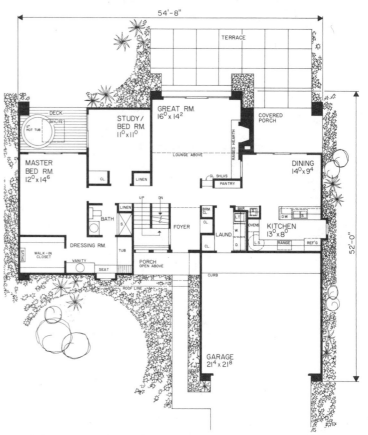

Design T92822
1,363 Sq. Ft. - First Floor
351 Sq. Ft. - Second Floor
36,704 Cu. Ft.

**Gable Roof
Version**

UPPER GREAT RM.

RAILING

CL.

LOUNGE / HOBBIES
16⁰ x 9²

SKYLITE

CL.

DN

RAILING

UPPER
FOYER

STOR. /
BATH

RAILING

BALCONY

LOUNGE / GUEST RM. /
GRANDCHILDREN'S RM.
16⁰ x 19²

CL.

CL.

DN

RAILING

UPPER
FOYER

BATH

S

RAILING

ALTERNATE SECOND FLOOR

... For the 80's and Decades to Come

● The full bath is planned to have easy access to the master bedroom and living areas. Note the stall shower, tub, seat and vanity. The second floor offers two optional layouts. It may serve as a lounge, studio or hobby area overlooking the great room. Or, it may be built to function as a complete private guest room. It would be a great place for the visiting grandchildren. Don't miss the outdoor balcony. Additional livability and storage facilities may be developed in the basement. Then, of course, there are two exteriors to choose from. Design T92821, with its horizontal frame siding and deep, attractive cornice detail, is an eye-catcher. For those with a preference for a contemporary fashioned gable roof and vertical siding, there is Design T92822. With the living areas facing the south, these designs will enjoy benefits of passive solar exposure. The overhanging roofs will help provide relief from the high summer sun. This is surely a modest-sized floor plan which will deliver new dimensions in small-family livability.

Design T91300
1,008 Sq. Ft.; 19,313 Cu. Ft.

● The projecting garage with its bulk storage area adds a full measure of design distinction. Behind the garage is a family room which functions with the kitchen.

Floor plan labels (Design T91300)

53'-4"
48'-0"

TERRACE

BED RM. 11⁸ x 11⁶
BED RM. 9⁰ x 11⁶
KIT. 8⁰ x 8⁰
FAMILY RM. 15⁸ x 11⁴

RANGE   REF'S

24'-0"
36'-0"

BED RM. 10⁰ x 11⁶
BATH
LIVING RM. 17⁴ x 11⁶
STORAGE

GARAGE 11⁴ x 23⁸

Design T93221
976 Sq. Ft.; 9,523 Cu. Ft.

● This hip-roof home has a wide overhang. The plan features excellent storage facilities. The kitchen-dining area is spacious and overlooks the rear yard. Note the optional carport with storage area.

Floor plan labels (Design T93221)

40'-0"

TERRACE
TERRACE

12'-0"
4'-0"   8'-0"

BED RM. 11⁴ x 10⁴
STORAGE 6⁸ x 5⁰
KITCHEN - DINING 15⁰ x 10⁴

STOR. 4⁰ x 5⁰
BATH
D W
HTR
RANGE   REF'G

KITCHEN-DINING RM.

STORAGE 7⁴ x 5⁴

24'-5"
26'-5"

BED RM. 11⁴ x 10⁴
BED RM. 10⁸ x 10⁰
LIVING RM. 14⁴ x 12⁸

LIN.

LIVING RM.

CARPORT 12⁰ x 26⁵

OPTIONAL CARPORT PLAN

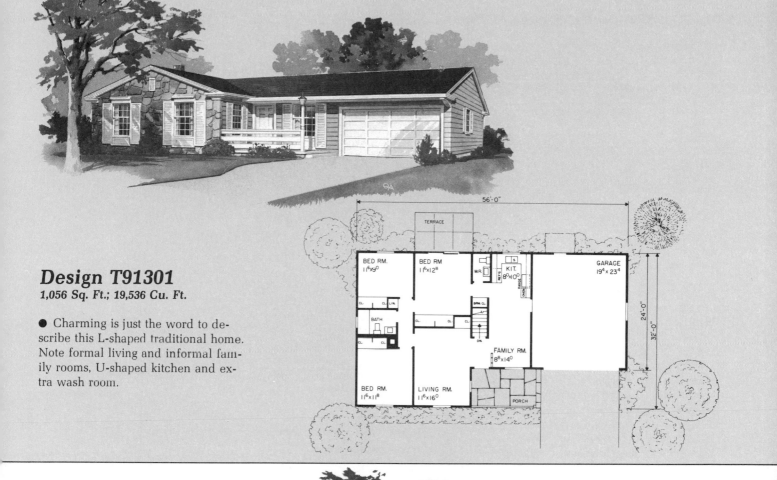

Design T91301
1,056 Sq. Ft.; 19,536 Cu. Ft.

● Charming is just the word to describe this L-shaped traditional home. Note formal living and informal family rooms, U-shaped kitchen and extra wash room.

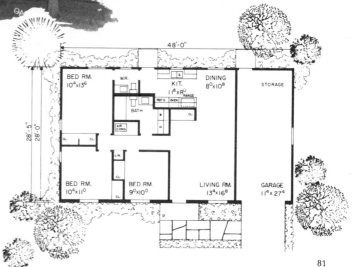

Design T93223
1,032 Sq. Ft.; 10,752 Cu. Ft.

● The master bedroom and kitchen of this efficient plan have direct access to the wash room. A full bath is convenient to all three bedrooms. The kitchen is but a few steps from the rear yard.

Design T91389
1,488 Sq. Ft.; 18,600 Cu. Ft.

● Your choice of exterior goes with this outstanding three bedroom, two bath floor plan. If your tastes include a liking for French Provincial, Design T91389, above, will provide a lifetime of satisfaction. On the other hand, should you prefer the simple straightforward lines of contemporary design, the exterior for Design T91387, below, will be your favorite. For those who enjoy the warmth of Colonial adaptations, the charming exterior for Design T91388, will be perfect. Of interest, is a comparison of these three exteriors. Observe the varying design treatment of the windows, the double front doors, the garage doors and the roof lines. Don't miss other architectural details. Study each exterior and the floor plan carefully. Three charming designs you won't want to miss.

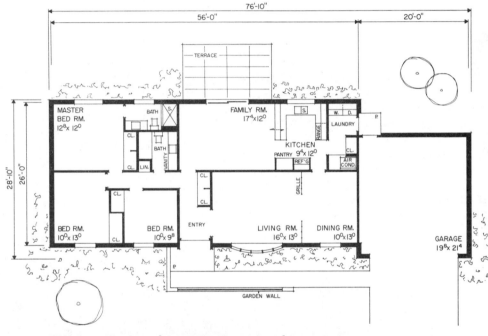

(One-Story Homes under 2000 Sq. Ft. continued on pg. 211)

Design T91387
1,488 Sq. Ft.; 16,175 Cu. Ft

Design T91388
1,488 Sq. Ft.; 18,600 Cu. Ft.

MULTI-LEVEL HOMES
Preferred Living Patterns for Sloping Sites

Design T92934
2,472 Sq. Ft. - Main Level; 2,145 Sq. Ft. - Lower Level
61,390 Cu. Ft.

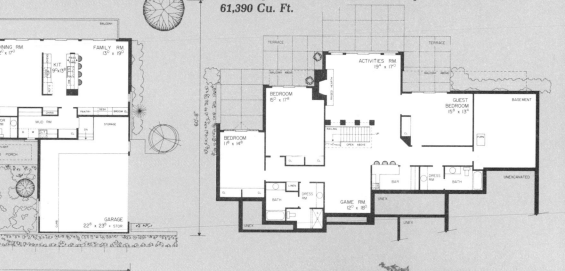

Design T92511

1,043 Sq. Ft. - Main Level; 703 Sq. Ft. - Upper Level
794 Sq. Ft. - Lower Level; 30,258 Cu. Ft.

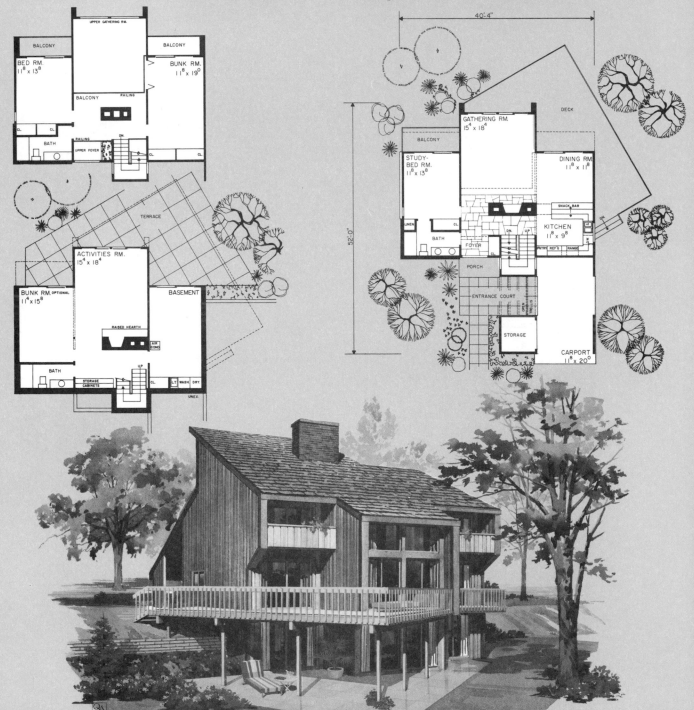

UPPER GATHERING RM.

BALCONY

BALCONY

BED RM.
11⁸ x 13⁸

BUNK RM.
11⁸ x 19⁰

BALCONY

RAILING

CL CL

BATH RAILING UPPER FOYER DN CL CL

TERRACE

ACTIVITIES RM.
15⁴ x 18⁴

BUNK RM. OPTIONAL
11⁴ x 15⁸

BASEMENT

RAISED HEARTH

AIR COND.

BATH

UP

STORAGE CABINETS CL LT WASH. DRY.

UNEX.

40'-4"

52'-0"

GATHERING RM.
15⁴ x 18⁴

DECK

BALCONY

STUDY-
BED RM.
11⁸ x 13⁸

DINING RM.
11⁸ x 11⁸

SNACK BAR

LINEN KITCHEN
11⁸ x 9⁸

BATH CL DN UP RANGE

FOYER ENTRY REF'G

CL

PORCH

ENTRANCE COURT OPEN TRELLIS

STORAGE

CARPORT
11⁸ x 20⁰

84

Design T92937 1,096 Sq. Ft. - Main Level
1,104 Sq. Ft. - Lower Level; 1,115 Sq. Ft. - Upper Level; 38,440 Cu. Ft.

● This contemporary multi-level home features an extended rear balcony that covers a rear patio, plus a master bedroom suite, complete with whirlpool and raised-hearth pass-thru. Two other bedrooms and a second bath are on the upper level.

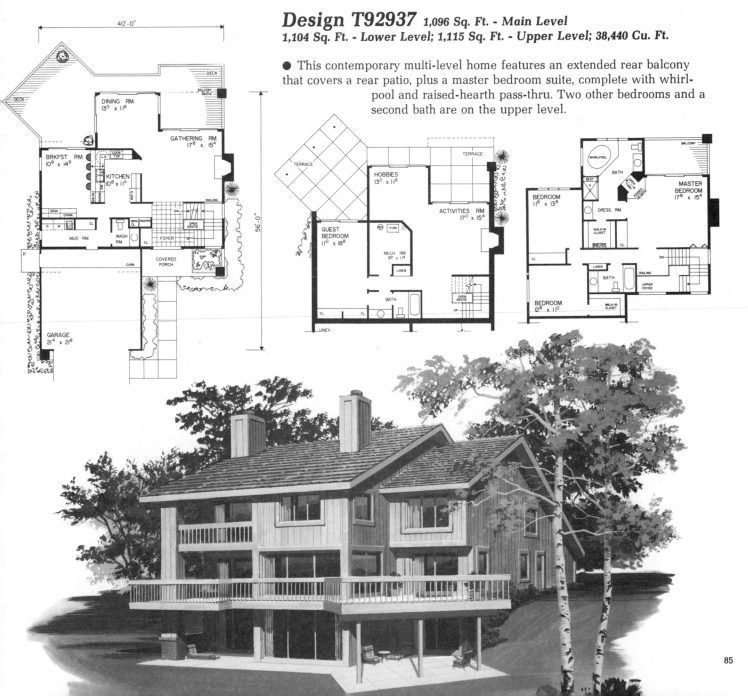

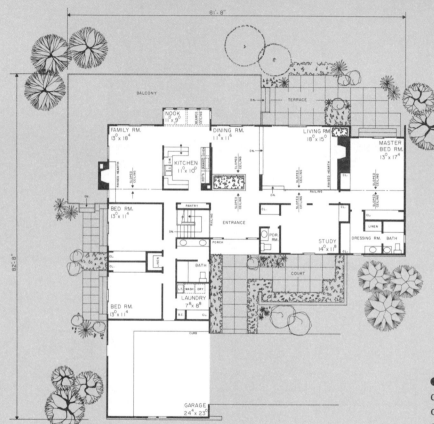

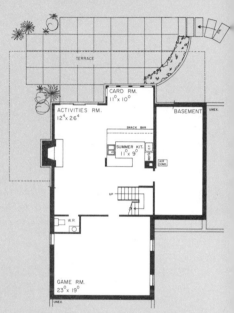

Design T92502
2,606 Sq. Ft. - Main Level
1,243 Sq. Ft. - Lower Level; 45,000 Cu. Ft.

● A home with two faces. From the street this design gives all the appearances of being a one-story, L-shaped home. One can only guess at the character of the rear elevation as dictated by the sloping terrain. A study of the interior of this design reveals a tremendous convenient living potential.

Design T92504
1,918 Sq. Ft. - Main Level
1,910 Sq. Ft. - Lower Level; 39,800 Cu. Ft.

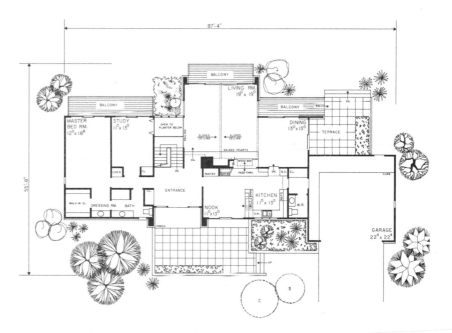

● Taking advantage of that sloping site can result in the opening up of a lower level which can double the available living area. Such has been the case in this hillside design. Study the interior carefully. This design offers tremendous living potential to the active family.

LAUNDRY
8⁰ x 12⁸

FAMILY RM.
18⁰ x 22⁴
BEAMED CEILING

SNACK BAR

BATH

TERRACE

BALCONY ABOVE

UP

DN.

UNEXCAVATED

GARAGE
26⁴ x 22⁰

76'-0"

12'-0"

64'-0"

32'-10"

48'-0"

11'-7"

TERRACE

BALCONY

SOLARIUM
11⁸ x 18⁰

DINING RM.
14⁰ x 12⁴ + BAY

KITCHEN
11⁰ x 15²
WORK ISLAND

BRKFST. RM.
10⁴ x 15²

WALK-IN CL.

DRESSING RM.

BATH

BATH

MASTER BED RM.
19⁰ x 15⁴

BED RM.
12⁸ x 10⁶

SHELVES

STOR.

B-B-Q

RANGE

OVENS

PANTRY

BUFFET CHINA

FOYER

PDR. RM.

LIVING RM.
23⁴ x 15⁶ + BAY

COVERED PORCH

BED RM.
13⁶ x 12⁸

BED RM.
13⁶ x 16⁰

ROOF

Design T92254
1,220 Sq. Ft. - Main Level; 1,344 Sq. Ft. - Upper Level
659 Sq. Ft. - Lower Level; 56,706 Cu. Ft.

Design T92847 1,874 Sq. Ft. - Main Level
1,131 Sq. Ft. - Lower Level; 44,305 Cu. Ft.

● This is an exquisitely styled Tudor, hillside design, ready to serve its happy occupants for many years. The contrasting use of material surely makes the exterior eye-catching.

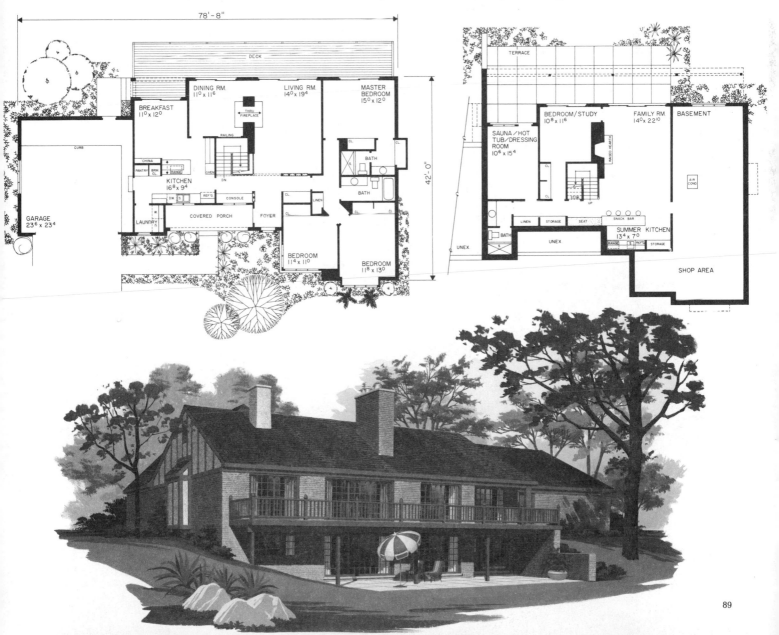

Design T92761
1,242 Sq. Ft. - *Main Level*
1,242 Sq. Ft. - *Lower Level*; 25,045 Cu. Ft.

● Here is another one-story that doubles its livability by exposing the lowest level at the rear. Formal living on the main level and informal living, the activity room and study, on the lower level. Observe the wonderful outdoor living facilities. The deck acts as a cover for the terrace.

Lower Level Plan:

TERRACE

ACTIVITIES RM. 14⁰ x 17⁶

STUDY 15¹⁰ x 10⁰

BED RM. 10¹⁰ x 13¹⁰

STORAGE

BED RM. 11² x 12⁸

LINEN

BATH

VANITY

MECH. RM.

AIR COND.

WALK IN CLOSET

UNEX.

Main Level Plan:

50'-0"

DECK

LIVING RM. 14⁴ x 17⁶

DINING RM. 10⁰ x 10⁰

NOOK 8⁸ x 10⁰

BALCONY

MASTER BED RM. 11⁸ x 15⁰

RAILING

KITCHEN 12⁰ x 13⁰

BATH

ENTRY

WASH RM.

OVEN RANGE

SERVICE ENTRANCE

LAUNDRY

PORCH

CURB

GARAGE 21⁴ x 21⁸

STORAGE

52'-0"

● Four bedrooms! Or three plus a study, it's your choice. A fireplace in the study/bedroom guarantees a cozy atmosphere. The warmth of a fireplace also will be enjoyed in the gathering room and activities room. Lots of living space, too. An exceptionally large gathering room with sliding glass doors that open onto the main terrace to enjoy the scenic outdoors. A formal dining room, too. And a kitchen that promises to turn a novice cook into a pro. Check out the counter space, the pantry and the island range. This house is designed to make living pleasant.

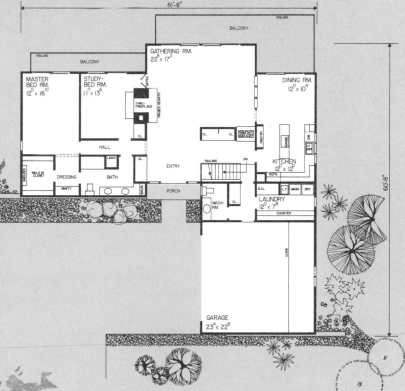

Design T92583 1,838 Sq. Ft. - Main Level
1,558 Sq. Ft. - Lower Level; 29,400 Cu. Ft.

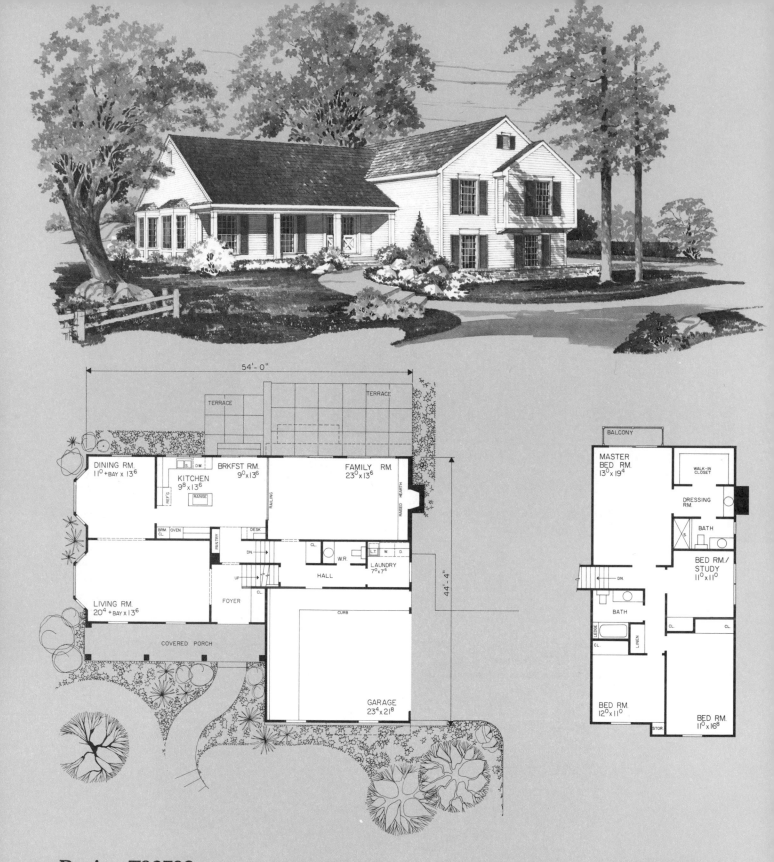

Design T92786 *871 Sq. Ft. - Main Level; 1,132 Sq. Ft. - Upper Level; 528 Sq. Ft. - Lower Level; 44,000 Cu. Ft.*

● A bay window in each the formal living room and dining room. A great interior and exterior design feature to attract attention to this tri-level home. The exterior also is enhanced by a covered front porch to further the Colonial charm. The interior livability is outstanding, too. An abundance of built-ins in the kitchen create an efficient work center. Features include an island range, pantry, broom closet, desk and breakfast room with sliding glass doors to the rear terrace. The lower level houses the informal family room, wash room and laundry. Further access is available to the outdoors by the family room to the terrace and laundry room to the side yard.

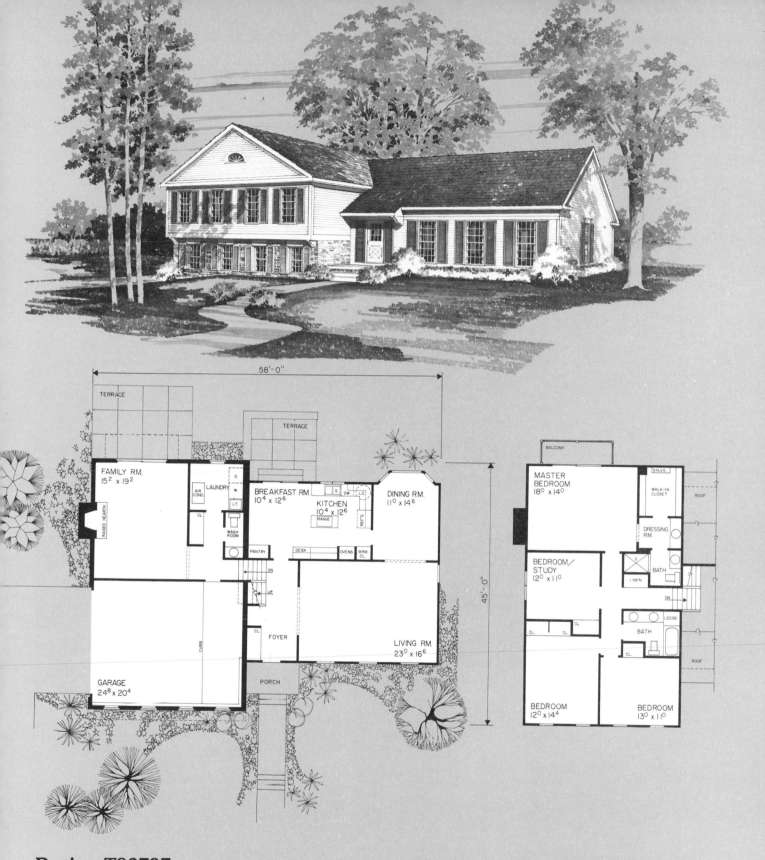

Design T92787
976 Sq. Ft. - Main Level; 1,118 Sq. Ft. - Upper Level; 524 Sq. Ft. - Lower Level; 36,110 Cu. Ft.

● Three level living! Main, upper and lower levels to serve you and your family with great ease. Start from the bottom and work your way up. Family room with raised hearth fireplace, laundry and washroom on the lower level. Formal living and dining rooms, kitchen and breakfast room on the main level. Stop and take note at the efficiency of the kitchen with its many outstanding extras. The upper level houses the three bedrooms, study (or fourth bedroom if you prefer) and two baths. This design has really stacked up its livability to serve its occupants to their best advantage. This design has great interior livability and exterior charm.

A Lifetime of Exciting, Contemporary Living Patterns

● Here is a home for those with a bold, contemporary living bent. The exciting exteriors give notice of an admirable flair for something delightfully different. The varying roof planes and textured blank wall masses are distinctive. Two sets of panelled front doors permit access to either level. The inclined ramp to the upper main level is dramatic, indeed. The rear exterior highlights a veritable battery of projecting balconies. This affords direct access to outdoor living for each of the major rooms in the house. Certainly an invaluable feature should your view be particularly noteworthy. Notice two covered outdoor balconies plus a covered terrace. Indoor-outdoor living at its greatest.

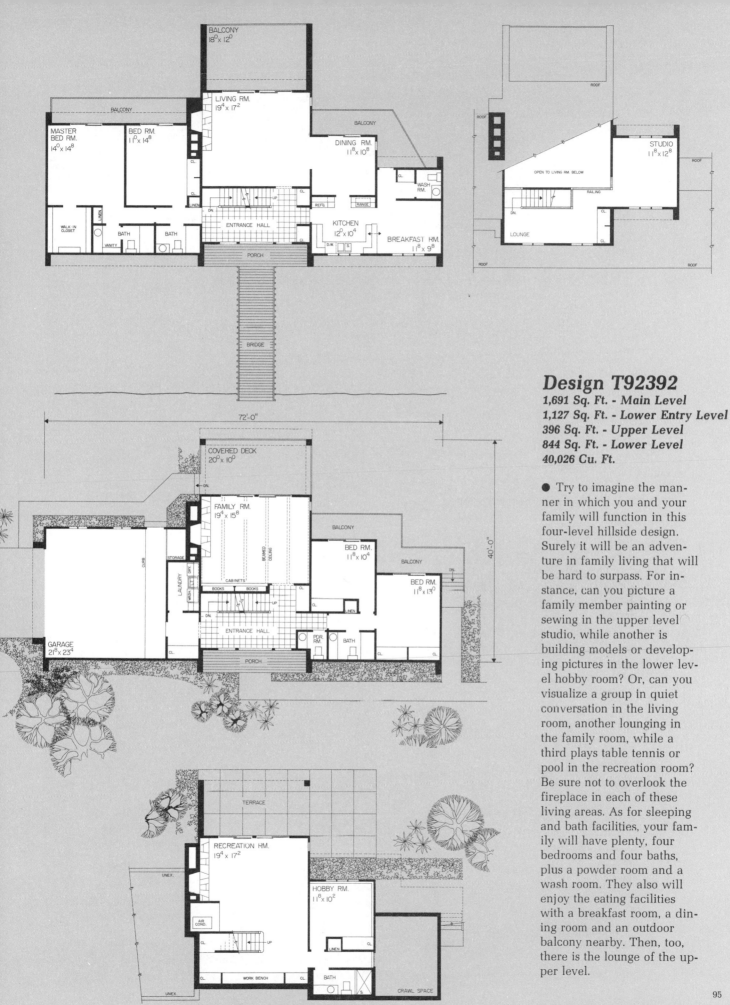

BALCONY
18⁰ x 12⁰

LIVING RM.
19⁴ x 17²

BALCONY

BALCONY

DINING RM.
11⁸ x 10⁸

WASH RM.

MASTER BED RM.
14⁰ x 14⁸

BED RM.
11⁰ x 14⁸

CL

CL

CL

REFG.

RANGE

UP

DN

LINEN

ENTRANCE HALL

KITCHEN
12⁰ x 10⁴

WALK IN CLOSET

LINEN

BATH

BATH

VANITY

PORCH

CL

D.W.

S

BREAKFAST RM.
11⁸ x 9⁸

BRIDGE

ROOF

ROOF

ROOF

ROOF

ROOF

STUDIO
11⁸ x 12⁸

OPEN TO LIVING RM. BELOW

RAILING

DN.

LOUNGE

CL

CL

72'-0"

40'-0"

COVERED DECK
20⁰ x 10⁰

DN.

FAMILY RM.
19⁴ x 15⁸

BALCONY

BALCONY

BED RM.
11⁸ x 10⁴

BED RM.
11⁸ x 13⁰

CURB

STORAGE

LAUNDRY

WASH

DRY.

BEAMED CEILING

CABINETS

BOOKS

BOOKS

UP

DN.

CL

LINEN

CL

DN.

ENTRANCE HALL

GARAGE
21⁸ x 23⁴

CL

PDR. RM.

BATH

CL

CL

PORCH

TERRACE

RECREATION RM.
19⁴ x 17²

UNEX.

AIR COND.

HOBBY RM.
11⁸ x 10²

UP

LINEN

CL

CL

WORK BENCH

CL

BATH

S

UNEX.

CRAWL SPACE

Design T92392

1,691 Sq. Ft. - Main Level
1,127 Sq. Ft. - Lower Entry Level
396 Sq. Ft. - Upper Level
844 Sq. Ft. - Lower Level
40,026 Cu. Ft.

● Try to imagine the manner in which you and your family will function in this four-level hillside design. Surely it will be an adventure in family living that will be hard to surpass. For instance, can you picture a family member painting or sewing in the upper level studio, while another is building models or developing pictures in the lower level hobby room? Or, can you visualize a group in quiet conversation in the living room, another lounging in the family room, while a third plays table tennis or pool in the recreation room? Be sure not to overlook the fireplace in each of these living areas. As for sleeping and bath facilities, your family will have plenty, four bedrooms and four baths, plus a powder room and a wash room. They also will enjoy the eating facilities with a breakfast room, a dining room and an outdoor balcony nearby. Then, too, there is the lounge of the upper level.

Design T91974 1,680 Sq. Ft. - Upper Level; 1,344 Sq. Ft. - Lower Level; 34,186 Cu.Ft.

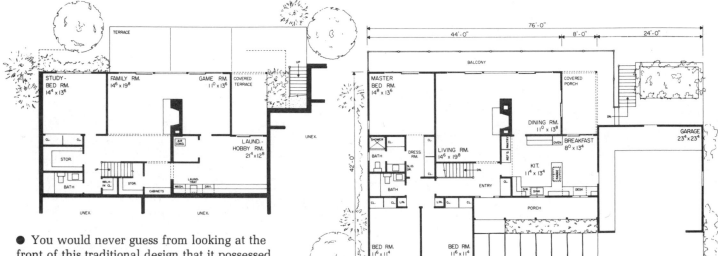

● You would never guess from looking at the front of this traditional design that it possessed such a strikingly different rear. From the front, you would guess that all of its livability is on one floor. Yet, just imagine the tremendous amount of livability that is added to the plan as a result of exposing the lower level – 1,344 square feet of it. Living in this hillside house will mean fun. Obviously, most popular spot will be the balcony.

Design T92218   889 Sq. Ft. - Main Level; 960 Sq. Ft. - Upper Level; 936 Sq. Ft. - Lower Level; 33,865 Cu. Ft.

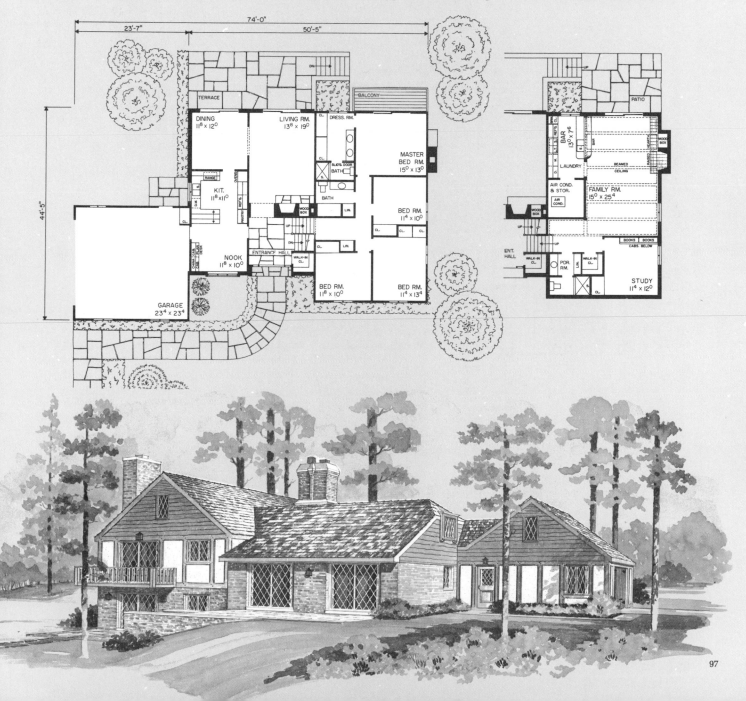

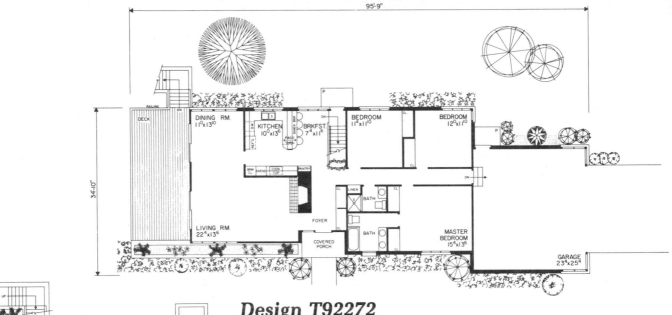

Design T92272
1,731 Sq. Ft. - Main Level
672 Sq. Ft. - Lower Level; 27,802 Cu. Ft.

● Certainly not a huge house. But one, nevertheless, that is long on livability and one that surely will be fun to live in. With its wide-overhanging hip roof, this unadorned facade is the picture of simplicity. As such, it has a quiet appeal all its own. The living-dining area is one of the focal points of the plan. It is wonderfully spacious. The large glass areas and the accessibility, through sliding glass doors, of the outdoor balcony are fine features. For recreation, there is the lower level area which opens onto a large terrace covered by the balcony above.

**(Multi-Level Homes
continued on pg. 237)**

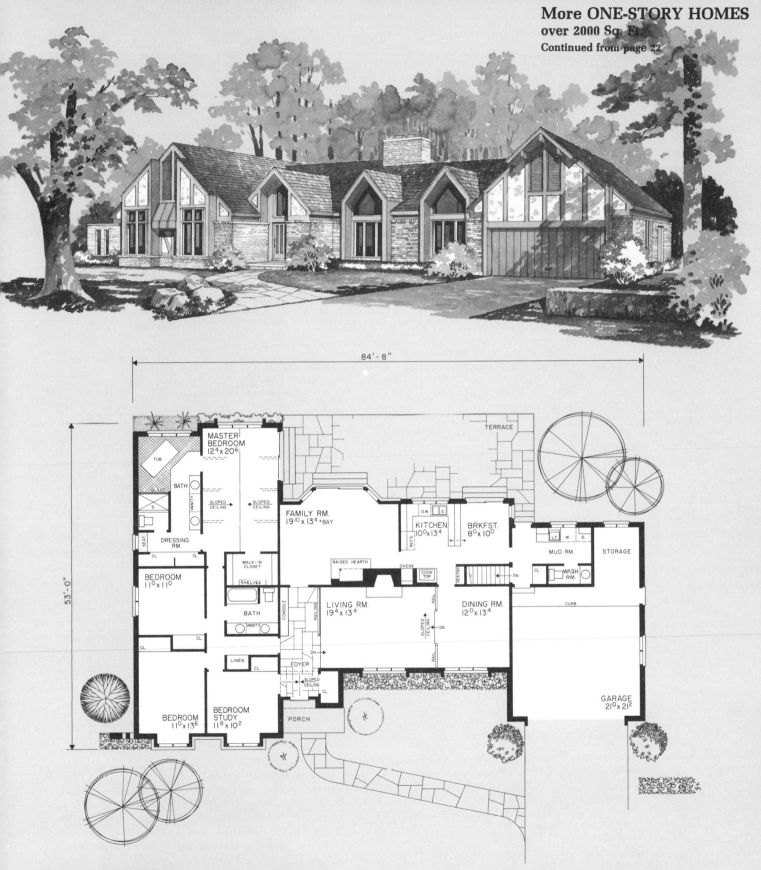

Design T92877 2,612 Sq. Ft.; 67,175 Cu. Ft.

● Here's a dramatic, Post-Modern exterior with a popular plan featuring an outstanding master bedroom suite. The bedroom itself is spacious, has a sloped ceiling, a large walk-in closet and sliding glass doors to the terrace. Now ex-

amine the bath and dressing area. Two large closets, twin vanities, built-in seat and a dramatically presented corner tub are present. The tub will be a great place to spend the evening hours after a long, hard day. Along with this bed-

room, there are three more served by a full bath. The living area of this plan has the formal areas in the front and the informal areas in the rear. Both have a fireplace. The spacious work center is efficiently planned.

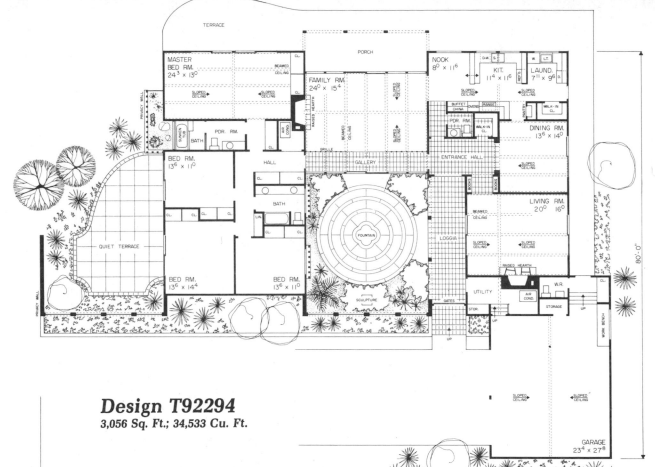

Design T92294
3,056 Sq. Ft.; 34,533 Cu. Ft.

● Here is a western ranch with an authentic Spanish flavor. Striking a note of distinction, the arched privacy walls provide a fine backdrop for the long, raised planter. The low-pitched roof features tile and has a wide overhang with exposed rafter tails. The interior is wonderfully zoned. The all-purpose family room is flanked by the sleeping wing and the living wing. Study each area carefully for the planning is excellent and the features are many. Indoor-outdoor integration is outstanding. At left – the spacious interior court. The covered passage to the double front doors is dramatic, indeed.

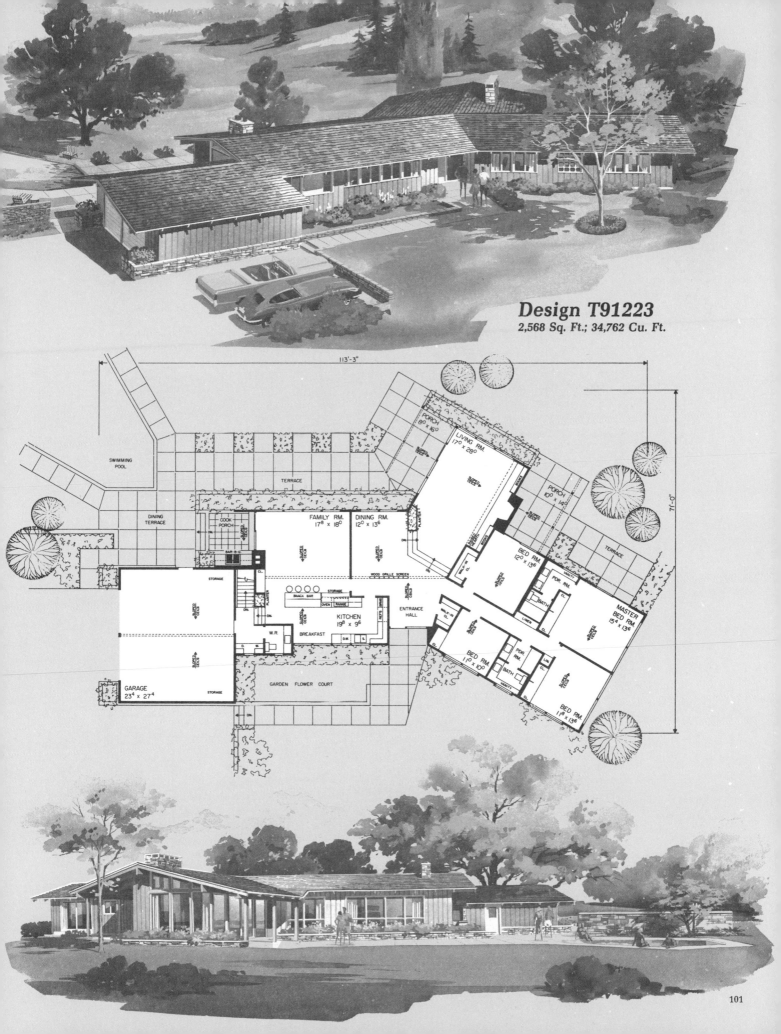

Design T91223

2,568 Sq. Ft.; 34,762 Cu. Ft.

113'-3"

71'-0"

SWIMMING POOL

TERRACE

DINING TERRACE

COOK PORCH

FAMILY RM.
17⁸ x 18⁰

DINING RM.
12⁰ x 13⁶

PORCH
18⁰ x 16⁰

LIVING RM.
17⁰ x 28⁰

PORCH
10⁰ x 14⁰

TERRACE

STORAGE

GARAGE
23⁴ x 27⁴

STORAGE

KITCHEN
19⁸ x 9⁶

BREAKFAST

SNACK BAR

OVEN | RANGE

STORAGE

W.R.

D.W.

ENTRANCE HALL

WOOD GRILLE SCREEN

BED RM.
12⁰ x 13⁶

PDR. RM.

BATH

LINEN

MASTER BED RM.
15⁴ x 13⁶

BED RM.
11⁰ x 10⁰

PDR. RM.

BATH

LIN.

VANITY

BED RM.
11⁸ x 13⁶

GARDEN FLOWER COURT

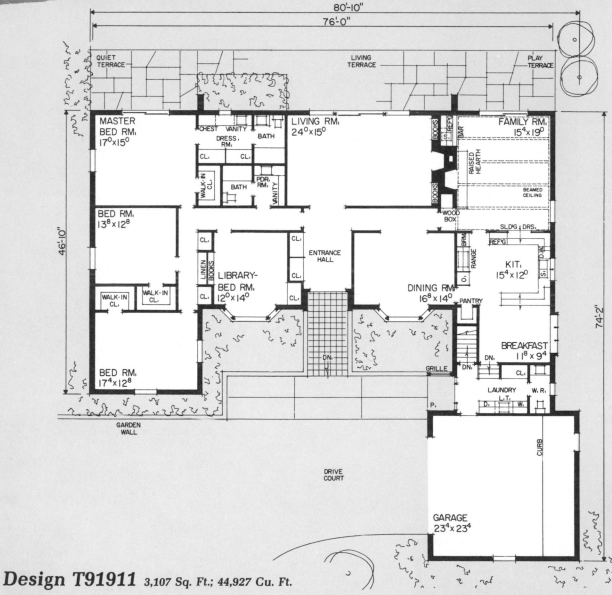

80'-10"

76'-0"

QUIET TERRACE

LIVING TERRACE

PLAY TERRACE

MASTER BED RM. 17⁰x15⁰

CHEST VANITY

DRESS. RM.

BATH

LIVING RM. 24⁰x15⁰

BOOKS

REF'G S.

BAR

FAMILY RM. 15⁴x19⁰

CL.

CL.

WALK-IN CL.

BATH

PDR. RM.

VANITY

RAISED HEARTH

BEAMED CEILING

BED RM. 13⁸x12⁸

BOOKS

WOOD BOX

SLD'G DRS.

REF'G

D.W.

46'-10"

CL.

LINEN

BOOKS

CL.

LIBRARY- BED RM. 12⁰x14⁰

CL.

CL.

CL.

ENTRANCE HALL

BRM

RANGE

O.

DINING RM. 16⁸x14⁰

KIT. 15⁴x12⁰

S.

74'-2"

WALK-IN CL.

WALK-IN CL.

PANTRY

DN.

DN.

BREAKFAST 11⁸x9⁴

BED RM. 17⁴x12⁸

DN.

GRILLE

CL.

LAUNDRY

W. R.

GARDEN WALL

D.

L.T.

W.

P.

CURB

DRIVE COURT

GARAGE 23⁴x23⁴

Design T91911 3,107 Sq. Ft.; 44,927 Cu. Ft.

● For luxurious, country-estate living it would be difficult to beat the livability offered by this impressive traditional design. To begin with, its exterior appeal is, indeed, gracious. Its floor plan highlights plenty of space, excellent room arrangements, fine traffic circulation and an abundance of convenient living features. It can function as either a three or four bedroom home. Either way, this is an outstanding one-story home.

Design T92768 *3,436 Sq. Ft.; 65,450 Cu. Ft.*

● Besides its elegant traditionally styled exterior with its delightfully long covered front porch, this home has an exceptionally livable interior. There is the outstanding four bedroom and two-bath sleeping wing. Note the extras in the master bedroom. Then, the effi-

cient front kitchen with island range flanked by the formal dining room and the informal breakfast nook. Separated by the two-way, thru fireplace are the living and family rooms which look out on the rear yard. Worthy of particular note is the development of a potential

live-in relative facility which is secluded for privacy. These two rooms would also serve the large family well as a hobby room and library or additional bedrooms. A full bath is adjacent as well as the laundry, basement stairs and service entrance.

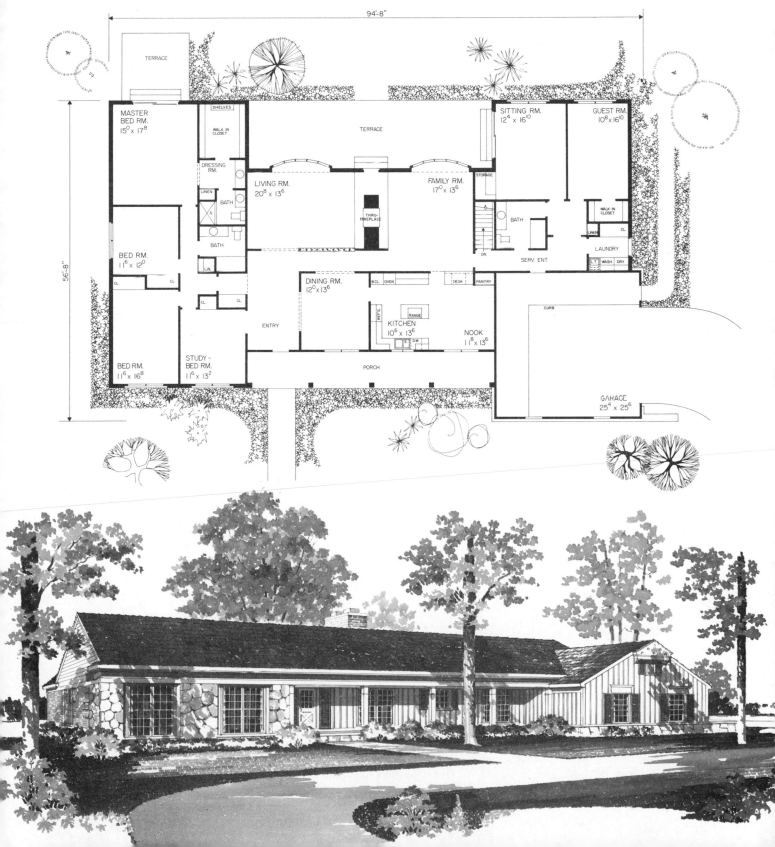

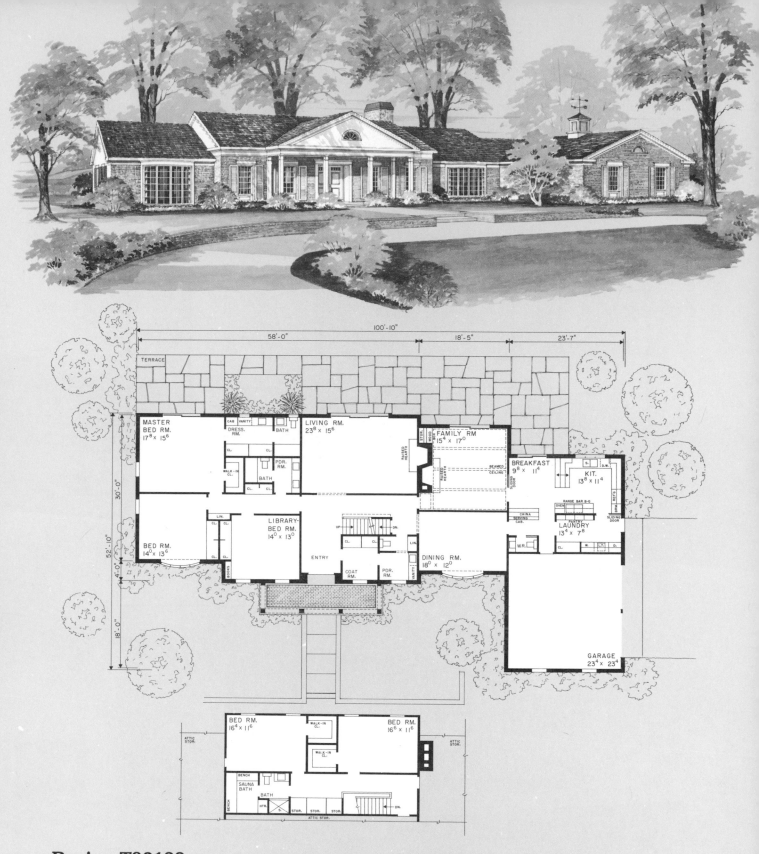

Design T92133 *3,024 Sq. Ft. - First Floor; 826 Sq. Ft. - Second Floor; 54,883 Cu. Ft.*

● A country-estate home which will command all the attention it truly deserves. The projecting pediment gable supported by the finely proportioned columns lends an aura of elegance. The window treatment, the front door detailing, the massive, capped chimney, the cupola, the brick veneer exterior, and the varying roof planes complete the characterization of an impressive home. Inside, there are 3,024 square feet on the first floor. In addition, there is a two bedroom second floor should its development be necessary. However, whether called upon to function as one, or 1-½ story home it will provide a lifetime of gracious living. Don't overlook the compartment baths, the big library, the coat room, the beamed ceiling family room, the two fireplaces.

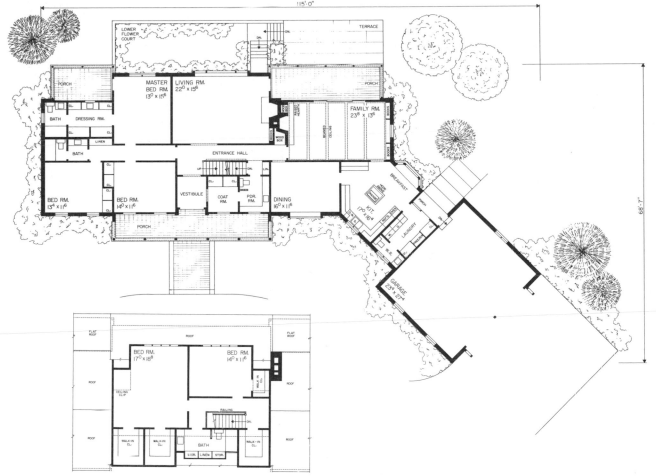

Design T91711 *2,580 Sq. Ft. - First Floor; 938 Sq. Ft. - Second Floor; 46,788 Cu. Ft.*

● If the gracious charm of the Colonial South appeals to you, this may be just the house you've been waiting for. There is something solid and dependable in its well-balanced facade and wide, pillared front porch. Much of the interest generated by this design comes from its interesting expanses of roof and angular projection of its kitchen and garage. The feeling of elegance is further experienced upon stepping inside, through double doors, to the spacious entrance hall where there is the separate coat room. Adjacent to this is the powder room, also convenient from the living areas. Work area of kitchen and laundry room is truly outstanding. Designed as a five bedroom house, each is large. Storage and bath facilities are excellent. Truly, an unforgettable family home!

Design T92756 2,652 Sq. Ft.; 51,540 Cu. Ft.

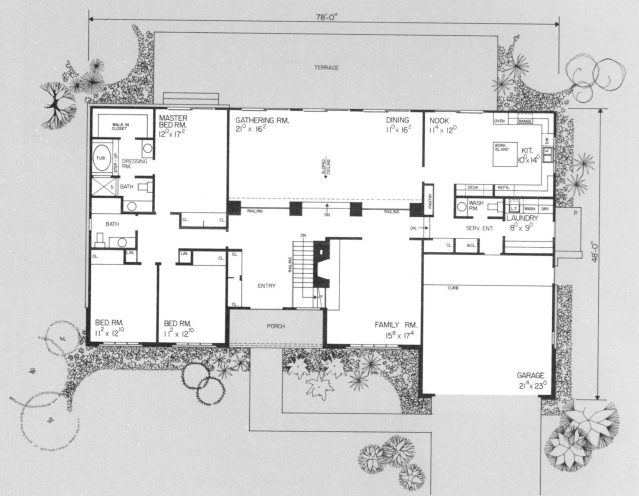

● This one-story contemporary is bound to serve your family well. With its many fine features it will assure the best in contemporary living. Notice the bath with tub and stall shower, dressing room and walk-in closet featured with the master bed-room. Two more family bedrooms. The sunken gathering room/dining room is highlighted by the sloped ceiling and sliding glass doors to the large rear terrace. This formal area is a full 32' x 16'. Imagine the great furniture placement that can be done in this area. In addition to the gathering room, there is an informal family room with fireplace. You will enjoy the efficient kitchen and get much use out of the work island, pantry and built-in desk. Note the service entrance with bath and laundry.

Design T92765 3,365 Sq. Ft.; 59,820 Cu. Ft.

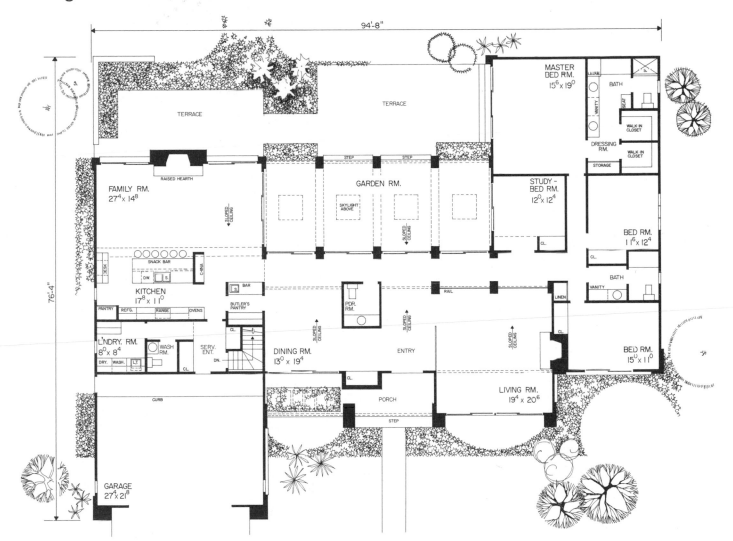

● This three (optional four) bedroom contemporary is a most appealing design. It offers living patterns that will add new dimensions to your everyday routine. The sloped ceilings in the family room, dining room and living room add much spaciousness to this home.

The efficient kitchen has many fine features including the island snack bar and work center, built-in desk, china cabinet and wet bar. Adjacent to the kitchen is a laundry room, washroom and stairs to the basement. Formal and informal living will each have its own

area. A raised hearth fireplace and sliding glass doors to the rear terrace are in the informal family room. Another fireplace is in the front formal living room. You will enjoy all that natural light in the garden room from the skylights in the sloped ceiling.

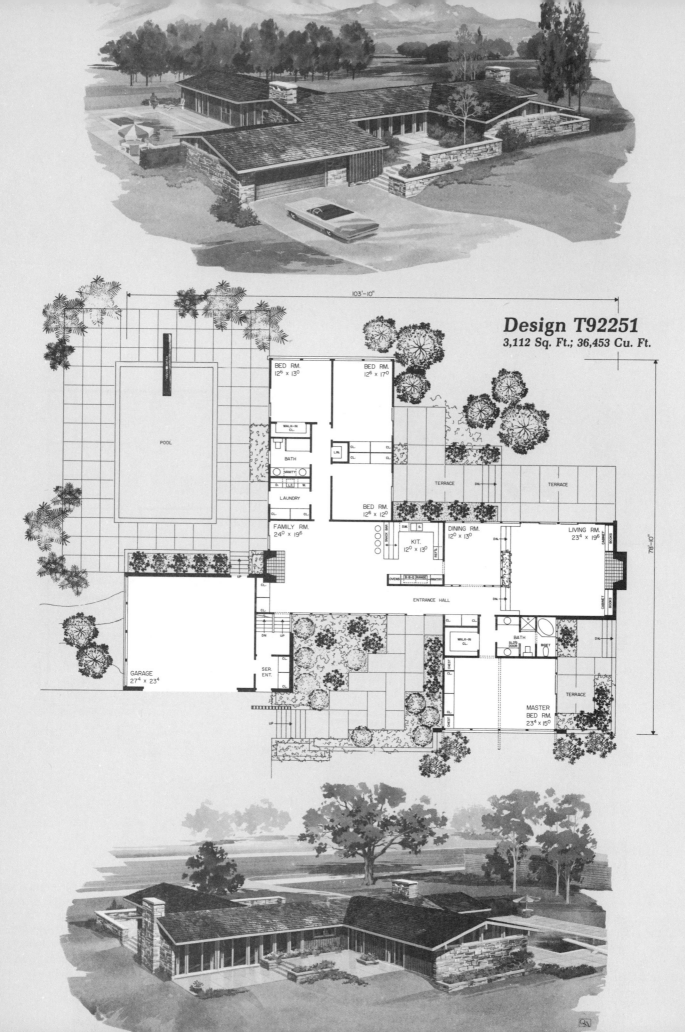

Design T92251
3,112 Sq. Ft.; 36,453 Cu. Ft.

103'-10"

78'-10"

POOL

BED RM.
12⁶ x 13⁰

BED RM.
12⁶ x 17⁰

WALK-IN CL.

BATH

VANITY

LAUNDRY

FAMILY RM.
24⁴ x 19⁶

CL.

CL.

CL.

L.IN.

CL.

CL.

BED RM.
12⁶ x 12⁰

TERRACE

DN.

TERRACE

DINING RM.
12⁰ x 13⁰

KIT.
12⁰ x 13⁰

SNACK BAR

OVENS

RANGE

PANTRY

LIVING RM.
23⁴ x 19⁶

CABINET

BOOKS

ENTRANCE HALL

DN.

DN.

GARAGE
27⁴ x 23⁴

UP

DN

UP

SER.
ENT.

CL.

CL.

WALK-IN CL.

CHEST

CHEST

CL.

SLDG.
DOOR

BATH

BIDET

DN.

TERRACE

MASTER
BED RM.
23⁴ x 15⁰

UP

108

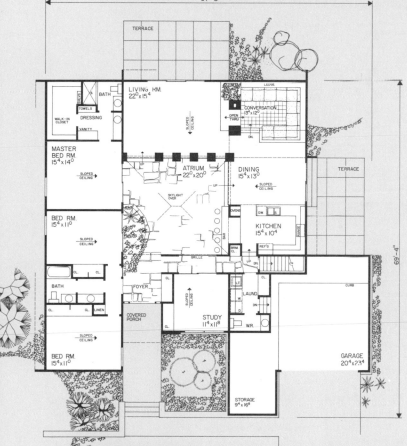

Design T92832
2,805 Sq. Ft. - Excluding Atrium
52,235 Cu. Ft.

● The advantage of passive solar heating is a significant highlight of this contemporary design. The huge skylight over the atrium provides shelter during inclement weather, while permitting the enjoyment of plenty of natural light to the atrium below and surrounding areas. Whether open to the sky, or sheltered by a glass or translucent covering, the atrium becomes a cheerful spot and provides an abundance of natural light to its adjacent rooms. The stone floor will absorb an abundance of heat from the sun during the day and permit circulation of warm air to other areas at night. During the summer, shades afford protection from the sun without sacrificing the abundance of natural light and the feeling of spaciousness. Sloping ceilings highlight each of the major rooms, three bedrooms, formal living and dining and study. The conversation area between the two formal areas will really be something to talk about. The broad expanses of roof can accommodate solar panels should an active system be desired to supplement the passive features of this design.

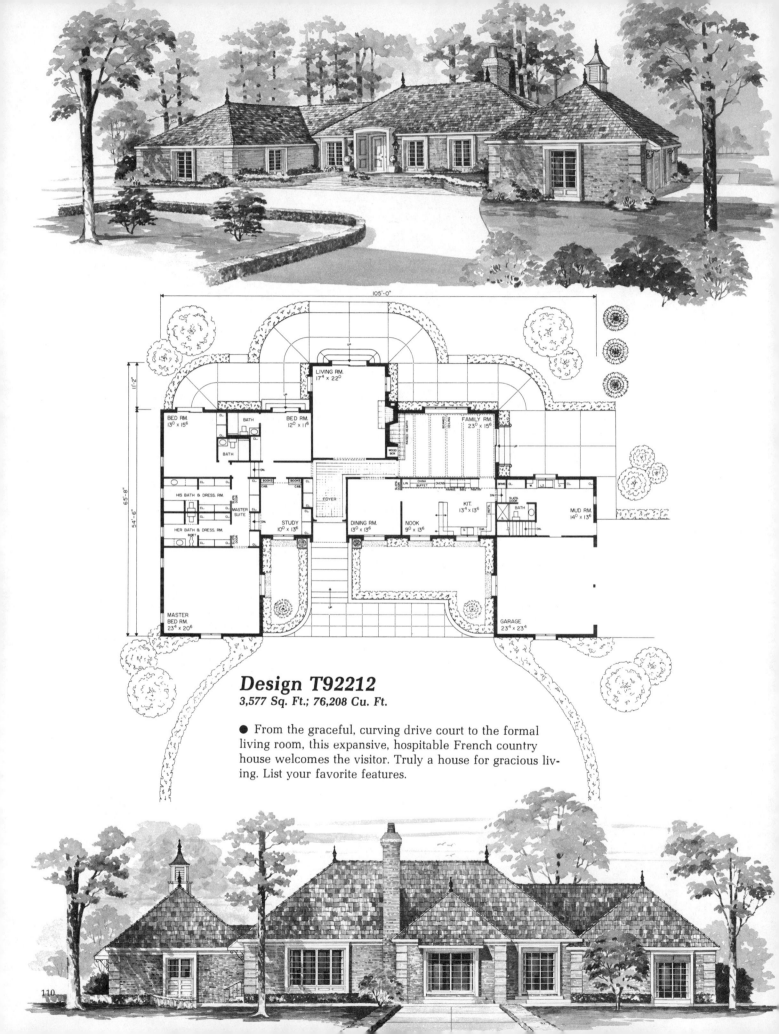

Design T92212
3,577 Sq. Ft.; 76,208 Cu. Ft.

● From the graceful, curving drive court to the formal living room, this expansive, hospitable French country house welcomes the visitor. Truly a house for gracious living. List your favorite features.

Design T92693
3,462 Sq. Ft.; 79,982 Cu. Ft.

● This elegant Georgian manor is reminiscent of historic Rose Hill, built 1818 in Lexington, Kentucky. It is typical of the classic manors with Greek Revival features built in Kentucky as the 19th Century dawned. Note the classical portico of four Ionic columns plus the fine proportions. Also noteworthy is the updated interior, highlighted by a large country kitchen with fireplace and an efficient work center that includes an island cooktop. The country kitchen leads directly into a front formal dining room, just off the foyer. On the other side of the foyer is a front living room. A large library is located in the back of the house. It features built-in bookcases plus a fireplace, one of four fireplaces.

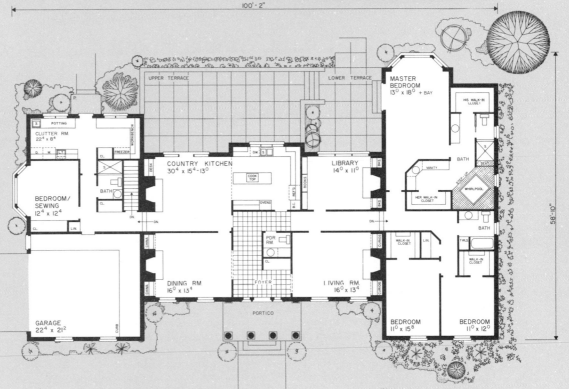

Clutter Room, Media Room To The Fore

Design T92915 2,758 Sq. Ft.; 60,850 Cu. Ft.

● The features of this appealing contemporary design go far beyond the clutter and media rooms. The country kitchen is spacious and caters to the family's informal living and dining activities. While it overlooks the rear yard it is just a step from the delightful greenhouse. Many happy hours will be spent here enjoying to the fullest the outdoors from within. The size of the greenhouse is 8'x18' and contains 149 sq. ft. not included in the square footage quoted above. The formal living and dining areas feature spacious open planning. Sloping ceiling in the living room, plus the sliding glass doors to the outdoor terrace enhance the cheerfulness of this area. The foyer is large and routes traffic efficiently to all areas. Guest coat closets and a powder room are handy. The sleeping zone is well-planned. Two children's bedrooms have fine wall space, good wardrobe facilities and a full bath. The master bedroom is exceptional. It is large enough to accommodate a sitting area and has access to the terrace. Two walk-in closets, a vanity area with lavatory and a compartmented bath are noteworthy features. Observe the stall shower in addition to the dramatic whirlpool installation.

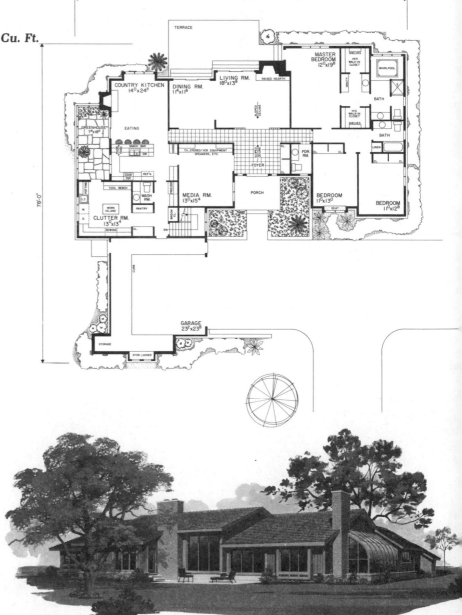

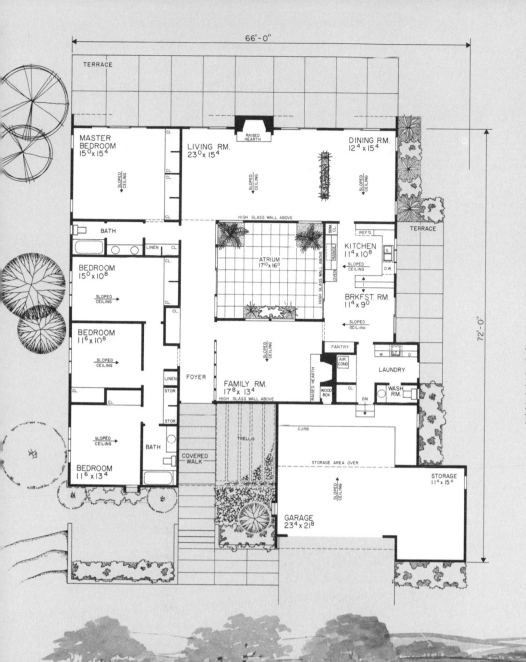

66'-0"

TERRACE

MASTER BEDROOM
15⁰ x 15⁴
SLOPED CEILING

LIVING RM.
23⁰ x 15⁴
SLOPED CEILING

RAISED HEARTH

DINING RM.
12⁴ x 15⁴
SLOPED CEILING

CL.
CL.
CL.
CL.

BATH

LINEN
CL.

HIGH GLASS WALL ABOVE

TERRACE

BEDROOM
15⁰ x 10⁸
SLOPED CEILING

CL.

ATRIUM
17¹⁰ x 16⁰

KITCHEN
11⁴ x 10⁸
SLOPED CEILING

REF'G
RANGE
OVEN
BRM. CL.
S.
D.W.

BEDROOM
11⁶ x 10⁸
SLOPED CEILING

CL.

HIGH GLASS WALL ABOVE

BRKFST. RM.
11⁴ x 9⁰
SLOPED CEILING

CL.
LINEN
STOR.
STOR.

FOYER

SLOPED CEILING

FAMILY RM.
17⁸ x 13⁴

PANTRY
AIR COND.

WOOD BOX
RAISED HEARTH
CL.

LAUNDRY
W L D

WASH. RM.

DN

BEDROOM
11⁶ x 13⁴
SLOPED CEILING

BATH

COVERED WALK

TRELLIS

HIGH GLASS WALL ABOVE

CURB

STORAGE AREA OVER

STORAGE
11⁴ x 15⁴

SLOPED CEILING

GARAGE
23⁴ x 21⁸

72'-0"

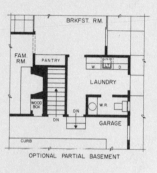

BRKFST. RM.

FAM. RM.

PANTRY

WOOD BOX
DN

DN

LAUNDRY
W L D
W.R.

GARAGE

CURB

OPTIONAL PARTIAL BASEMENT

Design T92135
2,495 Sq. Ft. - Excluding Atrium
28,928 Cu. Ft.

● For those seeking a new experience in home ownership. The proud occupants of this contemporary home will forever be thrilled at their choice of such a distinguished exterior and such a practical and exciting floor plan. The variety of shed roof planes contrast dramatically with the simplicity of the vertical siding. Inside there is a feeling of spaciousness resulting from the sloping ceilings. The uniqueness of this design is further enhanced by the atrium. Open to the sky, this outdoor area, indoors, can be enjoyed from all parts of the house. The sleeping zone has four bedrooms, two baths and plenty of closets. The informal living zone has a fine kitchen and breakfast room. The formal zone consists of a large living-dining area with fireplace.

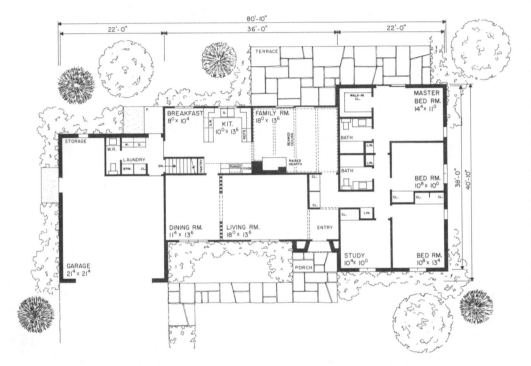

Design T92129
2,057 Sq. Ft.; 36,970 Cu. Ft.

● This four bedroom home is zoned for convenient living. The sleeping area, with its two full baths and plenty of closets, will have a lot of privacy. The formal living and dining rooms function together and may be completely by-passed when desired. The informal living areas are grouped together and overlook the rear yard. The family room with its beamed ceiling is but a step from the kitchen. The U-shaped kitchen is handy to both the breakfast and dining rooms.

Design T92851
2,739 Sq. Ft.; 55,810 Cu. Ft.

● This spacious one-story has a classic Country French hip roof. The front entrance creates a charming entry. Beyond the covered porch is an octagonal foyer. A closet, shelves and powder room are contained in the foyer. All of the living areas overlook the rear yard. Sliding glass doors open each of these areas to the rear terrace. Their features include a fireplace in the living room, skylight in the dining room and a second set of sliding glass doors in the family room leading to a covered porch.

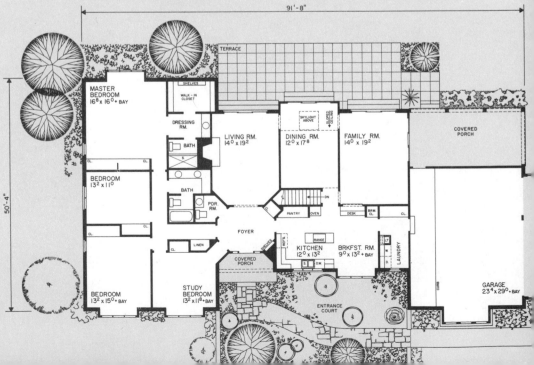

Design T92378
2,580 Sq. Ft.; 49,792 Cu. Ft.

● If yours is a preference for an exterior that exudes both warmth and formality, the styling of English Tudor may suit your fancy. A host of architectural features blend together to produce this delightfully appealing exterior. Notice the interesting use of contrasting exterior materials. Don't overlook the two stylish chimneys. The manner in which the interior functions to provide the fine living patterns is outstanding. Each of four main rooms — look out on the rear terrace.

Design T92318

2,029 Sq. Ft.; 31,021 Cu. Ft.

● Warmth and charm are characteristics of the Tudor adaptations. This modest sized home, with its twin front-facing gabled roofs, represents a great investment. While it will be an exciting and refreshing addition to any neighborhood, its appeal will never grow old. Study the plan carefully. It has much to offer with its sunken living room, formal dining room, and beamed ceiling family room. Notice the two fireplaces, plus the mud room and washroom.

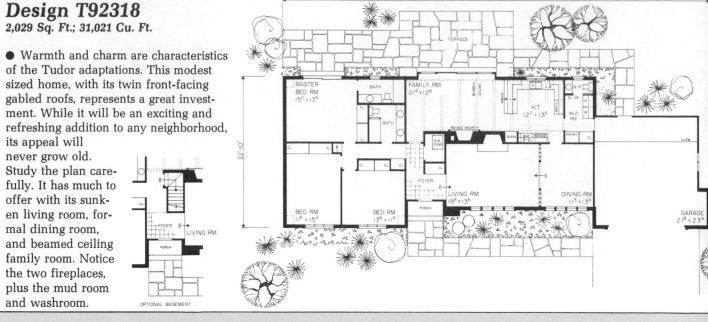

Design T92785

2,375 Sq. Ft.; 47,805 Cu. Ft.

● Exceptional Tudor design! Passersby will surely take a second glance at this fine home wherever it may be located. And the interior is just as pleasing. As one enters the foyer and looks around, the plan will speak for itself in the areas of convenience and efficiency. There is a hall leading to each of the three bedrooms and study of the sleeping wing and another leading to the living room, family room, kitchen and laundry. The formal dining room can be entered from both the foyer and the kitchen. Efficiency will be the by-word when describing the kitchen. Note the fine features: a built-in desk, pantry, island snack bar with sink and pass-thru to the family room.

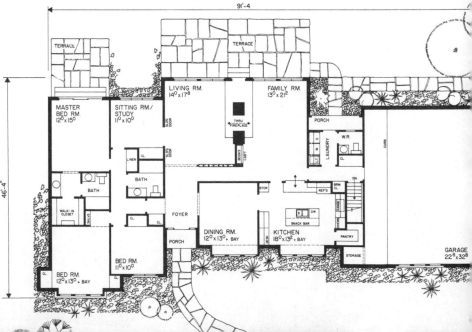

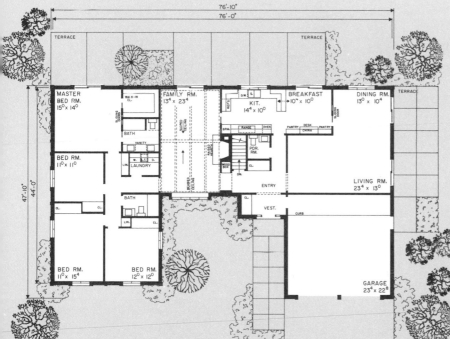

Design T92142
2,450 Sq. Ft.; 43,418 Cu. Ft.

● Adaptations of Old England have become increasingly popular in today's building scene. And little wonder, for many of these homes when well-designed have a very distinctive charm. Here is certainly a home which will be like no other in its neighborhood. Its very shape adds an extra measure of uniqueness. And inside, there is all the livability the exterior seems to foretell. The sleeping wing has four bedrooms, two full baths, and the laundry room – just where the soiled linen originates. The location of the family room is an excellent one. For with children there is usually traffic between family room and bedrooms. The spacious formal living and dining area will enjoy its privacy and be great fun to furnish.

Design T92766
2,711 Sq. Ft.; 59,240 Cu. Ft.

● A sizeable master bedroom with a dressing area featuring two walk-in closets, a twin lavatory and compartmented bath. Two-bedroom children's area with full bath and supporting study. Formal living and dining zone separated by a thru-fireplace. A spacious kitchen-nook with a cheerfully informal sun room just a step away through sliding glass doors. The service area has a laundry, storage, washroom and stairs to basement. An array of sliding glass doors leading to outdoor living on the various functional terraces. These are but some of the highlights of this appealing L-shaped traditional. Be sure to note the large number of sizeable closets for a variety of uses.

Design T92778
2,761 Sq. Ft.; 41,145 Cu. Ft.

● No matter what the occasion, family and friends alike will enjoy the sizeable gathering room. A spacious 20' x 23', this room has a thru fireplace to the study and two sets of sliding glass doors to the large rear terrace. Indoor-outdoor living can also be enjoyed from the dining room, study and master bedroom. There is also a covered porch accessible through sliding glass doors in the dining room and breakfast nook.

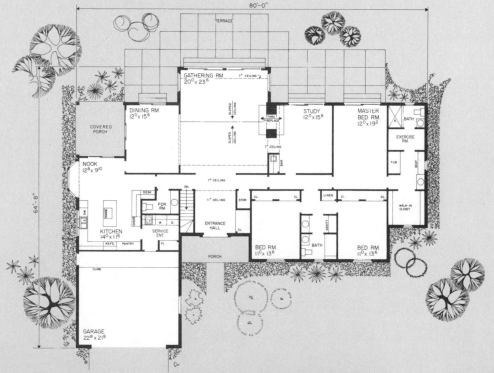

TERRACE

TERRACE

BED RM.
16⁸ x 13⁸

LIVING RM.
21⁴ x 14⁰

NOOK
11⁶ x 9⁸

FAMILY RM.
15¹⁰ x 21⁸

BATH

BED RM.
13⁰ x 12⁰

KITCHEN
11⁶ x 12⁰

RAISED HEARTH

LIN

DINING RM.
14⁰ x 13⁰

PANTRY

REF'S.

SNACK BAR

AIR COND.

LINEN

CL.

LAUNDRY

LINEN

CL.

LT

W

D.

GALLERY

STUDY
10⁸ x 10⁴

BATH

PORCH

DRESSING RM.

TUB

VANITY

WALK-IN CLOSET

MASTER BED RM.
13⁰ x 18⁴

GARAGE
21¹⁰ x 23⁸

76'-0"

66'-8"

Design T92784
2,980 Sq. Ft.; 41,580 Cu. Ft.

● The projection of the master bedroom and garage create an inviting U-shaped area leading to the covered porch of this delightful traditionally styled design. After entering through the double front doors, the gallery will lead to each of the three living areas: the sleeping wing of two bedrooms, full bath and study; the informal area of the family room with raised hearth fireplace and sliding glass doors to the terrace and the kitchen/nook area (the kitchen has a pass-thru snack bar to the family room); and the formal area consisting of a separate dining room with built-in china cabinets and the living room. Note the privacy of the master bedroom.

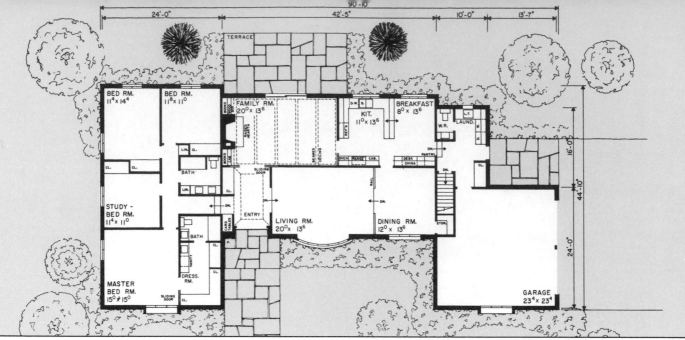

● Here are three delightful French Provincial adaptations, any one of which would surely be an impressive addition to a neighborhood. Each design features a sleeping wing of four bedrooms, two full baths, and plenty of closets. Further, each design has a separate first floor laundry with an adjacent wash room. Observe the sunken living room . . .

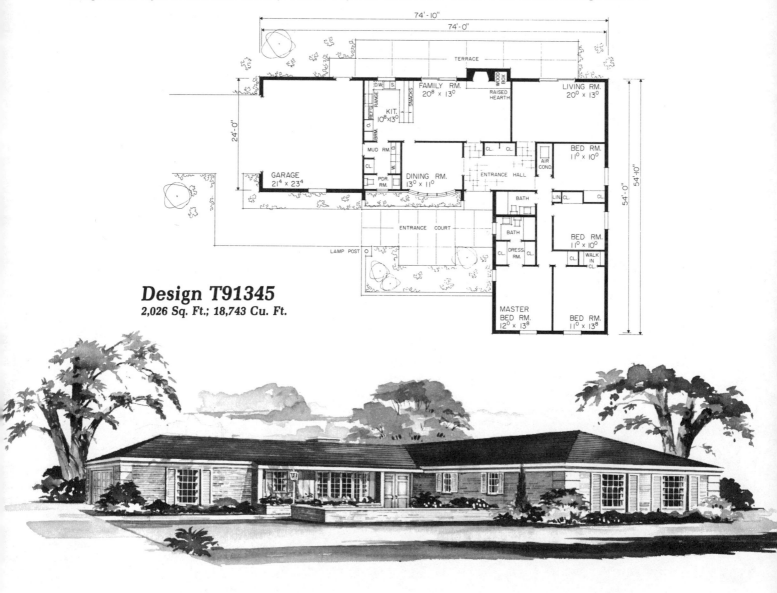

Design T91345
2,026 Sq. Ft.; 18,743 Cu. Ft.

Design T92134 2,530 Sq. Ft.; 44,458 Cu. Ft.

. . . and the beamed ceiling family room of Design T92134 above. Don't miss its big dressing room or raised hearth fireplace. Design T91345 has both its family and living rooms located to the rear and functioning with the terrace. Design T91054 has an efficient work area and a large formal dining room.

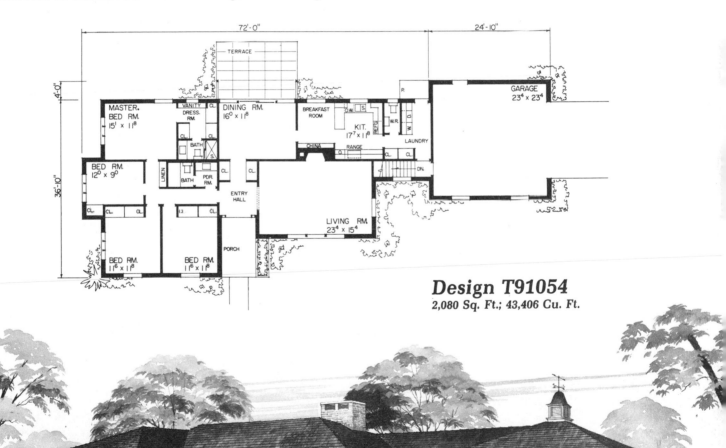

72'-0"   24'-10"

4'-0"

TERRACE

MASTER.
BED RM.
15' x 11⁸

VANITY
DRESS.
RM.

CL.

DINING RM.
16⁰ x 11⁸

BREAKFAST
ROOM

D.W. S.

KIT.
17⁷ x 11⁸

REFG.

W.R.

W D

P.

GARAGE
23⁴ x 23⁴

CL.

BATH

36'-10"

BED RM.
12⁰ x 9⁰

LINEN

BATH PDR.
RM.

CL.

CL.

CHINA

RANGE

CL. CL.

DN.

ENTRY
HALL

CL. CL. CL.

CL. CL.

LIVING RM.
23⁴ x 15⁴

BED RM.
11⁶ x 11⁸

BED RM.
11⁶ x 11⁸

PORCH

Design T91054
2,080 Sq. Ft.; 43,406 Cu. Ft.

Design T92220
2,646 Sq. Ft.; 46,880 Cu. Ft.

● The gracious formality of this home is reminiscent of a popularly accepted French styling. The hip-roof, the brick quoins, the cornice details, the arched window heads, the distinctive shutters, the recessed double front doors, the massive center chimney, and the delightful flower court are all features which set the dramatic appeal of this home. This floor plan is a favorite of many. The four bedroom, two bath sleeping wing is a zone by itself. Further, the formal living and dining rooms are ideally located.

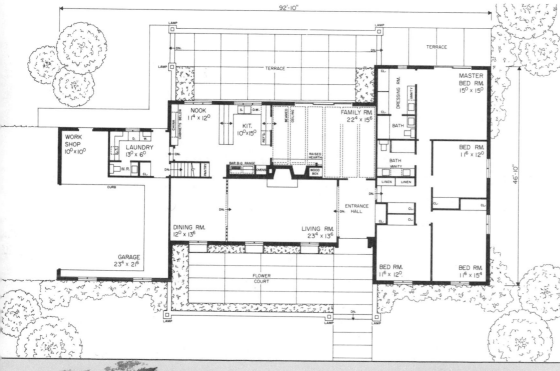

Design T92209
2,659 Sq. Ft.; 45,240 Cu. Ft.

Design T91892
2,036 Sq. Ft.; 26,575 Cu. Ft.

● The romance of French Provincial is captured here by the hip-roof masses, the charm of the window detailing, the brick quoins at the corners, the delicate dentil work at the cornices, the massive centered chimney, and the recessed double front doors. The slightly raised entry court completes the picture. The basic floor plan is a favorite of many. And little wonder, for all areas work well together, while still maintaining a fine degree of separation of functions. The highlight of the interior will be the sunken living room.

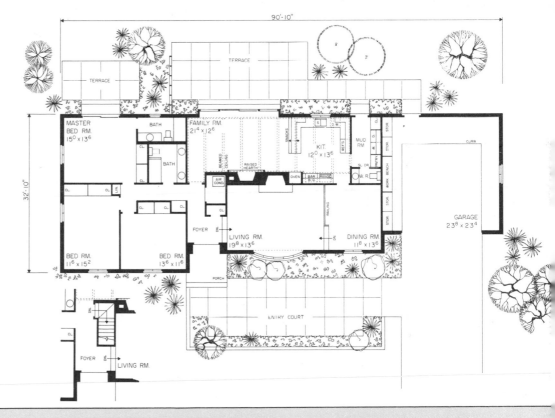

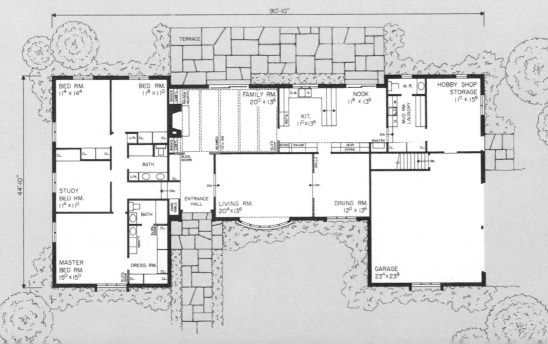

● Such an impressive home would, indeed, be difficult to top. And little wonder when you consider the myriad of features this one-story Colonial has going for it. Consider the exquisite detailing, the fine proportions, and the symmetry of the projecting wings. The gracious and inviting double front doors are a prelude to the exceptional interior. Formal entertaining will be enjoyed in the front living and dining rooms. For informal living there is the rear family room. The homemaker will find the work center a joy in which to function.

123

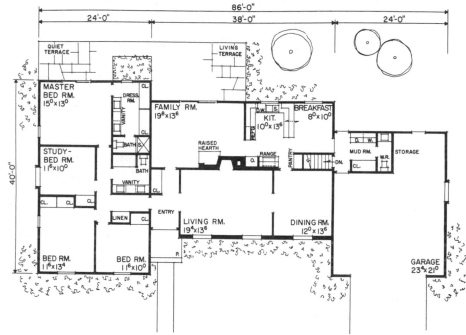

Design T91835
2,144 Sq. Ft.; 33,310 Cu. Ft.

● Cedar shakes and quarried natural stone are the exterior materials which adorn this irregularly shaped traditional ranch home. Adding to the appeal of the exterior are the cut-up windows, the shutters, the pediment gable, the cupola, and the double front doors. The detail of the garage door opening adds further interest. Inside, this favorite among floor plans, reflects all the features necessary to provide complete livability for the large family. The sleeping zone is a 24' x 40' rectangle which contains four bedrooms and two full baths.

Design T91929
2,312 Sq. Ft.; 26,364 Cu. Ft.

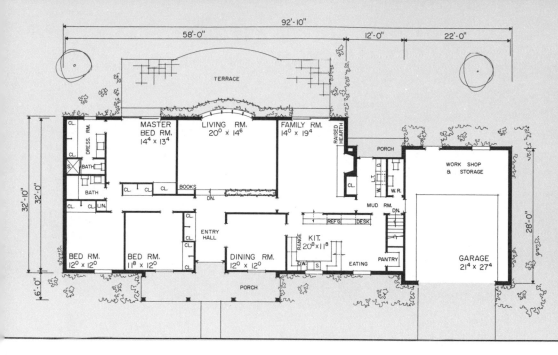

Design T91788
2,218 Sq. Ft.; 36,002 Cu. Ft.

● Charm, is but one of many words which may be used to correctly describe this fine design. In addition to its eye-appeal, it has a practical and smoothly functioning floor plan. The detail of the front entrance, highlighted by columns supporting the projecting pediment gable, is outstanding. Observe the window treatment and the double front doors. Perhaps the focal point of the interior will be the formal living room. It is, indeed, dramatic. Note mud room area.

Design T91929
2,312 Sq. Ft.; 26,364 Cu. Ft.

● This home will lead the hit parade in your new subdivision. Its sparkling, traditionally styled exterior will be the favorite of all that pass. And, once inside, friends will marvel at how the plan just seems to cater to your family's every activity. For formal entertaining, there is the sunken living room and the separate dining room. For informal livability, there's the beamed ceilinged family room and the outdoor terrace.

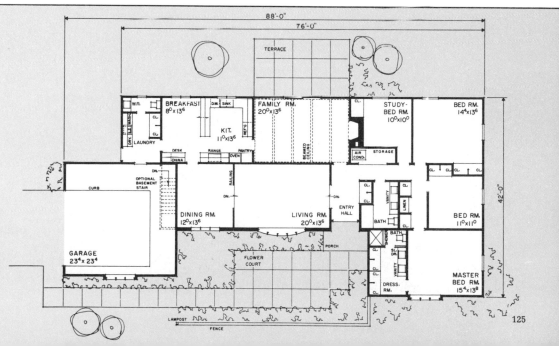

125

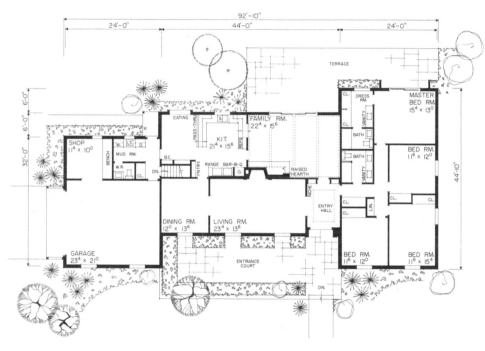

Design T91761
2,548 Sq. Ft.; 43,870 Cu. Ft.

● Low, strong roof lines and solid, enduring qualities of brick give this house a permanent, here-to-stay appearance. Bedroom wing is isolated, and the baths and closets deaden noise from the rest of the house. Center fireplaces in family and living rooms make furniture arrangement easy. There are a number of extras — a workshop, an unusually large garage, and an indoor barbecue. Garage has easy access to both basement and kitchen area. There are two eating areas — a formal dining room and a nook next to the delightful kitchen.

Design T92181
2,612 Sq. Ft.; 45,230 Cu. Ft.

● It is hard to imagine a home with any more eye-appeal than this one. It is the complete picture of charm. The interior is no less outstanding. Sliding glass doors permit the large master bedroom, the quiet living room, and the all-purpose family room to function directly with the outdoors. The two fireplaces, the built-in china cabinets, the bookshelves, the complete laundry, the kitchen pass-thru to breakfast room are extra features. Count the closets. There are all kinds of storage facilities.

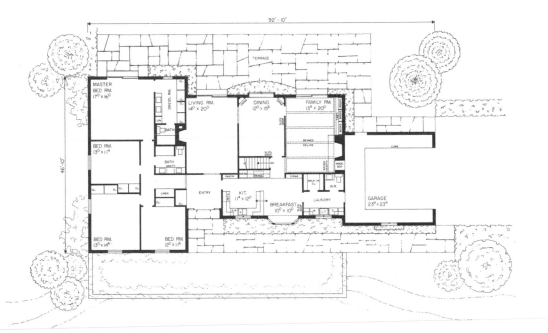

Design T92183
3,074 Sq. Ft.; 33,587 Cu. Ft.

● A great county-estate home with unsurpassed exterior appeal and positively outstanding interior livability. The enclosed front courtyard is just one of the many features that contribute to the air of distinction surrounding this pleasing traditional design. The floor plan includes everything one would require to guarantee his family the ultimate in gracious living.

Design T92746
2,790 Sq. Ft.; 57,590 Cu. Ft.

● This impressive one-story will surely be the talk-of-the-town. And not surprisingly, either. It embodies all the elements to assure a sound investment and years of happy family livability. The projecting living room with its stucco, simulated wood beams, and effective window treatment adds a dramatic note. The massive double front doors are sheltered by the covered porch. The spacious interior is particularly well-zoned. The sunken living room will enjoy its privacy. The gathering room on the other hand, will cater to the family's gregarious instincts.

Design T91989
2,282 Sq. Ft.; 41,831 Cu. Ft.

● High style with a plan as contemporary as today and tomorrow. There is, indeed, a feeling of coziness that emanates from the ground-hugging qualities of this picturesque home. Inside, there is livability galore. There's the four bedroom, two bath sleeping wing with a dressing room as a bonus. There's the sunken living room and the separate dining room to function as the family's formal living area. Then, overlooking the rear yard, there's the informal living area with its beamed ceiling family room.

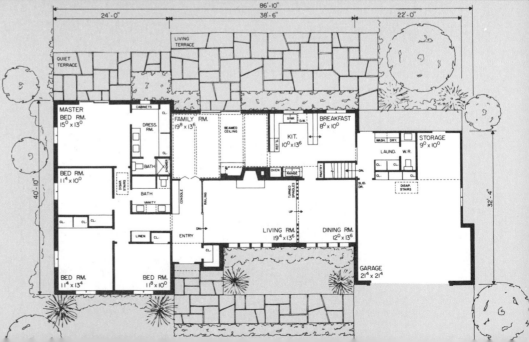

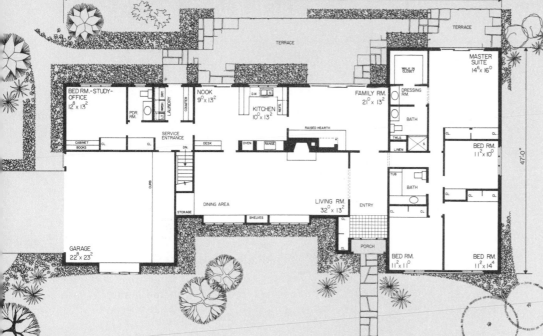

Design T92573
2,747 Sq. Ft.; 48,755 Cu. Ft.

● A Tudor ranch! Combining brick and wood for an elegant look. With a living/dining room measuring 32' by 13' (large indeed) fully appointed with a traditional fireplace and built-in shelves flanked by diagonally paned windows. The sleeping facilities consist of three family bedrooms plus an elegant master bedroom suite. A conveniently located laundry with a folding counter is in the service entrance. Adjacent to the laundry is a washroom and in the corner of the plan is a study or make it a fifth bedroom if you prefer.

Design T92335
2,674 Sq. Ft.; 41,957 Cu. Ft.

● Surely a winner for those who have a liking for the architecture of the Far West. With or without the enclosure of the front court, this home with its stucco exterior, brightly colored roof tiles and exposed rafter tails will be impressive, indeed. The floor plan reflects a wonderfully zoned interior. This results in a separation of functions which helps assure convenient living. The traffic patterns which flow from the spacious foyer are most efficient. While the sleeping wing is angled to the front line of the house, the sunken living room projects at an angle to the rear.

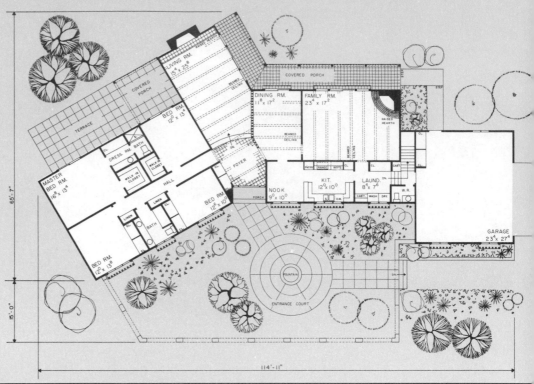

Design T92236
2,307 Sq. Ft.; 28,800 Cu. Ft.

● Living in this Spanish adaptation will truly be fun for the whole family. It will matter very little whether the backdrop matches the mountains below, becomes the endless prairie, turns out to be the rolling farmland, or is the backdrop of a suburban area. A family's flair for distinction will be satisfied by this picturesque exterior, while its requirements for everyday living will be gloriously catered to. The hub of the plan will be the kitchen-family room area. The beamed ceiling and raised hearth fireplace will contribute to the cozy, informal atmosphere. The separate dining room and the sunken living room function together formally.

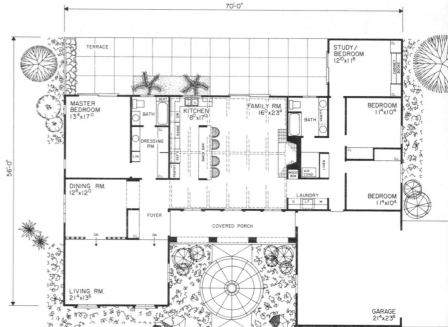

Design T92820
2,261 Sq. Ft.; 46,830 Cu. Ft.

● A privacy wall around the courtyard with pool and trellised planter area is a gracious area by which to enter this one-story design. The Spanish flavor is accented by the grillework and the tiled roof. Interior livability has a great deal to offer. The front living room has sliding glass doors which open to the entrance court; the adjacent dining room features a bay window. Informal activities will be enjoyed in the rear family room. Its many features include a sloped, beamed ceiling, raised hearth fireplace, sliding glass doors to the terrace and a snack bar for those very informal meals. Four bedrooms are in the private, sleeping wing of the house.

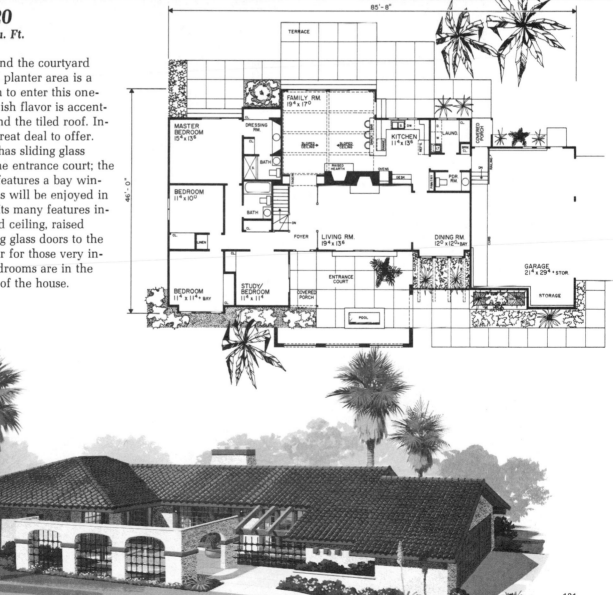

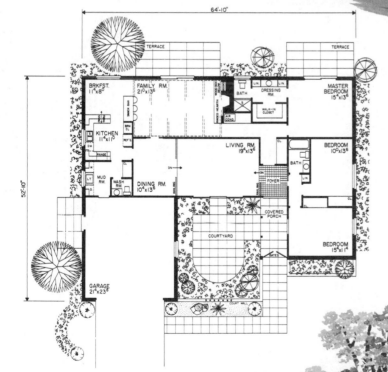

Design T92867
2,388 Sq. Ft.; 49,535 Cu. Ft.

78'-0"

TERRACE

COVERED PORCH

GATHERING RM.
20⁰ x 15⁴

SKYLIGHT ABOVE

MASTER BEDROOM
12⁸ x 15⁰

STUDY BEDROOM
10² x 11⁶

DINING RM.
9⁸ x 11⁴

LIVING RM.
13⁰ x 19⁶

BEDROOM
10⁰ x 10⁸

SLOPED CEILING
SLOPED CEILING

DRESSING RM.

STOR CL

CL

DESK

PANTRY

PANTRY

KITCHEN
10⁰ x 11⁴

BRM CL

DINING

BATH

BATH

KITCHENETTE

BATH

DN

BRKFST. RM.
8⁰ x 11⁴

FOYER

LAUND.

LINEN

COVERED PORCH

WASH RM.

CURB

ENTRANCE COURT

BEDROOM
11⁶ x 11⁰+BAY

BEDROOM
11⁶ x 11⁰+BAY

GARAGE
23⁴ x 24⁸

55'-4"

● A live-in relative would be very comfortable in this home. This design features a self-contained suite (473 sq. ft.) consisting of a bedroom, bath, living room and kitchenette with dining area. This suite is nestled behind the garage away from the main areas of the house. The rest of this traditional, one-story house, faced with fieldstone and vertical wood siding, is also livable.

Design T91754
2,080 Sq. Ft.; 21,426 Cu. Ft.

64'-10"

TERRACE

TERRACE

BRKFST.
11⁴ x 8⁰

FAMILY RM.
21⁰ x 13⁶

BATH

DRESSING RM

MASTER BEDROOM
15⁰ x 13⁶

RAISED HEARTH

RAISED HEARTH

WALK-IN CLOSET

KITCHEN
11⁴ x 11⁰

RANGE

AIR COND.

DW

REF'S

LIVING RM.
19⁴ x 13⁶

BEDROOM
10⁰ x 13⁶

DN

MUD RM.

WASH RM.

BATH

LT

DINING RM.
10⁰ x 13⁰

FOYER

LIN

CL

COVERED PORCH

COURTYARD

BEDROOM
15⁰ x 11⁰

GARAGE
21⁰ x 23⁶

COURT WALL

GATE

52'-10"

● Boasting a traditional Western flavor, this rugged U-shaped ranch home has all the features to assure grand living. The private front flower court, inside the high brick wall, creates a delightfully dramatic atmosphere which carries inside. The floor plan is positively unique and exceptionally livable. Wonderfully zoned, the bedrooms enjoy their full measure of privacy. The formal living and dining rooms function together in a most pleasing fashion. The areas of the laundry, kitchen, informal eating, and family room fit together in such a manner as to guarantee efficient living patterns.

Design T91394

832 Sq. Ft. - First Floor
512 Sq. Ft. - Second Floor
18,453 Cu. Ft.

● The growing family with a restricted building budget will find this a great investment - a convenient living floor plan inside an attractive facade.

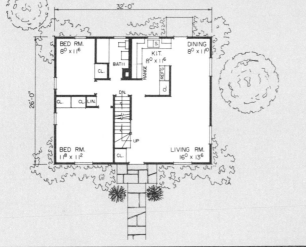

Design T92510

1,191 Sq. Ft. - First Floor
533 Sq. Ft. - Second Floor
27,500 Cu. Ft.

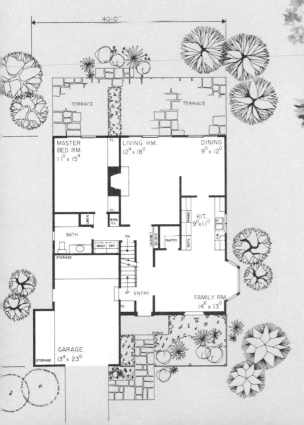

● The pleasant in-line kitchen is flanked by a separate dining room and a family room. The master bedroom is on the first floor with two more bedrooms upstairs.

133

Design T91701

1,344 Sq. Ft. - First Floor
948 Sq. Ft. - Second Floor
33,952 Cu. Ft.

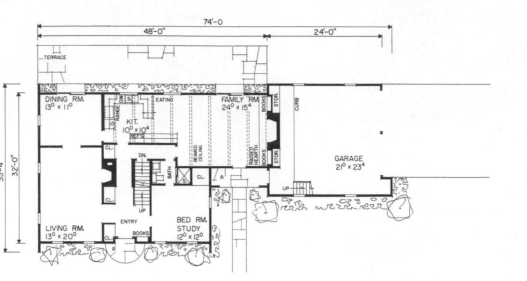

Design T91793

1,986 Sq. Ft. - First Floor
944 Sq. Ft. - Second Floor
35,800 Cu. Ft.

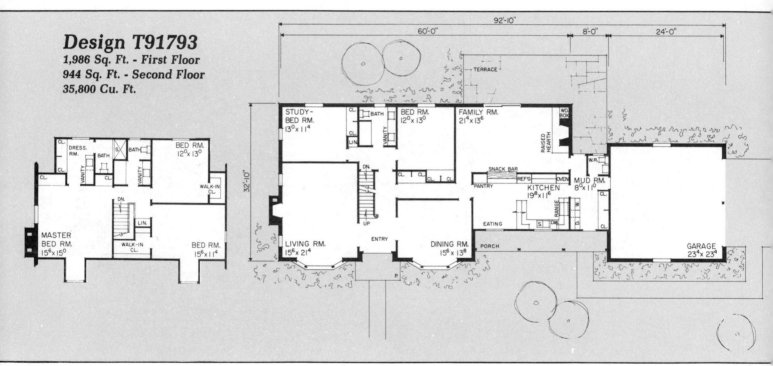

Design T91718

2,012 Sq. Ft. - First Floor
589 Sq. Ft. - Second Floor
45,405 Cu. Ft.

134

GARAGE 21⁴ x 25⁴

FAMILY RM. 15⁸ x 19⁴

DISAPPEAR'S STAIR

BREAKFAST 10⁴ x 13⁴

KIT. 10⁰ x 13⁴

BEAMED CEILING

ISLAND WORK CENTER

RANGE B-BQ PANTRY

BUFFET CHINA

OVENS

SLIDING DOOR

CL.

SERVICE

BATH

PDR. RM.

STUDY-BED RM. 13⁸ x 11⁶

DN.

DINING RM. 17⁸ x 13⁶

ENTRY

UP

LIVING RM. 20⁰ x 15⁶

22'-0"   18'-0"   52'-0"

93'-6"

29'-6"   28'-0"

STORAGE

STORAGE

ROOF

DISAPPEARING STAIR

DN.

ROOF

BED RM. 11⁶ x 12⁰

CL.

DN.

BATH

VANITY

UP   UP   DN.

BATH

DRESS. RM.

WALK-IN CL.

BED RM. 19⁰ x 11⁸

CL.   LIN.

CL.

LIN.   CL.

MASTER BED RM. 17⁸ x 15⁰

ROOF

Design T92132

1,958 Sq. Ft. - First Floor
1,305 Sq. Ft. - Second Floor
51,428 Cu. Ft.

● This Georgian adaptation gets its appeal from its formal facade. The exterior seems to reflect a certain way of life that, while formal is not necessarily devoid of fun and relaxation. The identifying characteristics of this exterior include the symmetry of the window arrangement, the detailing of the doorway, the massive end chimneys, the tight cornices, the delicate dentils, the raised level of the entrance. The dormers of the second floor with their gables and muntined windows are delightful indeed.

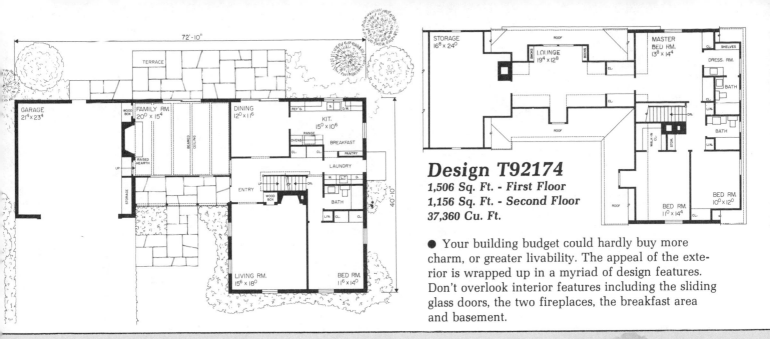

Design T92174

1,506 Sq. Ft. - First Floor
1,156 Sq. Ft. - Second Floor
37,360 Cu. Ft.

● Your building budget could hardly buy more charm, or greater livability. The appeal of the exterior is wrapped up in a myriad of design features. Don't overlook interior features including the sliding glass doors, the two fireplaces, the breakfast area and basement.

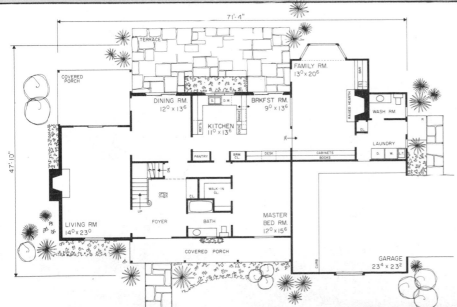

Design T92500

1,851 Sq. Ft. - First Floor
762 Sq. Ft. - Second Floor; 43,052 Cu. Ft.

● The large and active family will enjoy the living patterns this charming story-and-a-half design has to offer. Of course, the delightful exterior will ever be a source of pride.

Design T92615 2,563 Sq. Ft. - First Floor
552 Sq. Ft. - Second Floor; 59,513 Cu. Ft.

Second Floor Plan:
- ROOF
- BEDROOM 11⁰ x 13²
- BEDROOM 11² x 15⁶
- SKY LIGHT
- UPPER SOLARIUM
- ATTIC
- CL
- ROOF
- ROOF
- BATH
- OPEN
- LINEN
- DESK / VANITY
- LINEN
- ATTIC

First Floor Plan:
- 87'-8"
- 68'-8"
- TERRACE
- TERRACE
- MASTER BEDROOM 13⁰ x 19⁴
- SOLARIUM 14⁰ x 11⁸
- DINING RM. 12⁰ x 11⁸
- OVENS
- D.W.
- KITCHEN 12⁸ x 13⁶
- REF'G.
- FAMILY RM. 23⁸ x 18⁰
- TOWELS
- VANITY
- SEAT
- LDGE
- BATH
- SEAT
- WALK-IN CLOSET
- WALK-IN CLOSET
- COVERED PORCH
- PDR. RM.
- PANTRY
- DN.
- CL
- BAR
- W.R.
- SEAT
- FLOWER COURT
- LIVING RM. 14⁰ x 21⁴
- UP
- CL
- FOYER
- CL
- STUDY / BEDROOM / 14⁰ x 12⁰
- SERVICE HALL
- PORCH
- COVERED PORCH
- LAUNDRY
- CL
- W
- CURB
- GARAGE 23⁸ x 24⁰

● The exterior detailing of this design recalls 18th-Century New England architecture. Enter by way of the centered front door and you are greeted into the foyer. Directly to the right is the study or optional bedroom or to the left is the living room. This large formal room features sliding glass doors to the sun-drenched solarium. The beauty of the solarium will be appreciated from the master bedroom and the dining room along with the living room.

Design T91787

2,656 Sq. Ft. - First Floor
744 Sq. Ft. - Second Floor
51,164 Cu. Ft.

● Can't you picture this dramatic home sitting on your property? The curving front drive is impressive as it passes the walks to the front door and the service entrance. The roof masses, the centered masonry chimney, the window symmetry and the 108 foot expanse across the front are among the features that make this a distinctive home. Of interest are the living and family rooms — both similar in size and each having its own fireplace.

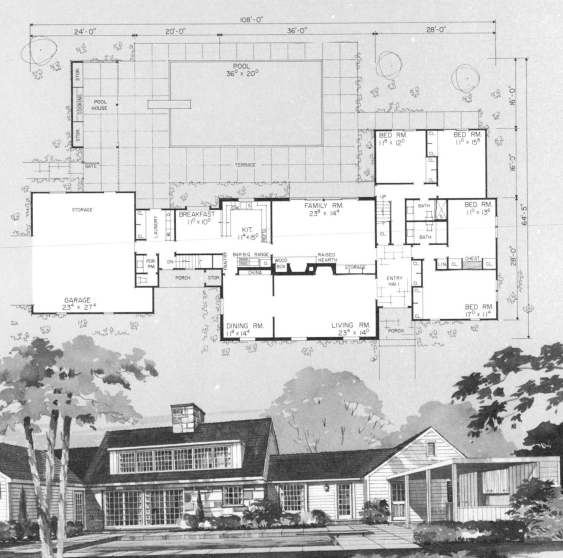

Design T92680

1,707 Sq. Ft. - First Floor
1,439 Sq. Ft. - Second Floor; 53,865 Cu. Ft.

● This Early American, Dutch Colonial not only has charm, but offers many fine features. The foyer allows easy access to all rooms on the first floor - excellent livability. Note the large country kitchen with beamed ceiling, fireplace and island cook top. A large, formal dining room and powder room are only a few steps away. A fireplace also will be found in the study and living room. The service area, mud room, wash room and laundry are tucked near the garage. Two bedrooms, full bath and master bedroom suite will be found on the second floor. A fourth bedroom and bath are accessible through the master bedroom or stairs in the service entrance.

Design T92890

1,612 Sq. Ft. - First Floor
1,356 Sq. Ft. - Second Floor
47,010 Cu. Ft.

● An appealing Farmhouse that is complimented by an inviting front porch. Many memorable summer evenings will be spent here. Entering this house, you will notice a nice-sized study to your right and spacious living room to the left. The adjacent dining room is enriched by an attractive bay window. Just a step away, an efficient kitchen will be found. Many family activities will be enjoyed in the large family room. The tavern/snack bar will make entertaining guests a joy. A powder room and laundry are also on the first floor. Upstairs you'll find a master bedroom suite featuring a bath with an oversized tub and shower and a dressing room. Also on this floor; two bedrooms, full bath and a large attic.

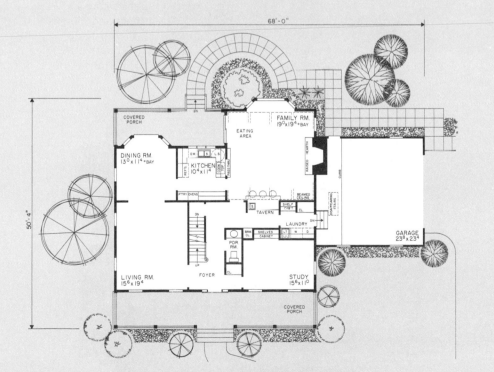

Design T92776

1,134 Sq. Ft. - First Floor
874 Sq. Ft. - Second Floor; 31,600 Cu. Ft.

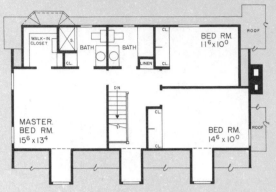

● The covered front porch of this one-and-a-half story will surely be a delight on those warm summer evenings. Basement included.

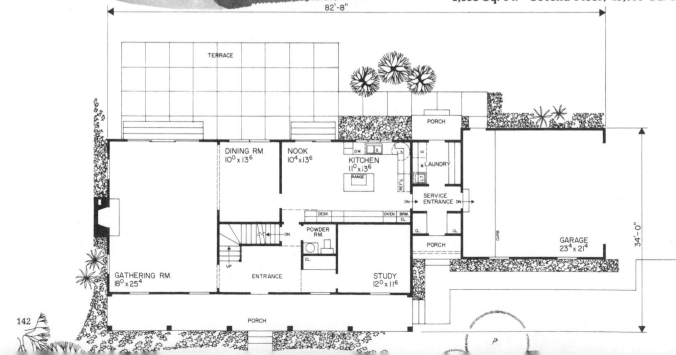

Design T92650

1,451 Sq. Ft. - First Floor
1,091 Sq. Ft. - Second Floor; 43,555 Cu. Ft.

● The rear view of this design is just as appealing as the front. The dormers and the covered porch with pillars is a charming way to introduce this house to the on-lookers. Inside, the appeal is also outstanding. Note the size (18 x 25 foot) of the gathering room which is open to the dining room. Kitchen-nook area is very spacious and features an island range, built-in desk and more. Great convenience having the laundry in service area close to the kitchen. Imagine, a fireplace in both the gathering room and the master bedroom! Make special note of the service entrance doors leading to both the front and back of the house.

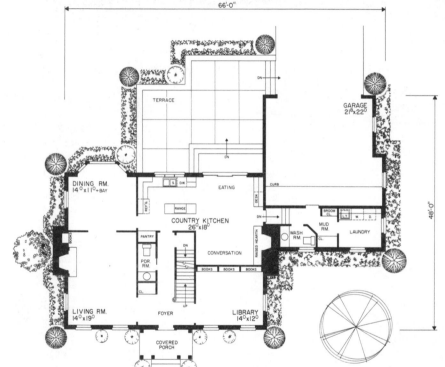

Design T92688 1,588 Sq. Ft. - First Floor
1,101 Sq. Ft. - Second Floor; 44,021 Cu. Ft.

● Here are two floors of excellent livability. Start at the country kitchen. It will be the center for family activities. It has an island, desk, raised hearth fireplace, conversation area and sliding glass doors to the terrace. Adjacent to this area is the washroom and laundry. Quieter areas are available in the living room and library. Three bedrooms are housed on the second floor.

Design T92686
1,683 Sq. Ft. - First Floor
1,541 Sq. Ft. - Second Floor; 57,345 Cu. Ft.

● This design has its roots in the South and is referred to as a raised cottage. This adaptation has front and rear covered porches whose columns reflect a modified Greek Revival style. Flanking the center foyer are the formal living areas of the living room and library and the informal country kitchen.

73'-8"

COVERED PORCH

GARAGE
21⁴x22⁰

LIBRARY
18⁸x12⁴

CURB

BRM
CL

CHINA

REF'S

PANTRY

COOK TOP

DN   DN

MUD RM

WASH RM

LAUNDRY

CHINA

BOOKS

BOOKS

COUNTRY KITCHEN
17⁰x27⁰

PDR RM

DN

LIVING RM.
18⁸x13⁴

UP   FOYER

DINING

COVERED PORCH

BEDROOM
16⁴x13⁴

BATH

WALK-IN CLOSET

WHIRLPOOL

CL

DN

RAILING

DRESSING RM

BATH

VANITY

CL

BEDROOM
16⁴x13⁴

LINEN

MASTER BEDROOM
19⁰x13⁴

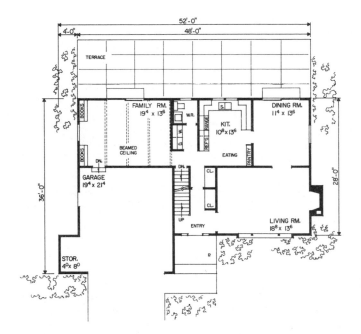

Design T91241
1,064 Sq. Ft. - First Floor
898 Sq. Ft. - Second Floor
24,723 Cu. Ft.

● You don't need a mansion to live graciously. What you do need is a practical floor plan which takes into consideration the varied activities of the busy family. This story-and-a-half design will not require a large piece of property. Its living potential is tremendous.

Design T92127
1,712 Sq. Ft. - First Floor
450 Sq. Ft. - Second Floor
39,435 Cu. Ft.

● Features aplenty – both inside and out. A list of the exterior design highlights is most interesting. It begins with the character created by the impressive roof surfaces. The U-shape creates a unique appeal and results in the formation of a garden court.

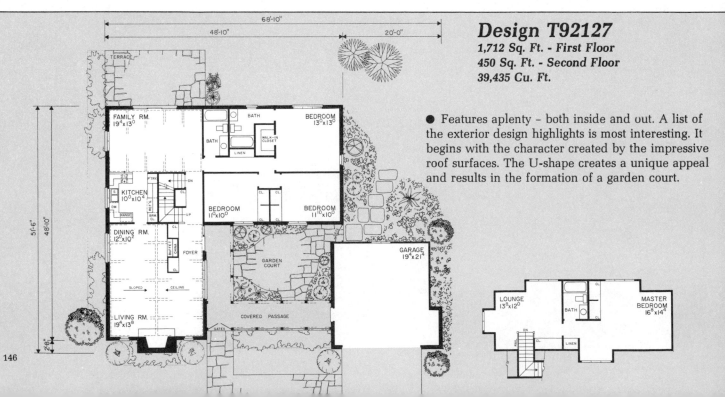

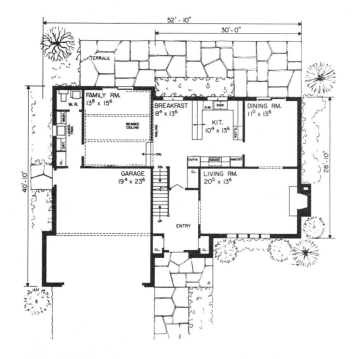

Design T91991

1,262 Sq. Ft. - First Floor
1,108 Sq. Ft. - Second Floor
31,073 Cu. Ft.

● Put yourself and your family in this English cottage adaptation and you'll all rejoice over your new home for many a year. The pride of owning and living in a home that is distinctive will be a constant source of satisfaction. Count the features that will serve your family for years.

Second Floor

DRESSING RM.

LOUNGE/
NURSERY
10⁰ x 9⁰

BEDROOM
12⁰ x 10⁰

CL

LIN.

MASTER
BEDROOM
13⁴ x 15⁴

DN

TUB

BATH

BEDROOM
10⁰ x 11⁰

BATH

ROOF

Design T92854
1,261 Sq. Ft. - First Floor
950 Sq. Ft. - Second Floor
36,820 Cu. Ft.

● The flair of old England has been captured in this outstanding one-and-a-half story design. Interior livability will efficiently serve the various needs of all family members. The first floor offers both formal and informal areas, along with the work centers. Note some of the various features which include a wet-bar in the dining room, the kitchen's snack bar, first floor laundry and rear covered porch to mention a few. Accommodations for sleeping will be found on the second floor. There are two family bedrooms and the master bedroom suite. Don't miss the uniqueness of the lounge/nursery area which is attached to the master bedroom.

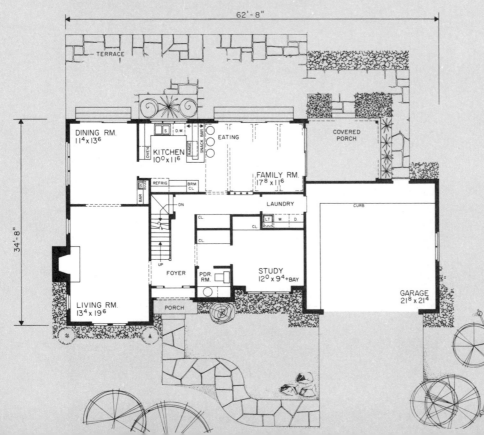

62' - 8"

34' - 8"

TERRACE

DINING RM.
11⁴ x 13⁶

KITCHEN
10⁰ x 11⁶

OVEN

D.W.

RANGE

SNACK BAR

EATING

COVERED
PORCH

BAR

REFRIG

BRM
CL

DN

FAMILY RM.
17⁸ x 11⁶

LAUNDRY

CURB

UP

CL

CL

LT W D

FOYER

PDR.
RM.

STUDY
12⁰ x 9⁴ +BAY

GARAGE
21⁸ x 21⁴

LIVING RM.
13⁴ x 19⁶

PORCH

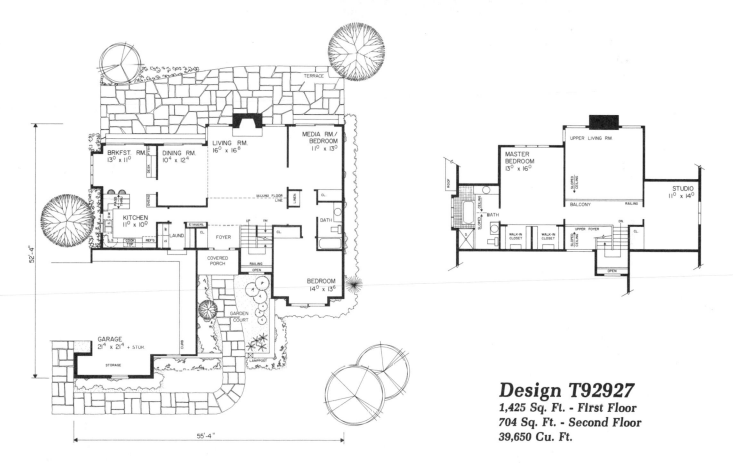

Design T92927
1,425 Sq. Ft. - First Floor
704 Sq. Ft. - Second Floor
39,650 Cu. Ft.

● This charming Early American design with stone and board exterior is just as warm on the inside. Features include a complete second-floor master bedroom suite with an upper living room, studio, upper foyer, and master bathroom. The upper living room and master bathroom feature sloped ceilings. The first floor features a convenience kitchen with pass-thru to a breakfast room. There's also a formal dining room just steps away in the rear of the house. An adjacent rear living room enjoys its own fireplace. Other features include a rear media room or optional third bedroom. This could be a great place for VCR's, computers, stereos, and even TV's. A downstairs bedroom enjoys an excellent front view. Other highlights include a garden court, covered porch, and large garage with extra storage. This is one well packaged house, indeed, with plenty to offer the entire family.

Design T92626

1,420 Sq. Ft. - First Floor
859 Sq. Ft. - Second Floor
34,974 Cu. Ft.

● This charming, one-and-a-half-story home surely elicits thoughts of an English countryside. It has a beckoning warmth that seems to foretell a friendly welcome. The exterior features are appealing, indeed. The window treatment, the stylish chimneys, the varying roof planes and the brick veneer and stucco exterior, are among the distinguishing characteristics. Inside, the family living potential is outstanding. Notice the extra first floor bedroom with its adjacent full bath. The kitchen overlooks the front yard and is flanked by informal and formal dining areas. Nearby is the laundry and the convenient washroom. The family room, which functions with the rear terrace, will be the favorite gathering spot. Upstairs, a fine master bedroom with private bath and dressing room. A second bath caters to the two large children's bedrooms.

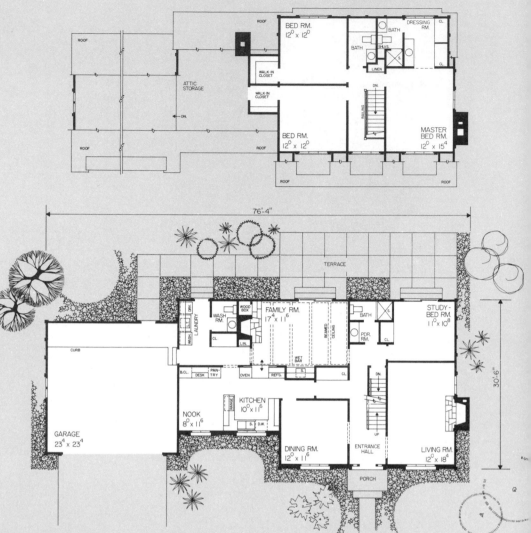

Design T92278 1,804 Sq. Ft. - First Floor; 939 Sq. Ft. - Second Floor; 44,274 Cu. Ft.

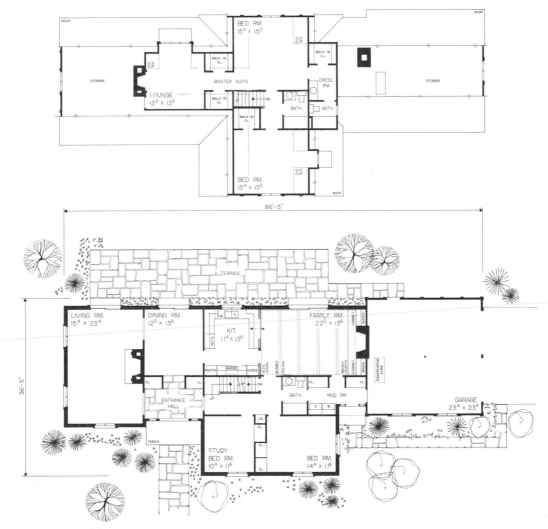

● This cozy Tudor adaptation is surely inviting. Its friendly demeanor seems to say, "welcome". Upon admittance to the formal front entrance hall, even the most casual of visitors will be filled with anticipation at the prospect of touring the house. And little wonder, too. Traffic patterns are efficient. Room relationships are excellent. A great feature is the location of the living, dining, kitchen, and family rooms across the back of the house. Each enjoys a view of the rear yard and sliding glass doors provide direct access to the terrace. Another outstanding feature is the flexibility of the sleeping patterns. This may be a five bedroom house, or one with three bedrooms with study and lounge. Don't miss the three baths. The mud room is handy from both garage and service entrances.

Design T91228

2,583 Sq. Ft. - First Floor
697 Sq. Ft. - Second Floor
51,429 Cu. Ft.

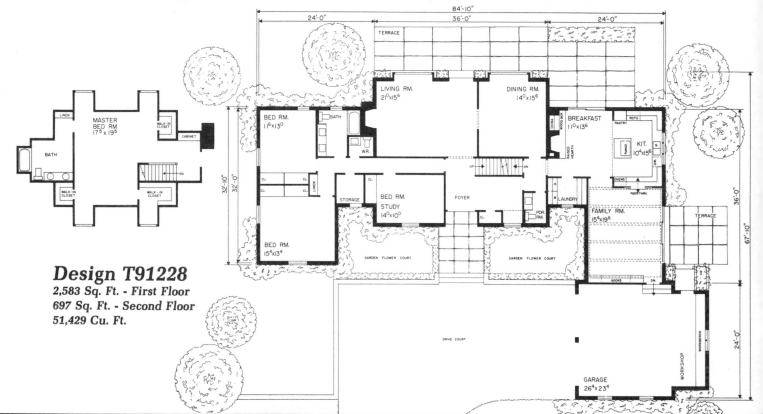

Second floor plan:
LINEN
MASTER BED RM. 17⁵ x 19⁵
WALK-IN CLOSET
CABINET
BATH
WALK-IN CLOSET
WALK-IN CLOSET
DN

First floor plan:
84'-10"
24'-0"
36'-0"
24'-0"
TERRACE
LIVING RM. 21⁰ x 15⁶
DINING RM. 14⁰ x 15⁶
BREAKFAST 11⁰ x 13⁶
WOOD BOX
CHINA
RAISED HEARTH
PANTRY
REFG.
KIT. 10⁴ x 15⁶
RANGE
BED RM. 11⁶ x 13⁰
BATH
W.R.
32'-10"
CL.
CL.
CL.
CL.
CL.
LINEN
CL.
STORAGE
BED RM. STUDY 14⁰ x 10⁰
FOYER
UP
DN
OVENS
PASS-THRU
DW.
LAUNDRY
PDR. RM.
W.
D.
FAMILY RM. 15⁴ x 19⁸
TERRACE
BED RM. 15⁴ x 13⁴
GARDEN FLOWER COURT
GARDEN FLOWER COURT
BOOKS
DN.
36'-0"
67'-10"
DRIVE COURT
WORKBENCH
WORKSHOP
24'-0"
GARAGE 26⁴ x 23⁴

Design T91060
3,190 Sq. Ft. - First Floor
1,024 Sq. Ft. - Second Floor
52,189 Cu. Ft.

Design T92718
1,941 Sq. Ft. - First Floor
791 Sq. Ft. - Second Floor; 49,895 Cu. Ft.

● You and your family will just love the new living patterns you'll experience in this story-and-a-half home. Livability will be equally as great on the second floor as well as the first.

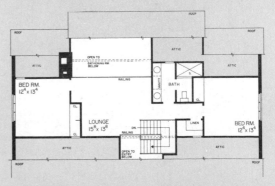

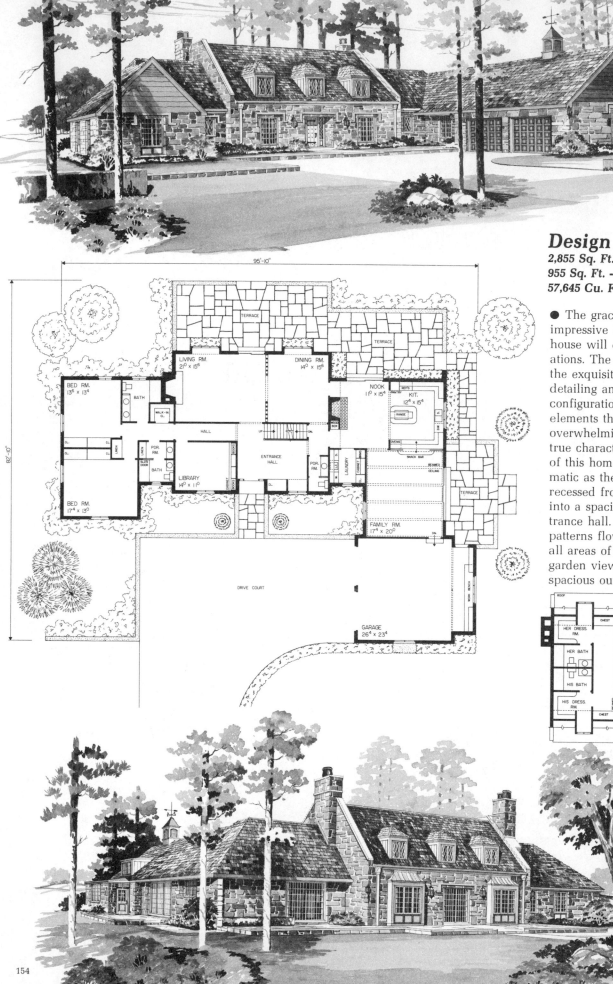

Design T92245

2,855 Sq. Ft. - First Floor
955 Sq. Ft. - Second Floor
57,645 Cu. Ft.

● The graciousness of this impressive English country house will endure for generations. The fine proportions, the exquisite architectural detailing and the interesting configuration are among the elements that create such an overwhelming measure of true character. The interior of this home will be as dramatic as the exterior. The recessed front entrance opens into a spacious, formal entrance hall. From here traffic patterns flow efficiently to all areas of the house. The garden view shows the three spacious outdoor terrace areas.

● The elegance of pleasing proportion and delightful detailing has seldom been better exemplified than by this classic French country manor adaptation. Approaching the house across the drive court, the majesty of this multi-roofed structure is breathtaking, indeed. An outstanding feature is the maid's suite. It is located above the garage and is easily reached by use of the covered porch connecting the laundry room's service entrance to the garage. If desired, it would make an excellent studio, quiet retreat or even a game room.

Design T91993
2,658 Sq. Ft. - *First Floor*
840 Sq. Ft. - *Master Suite*
376 Sq. Ft. - *Maid's Suite*
57,057 Cu. Ft.

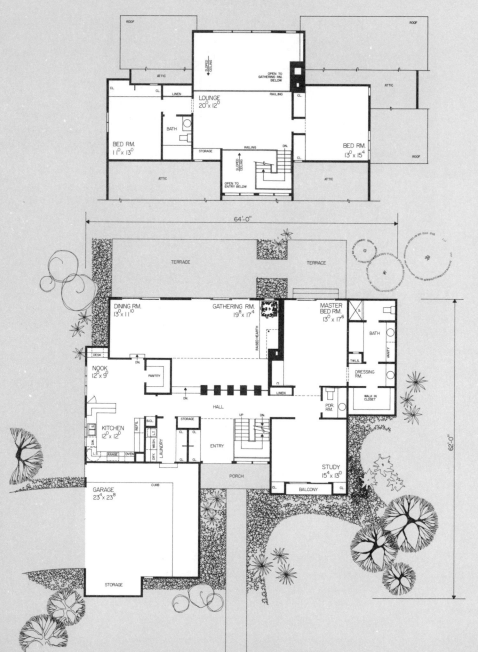

Design T92708
2,108 Sq. Ft. - First Floor
824 Sq. Ft. - Second Floor
52,170 Cu. Ft.

● Here is a one-and-a-half story home whose exterior is distinctive. It has a contemporary feeling, yet it retains some of the fine design features and proportions of traditional exteriors. Inside the appealing double front doors there is livability galore. The sunken rear living-dining area is delightfully spacious and is looked down into from the second floor lounge. The open end fireplace, with its raised hearth and planter, is another focal point. The master bedroom features a fine compartmented bath with both shower and tub. The study is just a couple steps away. The U-shaped kitchen is outstanding. Notice the pantry and laundry. Upstairs provides children with their own sleeping, studying and TV quarters. Absolutely a great design! Study all the fine details closely with your family.

Design T92782

2,060 Sq. Ft. - First Floor
897 Sq. Ft. - Second Floor
47,750 Cu. Ft.

● What makes this such a distinctive four bedroom design? Let's list some of the features. This plan includes great formal and informal living for the family at home or when entertaining guests. The formal gathering room and informal family room share a dramatic raised hearth fireplace. Other features of the sunken gathering room include: high, sloped ceilings, built-in planter and sliding glass doors to the front entrance court. The kitchen has a snack bar, many built-ins, a pass-thru to dining room and easy access to the large laundry/washroom. The master bedroom suite is located on the main level for added privacy and convenience. There's even a study with a built-in bar. The upper level has three more bedrooms, a bath and a lounge looking down into the gathering room.

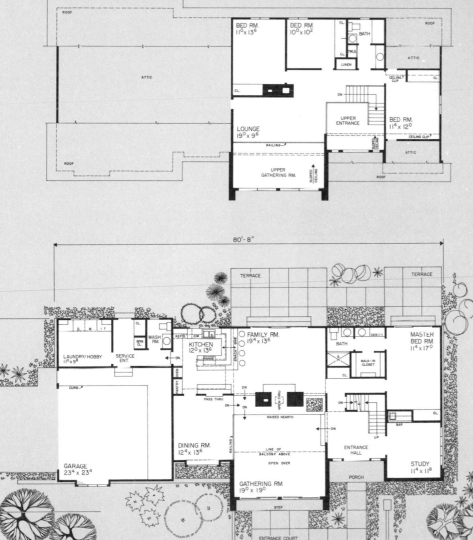

Design T92309 1,719 Sq. Ft. - First Floor; 456 Sq. Ft. - Second Floor; 22,200 Cu. Ft.

● Here's proof that the simple rectangle (which is relatively economical to build, naturally) can, when properly planned, result in unique living patterns. The exterior can be exceedingly appealing, too. Study the floor plan carefully. The efficiency of the kitchen could hardly be improved upon. It is strategically located to serve the formal dining room, the family room, and even the rear terrace. The sleeping facilities are arranged in a most interesting manner. The master bedroom with its attached bath and dressing room enjoys a full measure of privacy on the first floor. A second bedroom is also on this floor and has a full bath nearby. Then, upstairs there are two more bedrooms. Don't miss the laundry, the snack bar, the beamed ceiling, or the sliding glass doors. Note the big garage storage closet.

Design T92906 2,121 Sq. Ft. - First Floor
913 Sq. Ft. - Second Floor; 45,180 Cu. Ft.

● This striking Contemporary with Spanish good looks offers outstanding living for lifestyles of today. A three-car garage opens to a mudroom, laundry, and washroom to keep the rest of the house clean. An efficient, spacious kitchen opens to a spacious dining room, with pass-thru also leading to a family room. The family room and adjoining master bedroom suite overlook a backyard terrace. Just off the master bedroom is a sizable study that opens to a foyer. Steps just off the foyer make upstairs access quick and easy. The center point of this modern Contemporary is a living room that faces a front courtyard and a lounge above the living room. Three second-story bedrooms and an upper foyer join the upstairs lounge.

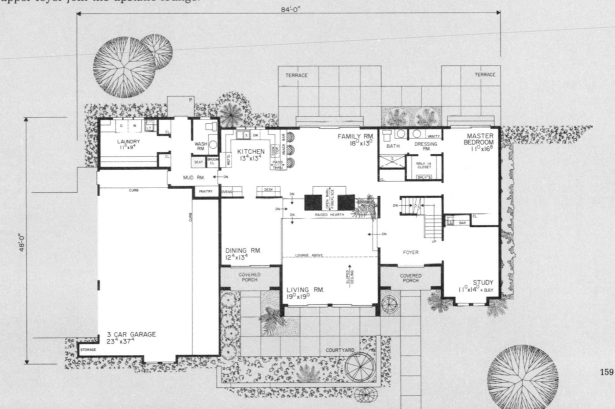

Design T92780
2,006 Sq. Ft. - First Floor
718 Sq. Ft. - Second Floor; 42,110 Cu. Ft.

● This 1½-story contemporary has more fine features than one can imagine. The livability is outstanding and can be appreciated by the whole family. Note the fine indoor-outdoor living relationships.

Design T92772
1,579 Sq. Ft. - First Floor
1,240 Sq. Ft. - Second Floor; 39,460 Cu. Ft.

● This four-bedroom two-story contemporary design is sure to suit your growing family needs. The rear U-shaped kitchen, flanked by the family and dining rooms, will be very efficient to the busy homemaker. Parents will enjoy all the convenience of the master bedroom suite.

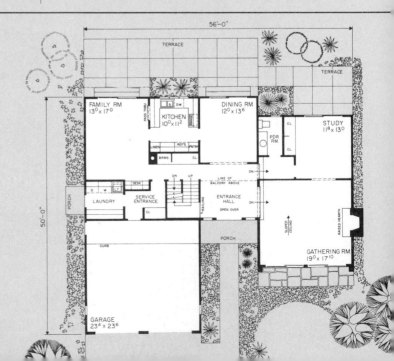

Design T92771
2,087 Sq. Ft. - First Floor
816 Sq. Ft. - Second Floor; 53,285 Cu. Ft.

● This design will provide an abundance of livability for your family. The second floor is highlighted by an open lounge which overlooks both the entry and the gathering room below.

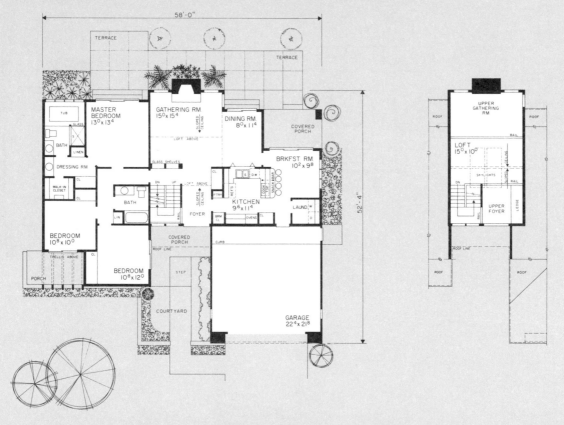

Design T92892 *1,623 Sq. Ft. - First Floor; 160 Sq. Ft. - Second Floor; 38,670 Cu. Ft.*

● What a striking contemporary! It houses an efficient floor plan with many outstanding features. The foyer has a sloped ceiling and an open staircase to the basement. To the right of the foyer is the work center. Note the snack bar, laundry and covered dining porch, along with the step-saving kitchen. Both the gathering and dining rooms overlook the back yard. Each of the three bedrooms has access to an outdoor area. Now, just think of the potential use of the second floor loft. It could be used as a den, sewing room, lounge, TV room or anything else you may need. It overlooks the gathering room and front foyer. Two large skylights will brighten the interior.

Design T92887 *1,338 Sq. Ft. - First Floor; 661 Sq. Ft. - Second Floor; 36,307 Cu. Ft.*

● This attractive, contemporary one-and-a-half story will be the envy of many. First, examine the efficient kitchen. Not only does it offer a snack bar for those quick meals but also a large dining room. Notice the adjacent dining porch. The laundry and garage access are also adjacent to the kitchen.

An exciting feature is the gathering room with fireplace. The first floor also offers a study with a wet bar and sliding glass doors that open to a private porch. This will make those quiet times cherishable. Adjacent to the study is a full bath followed by a bedroom. Up-stairs a large master bedroom suite oc-

cupies the entire floor. It features a bath with an oversized tub and shower, a large walk-in closet with built-ins and an open lounge with fireplace. Both the lounge and master bedroom, along with the gathering room, have sloped ceilings. Develop the lower level for additional space.

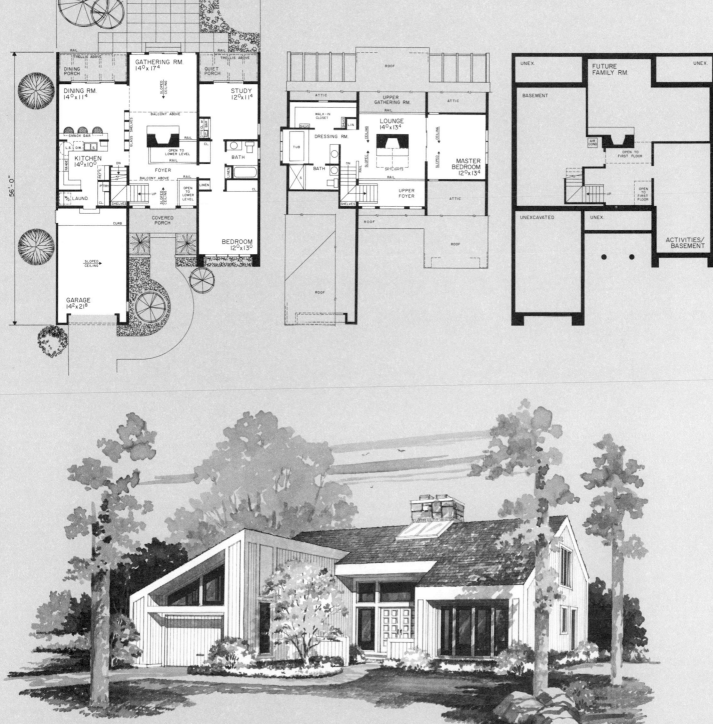

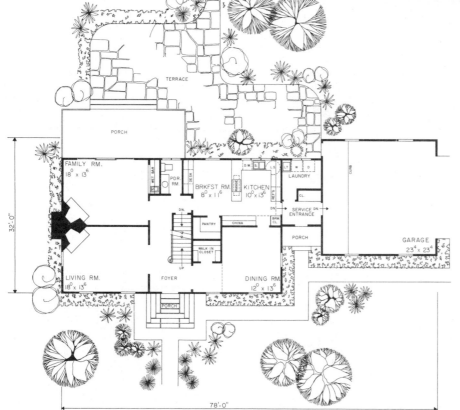

Design T92520

1,419 Sq. Ft. - First Floor
1,040 Sq. Ft. - Second Floor
39,370 Cu. Ft.

● From Tidewater Virginia comes this historic adaptation, a positive reminder of the charm of Early American architecture. Note how the center entrance gives birth to fine traffic circulation. List the numerous features.

Design T91986
896 Sq. Ft. - First Floor
1,148 Sq. Ft. - Second Floor; 28,840 Cu. Ft.

● This Gambrel roof design has a distinctive appearance and spells charm wherever it may be situated – far out in the country, or on a busy thoroughfare. It has a bonus room on the second floor, being a big family room over the garage.

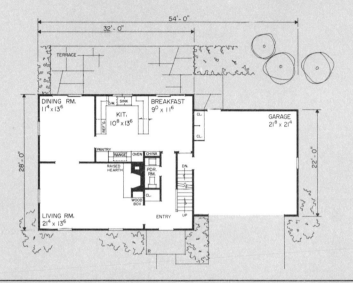

Design T91719
864 Sq. Ft. - First Floor
896 Sq. Ft. - Second Floor; 26,024 Cu. Ft.

● Truly a picture house. This attractive home with its authentic detailing illustrates how good, good floor planning really can be. All the elements are present for efficient and comfortable living. Try to envision how your family will function here.

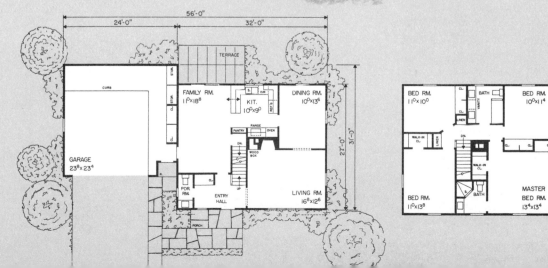

Design T92558
1,030 Sq. Ft. - First Floor
840 Sq. Ft. - Second Floor; 27,120 Cu. Ft.

● This relatively low-budget house
is long on exterior appeal and interior livability. It has all the features
to assure years of convenient living.
Make a list of your favorite features.

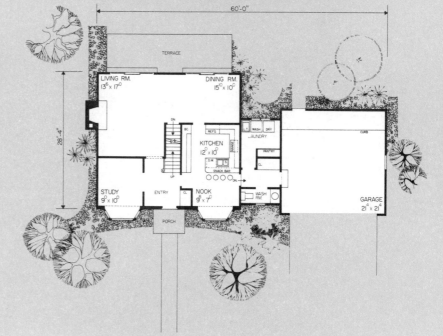

Design T92540
1,306 Sq. Ft. - First Floor
1,360 Sq. Ft. - Second Floor; 57,792 Cu. Ft.

● This efficient Colonial abounds in features. A
spacious entry flanked by living areas. A kitchen
flanked by eating areas. Upstairs, four bedrooms
including a sitting room in the master suite.

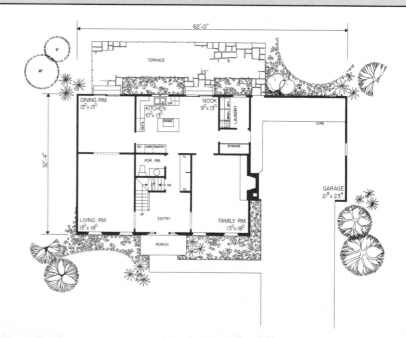

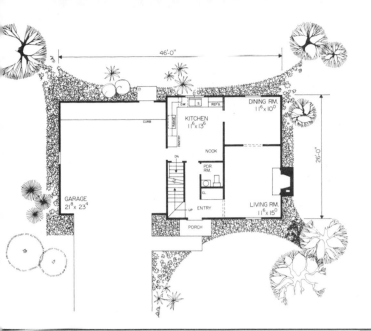

Design T92622
624 Sq. Ft. - First Floor
624 Sq. Ft. - Second Floor; 19,864 Cu. Ft.

● Appealing design can envelop little packages, too. Here is a charming, Early Colonial adaptation with an attached two-car garage to serve the young family with a modest building budget.

Design T91767

1,510 Sq. Ft. - First Floor
1,406 Sq. Ft. - Second Floor
42,070 Cu. Ft.

● An impressive Georgian adaptation that even at first glance seems to have a story of livability to tell. From the spacious center entry hall traffic can flow conveniently to all areas. And what delightful areas they are!

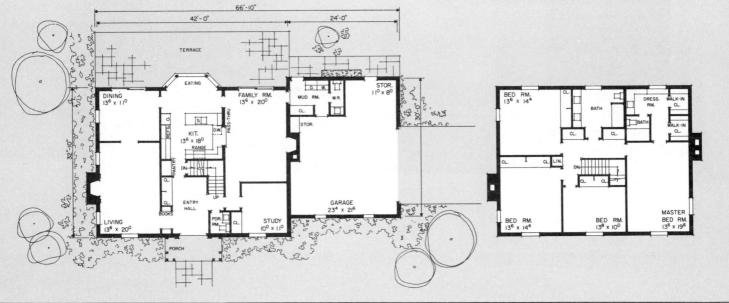

Design T92610

1,505 Sq. Ft. - First Floor
1,344 Sq. Ft. - Second Floor; 45,028 Cu. Ft.

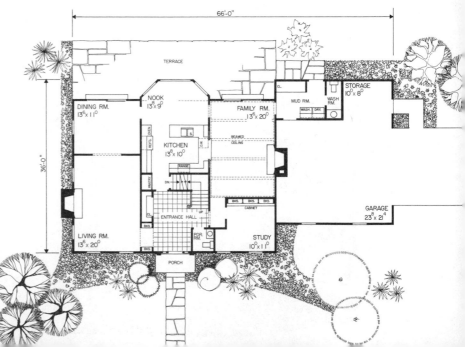

You'll never regret your choice of this Georgian design. Its stately facade seems to foretell all of the exceptional features to be found inside. From the delightfully spacious front entry hall, to the studio or maid's room over the garage this home is unique all along the way.

Design T91858
1,794 Sq. Ft. - First Floor
1,474 Sq. Ft. - Second Floor
424 Sq. Ft. - Studio; 54,878 Cu. Ft.

Design T92192

1,884 Sq. Ft. - First Floor
1,521 Sq. Ft. - Second Floor
58,380 Cu. Ft.

● This is surely a fine adaptation from the 18th-Century when formality and elegance were by-words. The authentic detailing of this design centers around the fine proportions, the dentils, the window symmetry, the front door and entranceway, the massive chimneys and the masonry work. The rear elevation retains all the grandeur exemplary of exquisite architecture. The appeal of this outstanding home does not end with its exterior elevations. Consider the formal living room with its corner fireplace. Also, the library with its wall of bookshelves and cabinets. Further, the dining room highlights corner china cabinets. Continue to study this elegant plan.

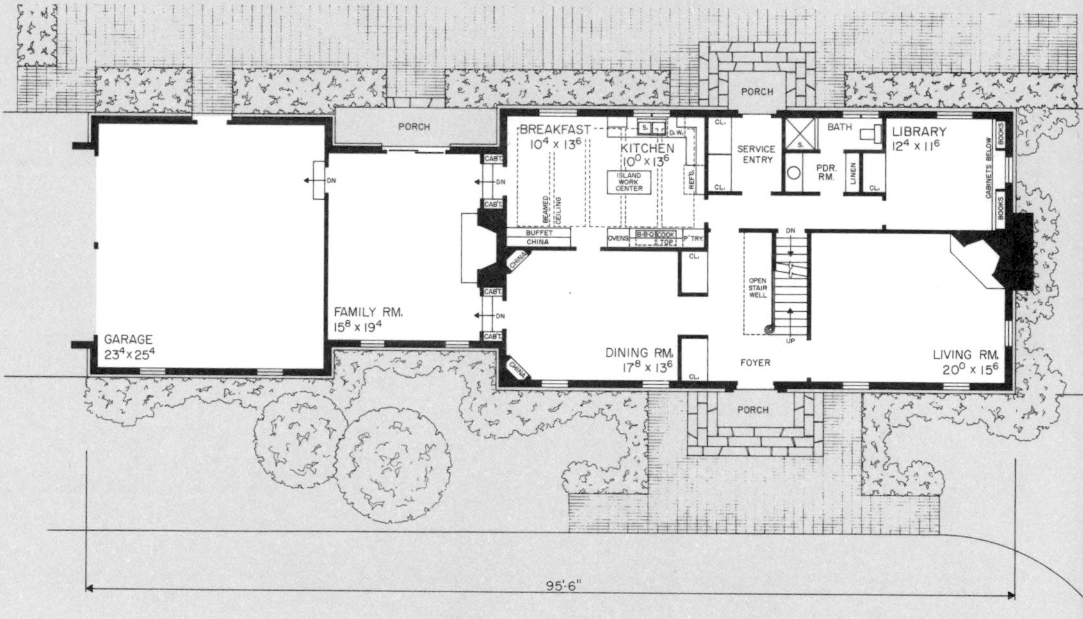

PORCH
PORCH
BREAKFAST
10⁴ x 13⁶
KITCHEN
10⁰ x 13⁶
ISLAND WORK CENTER
BEAMED CEILING
BUFFET
CHINA
OVENS
COOK TOP
SERVICE ENTRY
BATH
PDR. RM.
LINEN
LIBRARY
12⁴ x 11⁶
CABINETS BELOW
BOOKS
GARAGE
23⁴ x 25⁴
FAMILY RM.
15⁸ x 19⁴
CHINA
DINING RM.
17⁸ x 13⁶
OPEN STAIR WELL
FOYER
LIVING RM.
20⁰ x 15⁶
PORCH
95'-6"

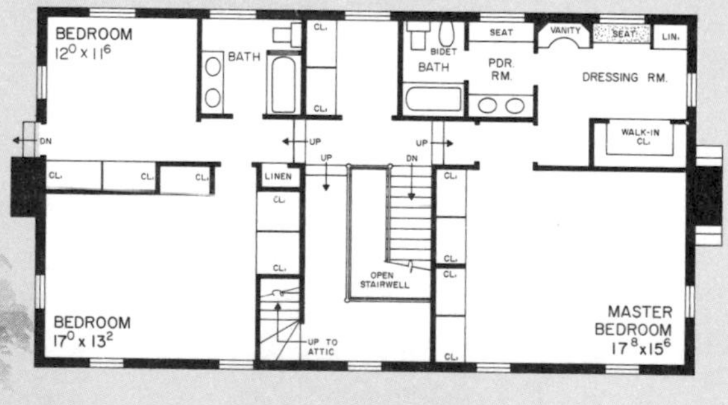

BEDROOM
12⁰ x 11⁶
BATH
BIDET
BATH
PDR. RM.
SEAT
VANITY
SEAT
LIN.
DRESSING RM.
WALK-IN CL.
LINEN
OPEN STAIRWELL
BEDROOM
17⁰ x 13²
UP TO ATTIC
MASTER BEDROOM
17⁸ x 15⁶

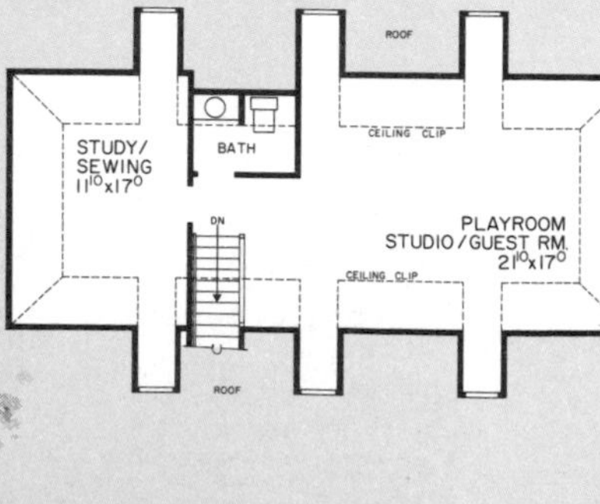

ROOF
STUDY/ SEWING
11¹⁰ x 17⁰
BATH
CEILING CLIP
PLAYROOM
STUDIO / GUEST RM.
21¹⁰ x 17⁰
CEILING CLIP
ROOF

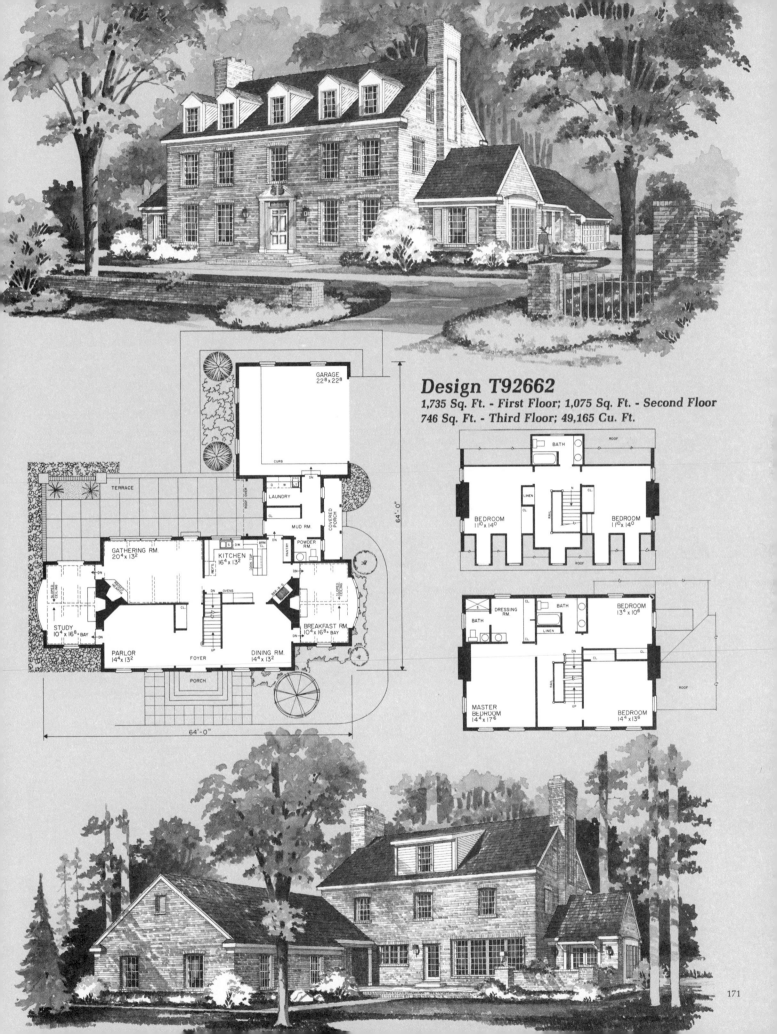

Design T92662

1,735 Sq. Ft. - First Floor; 1,075 Sq. Ft. - Second Floor
746 Sq. Ft. - Third Floor; 49,165 Cu. Ft.

GARAGE
22⁸ x 22⁸

CURB

ROOF OVER

LAUNDRY

CL

MUD RM.

COVERED PORCH

POWDER RM.

PANTRY

TERRACE

GATHERING RM.
20⁴ x 13²

KITCHEN
16⁴ x 13²

D.W.

BRM. CL

COOK TOP

OVENS

SLOPED CEILING

CL

STUDY
10⁴ x 16⁸ BAY

BREAKFAST RM.
10⁴ x 16⁸ BAY

PARLOR
14⁴ x 13²

FOYER

UP

DINING RM.
14⁴ x 13²

PORCH

64'-0"

64'-0"

BATH

ROOF

BEDROOM
11¹⁰ x 14⁰

LINEN

CL

RAIL

CL

BEDROOM
11¹⁰ x 14⁰

ROOF

DRESSING RM.

BATH

BATH

LINEN

CL

BEDROOM
13⁴ x 10⁶

CL

DN

CL

RAIL

CL

ROOF

MASTER BEDROOM
14⁴ x 17⁶

UP

BEDROOM
14⁴ x 13⁶

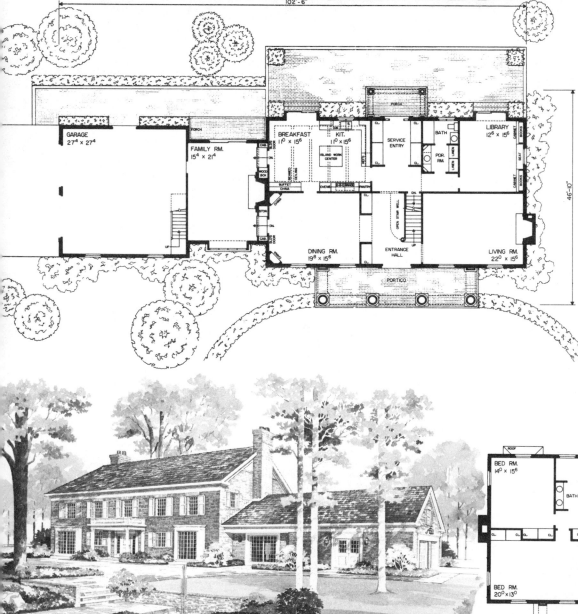

Design T92230
2,288 Sq. Ft. - First Floor
1,863 Sq. Ft. - Second Floor
79,736 Cu. Ft.

● The gracefulness and appeal of this southern adaptation will be everlasting. The imposing two-story portico is truly dramatic. Notice the authentic detailing of the tapered Doric columns, the balustraded roof deck, the denticulated cornice, the front entrance and the shuttered windows. The architecture of the rear is no less appealing. The spacious, formal front entrance hall provides a fitting introduction to the scale and elegance of the interior. The openness of the stairwell provides a view of the curving balusters above.

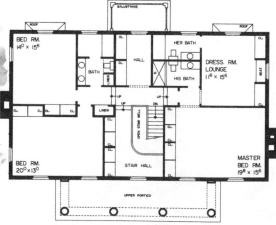

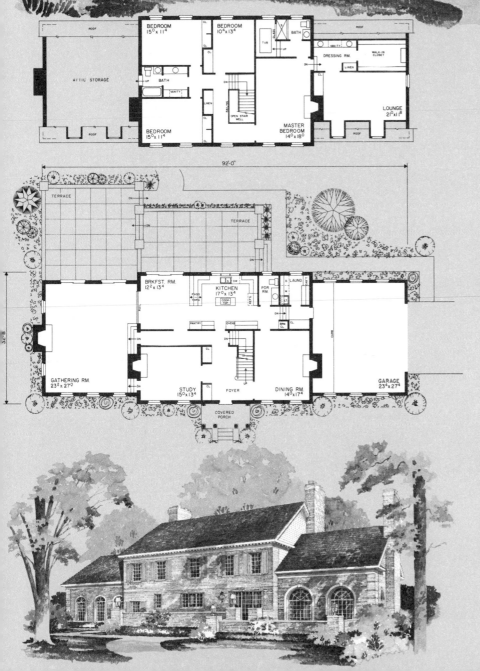

Design T92683
2,126 Sq. Ft. - First Floor
1,424 Sq. Ft. - Second Floor
78,828 Cu. Ft.

● This historical Georgian home has its roots in the 18th-Century. Dignified symmetry is a hallmark of both front and rear elevations. The full two-story center section is delightfully complimented by the 1½-story wings. Interior livability has been planned to serve today's active family. The elegant gathering room, three steps down from the rest of the house, has ample space for entertaining on a grand scale. It fills an entire wing and is dead-ended so that traffic does not pass through it. Guests and family alike will enjoy the two rooms flanking the foyer, the study and formal dining room. Each of these rooms will have a fireplace as its highlight. The breakfast room, kitchen, powder room and laundry are arranged for maximum efficiency. This area will always have that desired light and airy atmosphere with the sliding glass door and the triple window over the kitchen sink. The second floor houses the family bedrooms. Take special note of the spacious master bedroom suite. It has a deluxe bath, fireplace and sunken lounge with dressing room and walk-in closet. Surely an area to be appreciated.

173

Design T92107
1,020 Sq. Ft. - First Floor
720 Sq. Ft. - Second Floor
25,245 Cu. Ft.

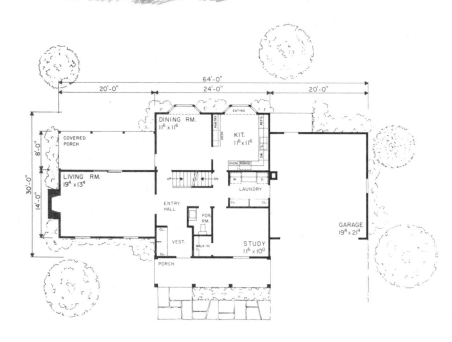

● There is no reason why it must take a fortune to build a Southern Colonial adaptation. This handsome exterior houses a plan under 2,000 square feet.

Design T92524
994 Sq. Ft. - First Floor
994 Sq. Ft. - Second Floor; 32,937 Cu. Ft.

● This small two-story, with a modest investment, will result in an impressive exterior and an outstanding interior which will provide exceptional livability. Your list of features will be long and surely impressive.

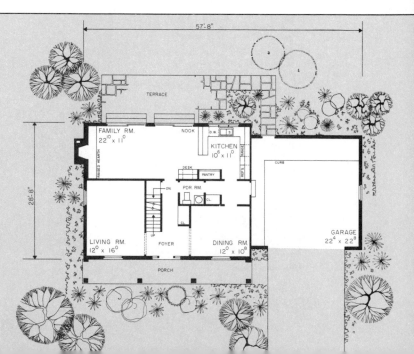

Design T92140 1,822 Sq. Ft. - First Floor; 1,638 Sq. Ft. - Second Floor; 52,107 Cu. Ft.

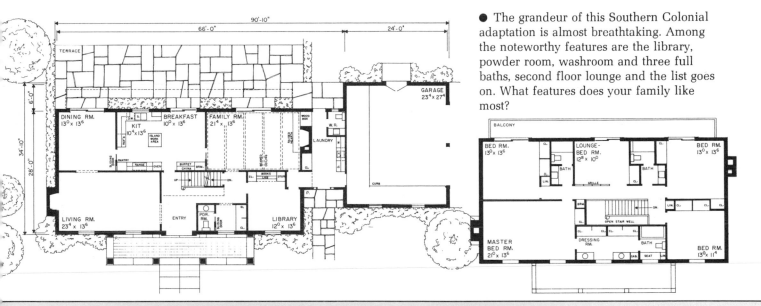

● The grandeur of this Southern Colonial adaptation is almost breathtaking. Among the noteworthy features are the library, powder room, washroom and three full baths, second floor lounge and the list goes on. What features does your family like most?

Design T92668 1,206 Sq. Ft. - First Floor
1,254 Sq. Ft. - Second Floor; 47,915 Cu. Ft.

● This elegant exterior houses a very livable plan. Every bit of space has been put to good use. The front country kitchen is a good place to begin. It is efficiently planned with its island cook top, built-ins and pass-thru to the dining room. The large great room will be the center of all family activities. Quiet times can be enjoyed in the front library. Study the second floor sleeping areas.

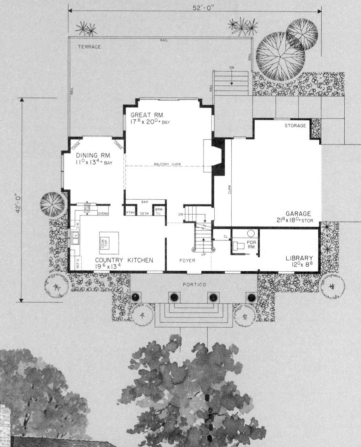

Design T92283

1,559 Sq. Ft. - First Floor
1,404 Sq. Ft. - Second Floor
48,606 Cu. Ft.

● Reminiscent of the stately character of Federal architecture during an earlier period in our history, this two-story is replete with exquisite detailing. The cornice work, the pediment gable, the dentils, the brick quoins at the corners, the beautifully proportioned columns, the front door detailing, the window treatment and the massive twin chimneys are among the features which make this design so unique.

Design T92281 1,961 Sq. Ft. - First Floor
1,472 Sq. Ft. - Second Floor; 49,974 Cu. Ft.

● Regal in character, this French design is a fine example of excellent proportion and perfect symmetry. The distinctiveness of this home continues right through the front doors into the spacious entrance hall with its curving staircase.

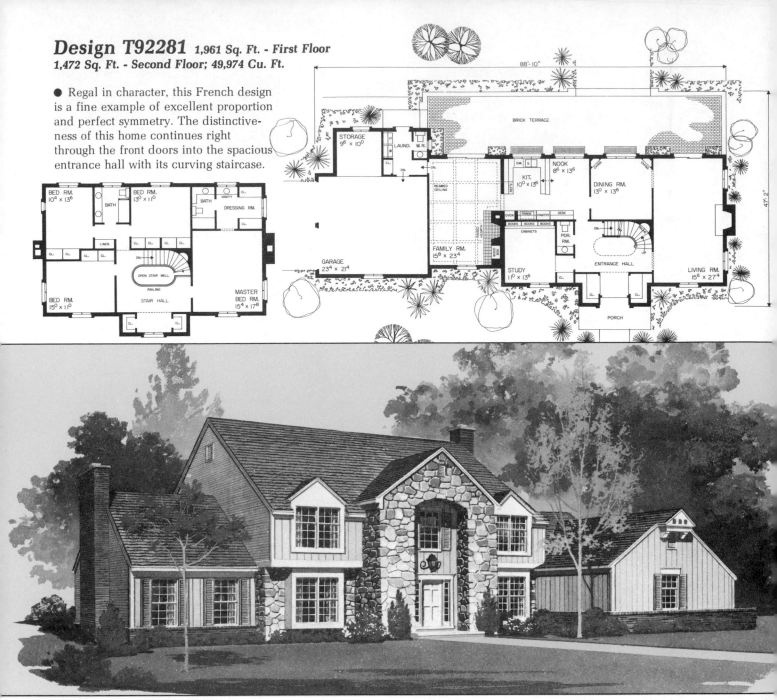

Design T92889 2,529 Sq. Ft. - First Floor
1,872 Sq. Ft. - Second Floor; 80,670 Cu. Ft.

● This is truly classical, Georgian design at its best. Some of the exterior highlights of this two-story include the pediment gable with cornice work and dentils, beautifully proportioned columns, front door detailing and window treatment.

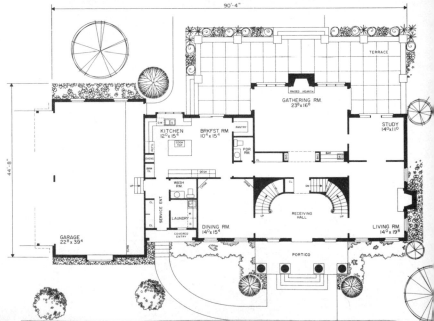

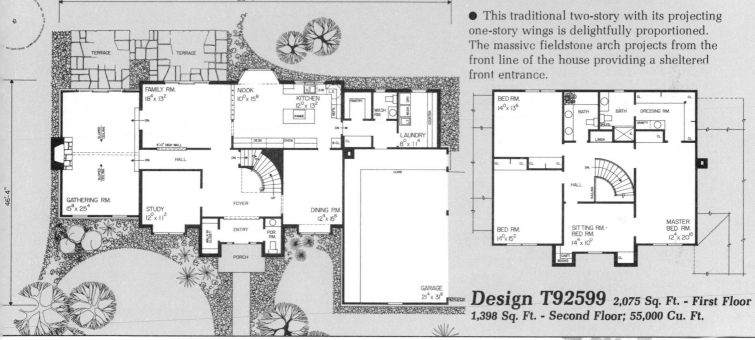

TERRACE TERRACE

FAMILY RM.
18⁴ x 13²

NOOK
10⁰ x 15⁸

KITCHEN
12⁰ x 13²

PANTRY

WASH RM.

LAUNDRY
8⁰ x 11⁴

SLOPED CEILING

4'-0" HIGH WALL

HALL

SLOPED CEILING

DESK

OVEN

B.CL.

CL.

GATHERING RM.
15⁸ x 25⁴

STUDY
12⁰ x 11²

FOYER

UP

DINING RM.
12⁰ x 15⁶

CURB

WALK IN CLOSET

ENTRY

PDR. RM.

PORCH

GARAGE
21⁴ x 31⁸

80'-4"

46'-4"

BED RM.
14⁰ x 13⁶

BATH

BATH

DRESSING RM.

VANITY

LINEN

CL.

HALL

DN.

RAILING

BED RM.
14⁰ x 15²

SITTING RM.-
BED RM.
14⁰ x 10⁰

MASTER
BED RM.
12⁴ x 20⁰

CAB'T
BOOKS

CL.

● This traditional two-story with its projecting one-story wings is delightfully proportioned. The massive fieldstone arch projects from the front line of the house providing a sheltered front entrance.

Design T92599 2,075 Sq. Ft. - First Floor
1,398 Sq. Ft. - Second Floor; 55,000 Cu. Ft.

Design T92687 1,819 Sq. Ft. - First Floor
1,472 Sq. Ft. - Second Floor; 56,820 Cu. Ft.

● Exterior styling of this home is reminiscent of the past but its floor plan is as up-to-date as it can get. Its many unique features include: a greenhouse, 78 square feet, off the country kitchen, a media room for all the modern electronic equipment, a hobby/laundry room with a washroom and a deluxe master bath. Imagine how your family will utilize each of these areas.

Design T92176 1,485 Sq. Ft. - First Floor; 1,175 Sq. Ft. - Second Floor; 41,646 Cu. Ft.

● This Georgian adaptation with its twin chimneys, brick quoins at the corners of the building, recessed panelled front entrance, twin carriage lamps, covered porch, pleasing window treatment and garage cupola will serve your family well. First of all, it will be one of the soundest investments you'll make in your lifetime. Then, it'll provide your family with years of wonderful living patterns. The big, end-living room features a fireplace and sliding glass doors to the rear terrace. Adjacent is the formal dining room strategically located but a couple of steps from the efficient kitchen. For informal eating there is the snack bar. Functioning closely with the kitchen is the family room. This will be the hub of activities. In addition to the beamed ceiling, there is the raised hearth fireplace, and built-in wood box, bookshelves and cabinets. Two sets of sliding glass doors provide access to both front and rear yards.

Design T92909 1,221 Sq. Ft. - First Floor
767 Sq. Ft. - Second Floor; 38,954 Cu. Ft.

● This charming traditional home with striking good looks offers the modern family plenty of contemporary amenities. The first floor features a large gathering room with fireplace, media room for stereos and VCRs, a convenient kitchen with breakfast room, plus a dining room.

Design T92826

1,112 Sq. Ft. - First Floor
881 Sq. Ft. - Second Floor; 32,770 Cu. Ft.

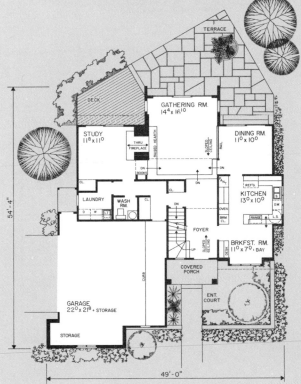

ALTERNATE KITCHEN / DINING RM /
BREAKFAST RM. FLOOR PLAN

● This is an outstanding example of the type of informal, traditional-style architecture that has captured the modern imagination. The interior plan houses all the features that people want most - a spacious gathering room, formal and informal dining areas, efficient, U-shaped kitchen, master bedroom, two children's bedrooms, second-floor lounge, entrance court and rear terrace and deck. Study all areas of this plan carefully.

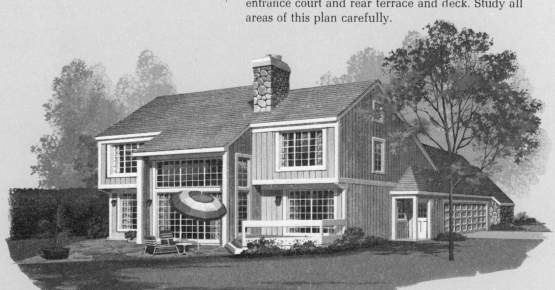

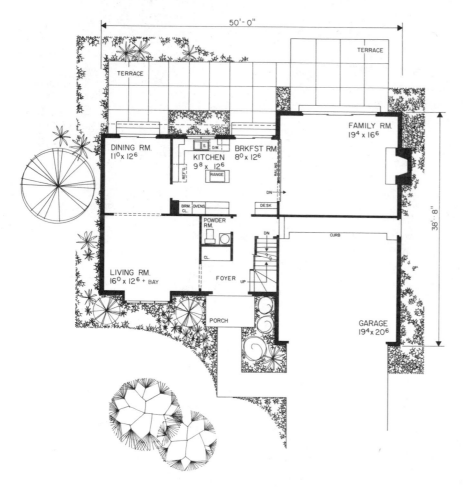

TERRACE

TERRACE

DINING RM.
11⁰ x 12⁶

KITCHEN
9⁸ x 12⁶

BRKFST RM.
8⁰ x 12⁶

FAMILY RM.
19⁴ x 16⁶

REF'G.

RANGE

BRM. OVENS
CL.

POWDER RM.

DESK

DN

DN

CURB

CL.

LIVING RM.
16⁰ x 12⁶ + BAY

FOYER

UP

PORCH

GARAGE
19⁴ x 20⁶

50'-0"

38'-8"

MASTER BEDROOM
11⁰ x 16⁸

BATH

BEDROOM/ STUDY
10² x 11⁰

CL.

BATH

CL.

HALL

LINEN

BEDROOM
13⁸ x 10⁴

CL.

BEDROOM
9³ x 10⁴

DN

CL.

Design T92798
1,149 Sq. Ft. - First Floor
850 Sq. Ft. - Second Floor
28,450 Cu. Ft.

● An island range in the kitchen is a great feature of the work center in this two-story French designed home. The breakfast room has an open railing to the sunken family room so it can enjoy the view of the family room's fireplace.

Sliding glass doors in each of the major rear rooms, dining, breakfast and family rooms, lead to the terrace for outdoor enjoyment. The front, formal living room is highlighted by a bay window. A powder room is conven-

iently located on the first floor near all of the major areas. All of the sleeping facilities are housed on the second floor. Each of the four bedrooms will serve its occupants ideally. A relatively narrow lot can house this design.

● Certainly a dramatic French adaptation highlighted by effective window treatment, delicate cornice detailing, appealing brick quoins and excellent proportion. Stepping through the double front doors the drama is heightened by the spacious entry hall with its two curving staircases to the second floor. The upper hall is open and looks down to the hall below. There is a study and a big gathering room which looks out on the raised terrace.

Design T92543

2,345 Sq. Ft. - First Floor
1,687 Sq. Ft. - Second Floor
76,000 Cu. Ft.

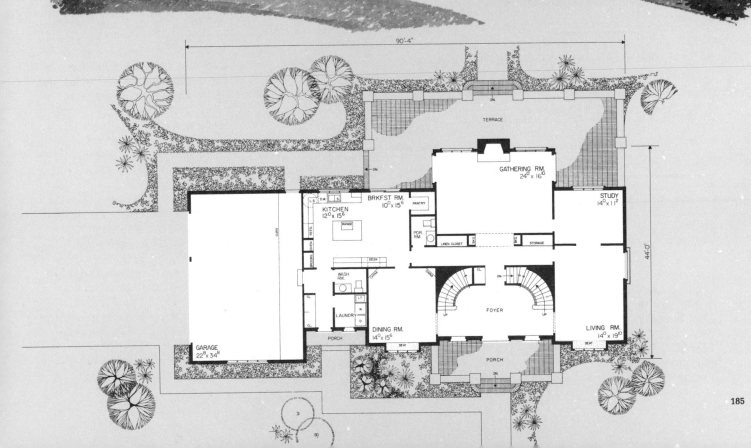

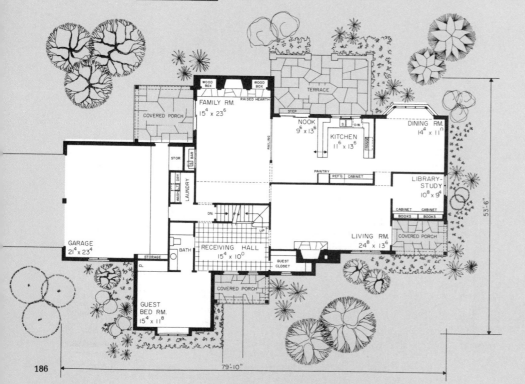

Design T92356

1,969 Sq. Ft. - First Floor
1,702 Sq. Ft. - Second Floor
55,105 Cu. Ft.

● Here is truly an exquisite Tudor adaptation. The exterior, with its interesting roof lines, its window treatment, its stately chimney and its appealing use of brick and stucco, could hardly be more dramatic. Inside, the drama really begins to unfold as one envisions his family's living patterns. The delightfully large receiving hall has a two story ceiling and controls the flexible traffic patterns. The living and dining rooms, with the library nearby, will cater to the formal living pursuits. The guest room offers another haven for the enjoyment of peace and quiet. Observe the adjacent full bath. Just inside the entrance from the garage is the laundry room. For the family's informal living activities there are the interactions of the family room - covered porch - nook - kitchen zone. Notice the raised hearth fireplace, the wood boxes, the sliding glass doors, built-in bar, and the kitchen pass-thru. Adding to the charm of the family room is its high ceiling. From the second floor hall one can look down and observe the activities below.

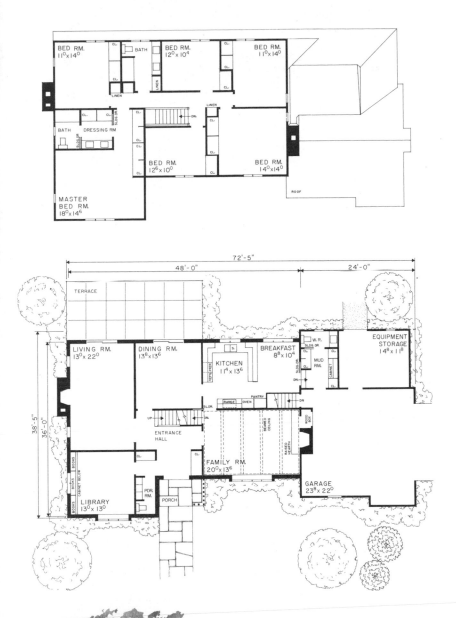

Design T92148
1,656 Sq. Ft. - First Floor
1,565 Sq. Ft. - Second Floor
48,292 Cu. Ft.

● The charm of this Tudor adaptation could hardly be improved upon. Its fine proportion and exquisite use of materials result in a most distinctive home. However, the tremendous exterior appeal tells only half of the story. Inside there is a breathtaking array of highlights which will cater to the whims of the large family. Imagine six large bedrooms, two full baths and plenty of closets on the second floor! The first floor has a formal living zone made up of the big living room, the separate dining room, and the sizeable library. A second zone is comprised of the U-shaped kitchen, the breakfast room and the family room — all contributing to fine informal family living patterns. Behind the garage is the mud room, wash room and the practical equipment storage room. Don't miss beamed ceiling, powder room, two fireplaces and two flights of stairs to basement.

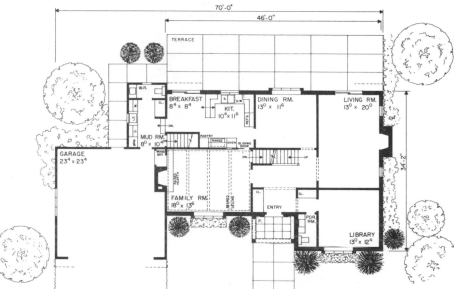

Design T92141 1,490 Sq. Ft. - First Floor
1,474 Sq. Ft. - Second Floor; 50,711 Cu. Ft.

● Imagine, six bedrooms on the second floor. The first floor houses the living areas: family room, living room, dining areas plus a library. Not much more livability could be packed into this spaciously designed home.

Design T92276 1,273 Sq. Ft. - First Floor
1,323 Sq. Ft. - Second Floor; 40,450 Cu. Ft.

● What a great home for the large, growing family. Five bedrooms and three baths are on the second floor. Both the formal and informal areas on the first floor are outstanding.

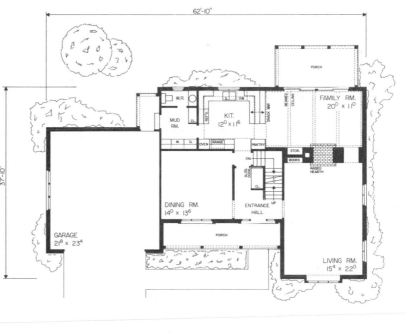

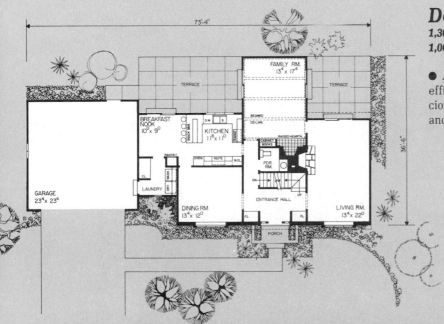

Design T92637
1,308 Sq. Ft. - First Floor
1,063 Sq. Ft. - Second Floor; 34,250 Cu. Ft.

● A generous, centered entrance hall routes traffic efficiently to all areas. And what wonderfully spacious areas they are. Note living, dining, sleeping and bath facilities. Don't miss first floor laundry.

Design T92391 2,496 Sq. Ft. - First Floor; 958 Sq. Ft. - Second Floor; 59,461 Cu. Ft.

● Here is a stately English adaptation that is impressive, indeed. The two-story octagonal foyer strikes a delightfully authentic design note. The entrance hall with open staircase and two-story ceiling is spacious. Clustered around the efficient kitchen are the formal living areas and those catering to informal activities. The family room with its beamed ceiling and raised hearth fireplace functions, like the formal living/dining zone, with the partially enclosed outdoor terrace. Three bedrooms with two baths comprise the first floor sleeping zone. Each room will enjoy its access to the terrace. Upstairs there are two more bedrooms and a study. Notice the sliding glass doors to the balcony and how the study looks down into the entrance hall. The three-car garage is great.

Design T91988

1,650 Sq. Ft. - First Floor
1,507 Sq. Ft. - Second Floor
49,474 Cu. Ft.

● A charming English Tudor adaptation which retains all the appeal of yesteryear, yet features an outstanding and practical contemporary floor plan. With all those rooms to serve a myriad of functions, the active family will lead a glorious existence. Imagine a five bedroom second floor. Or, make it a four bedroom, plus study, upstairs. In addition to the two full baths and fine closet facilities, there is convenient access to the huge storage area over the garage. Downstairs, flanking the impressive, formal front entry hall, there is space galore. The twenty-six foot, end living room will certainly be a favorite feature. The family room is large and will be lots of fun to furnish. The excellent kitchen is strategically located between the formal dining room and the informal breakfast room. The mud room is ideally located to receive traffic from the garage as well as from the rear yard. Don't miss the wash room and the powder room. Note pass-thru from kitchen to family room and abundance of storage available in garage.

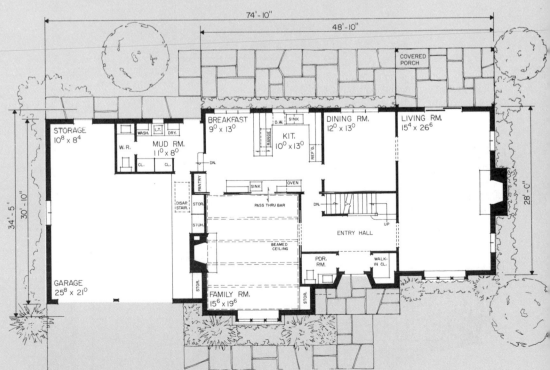

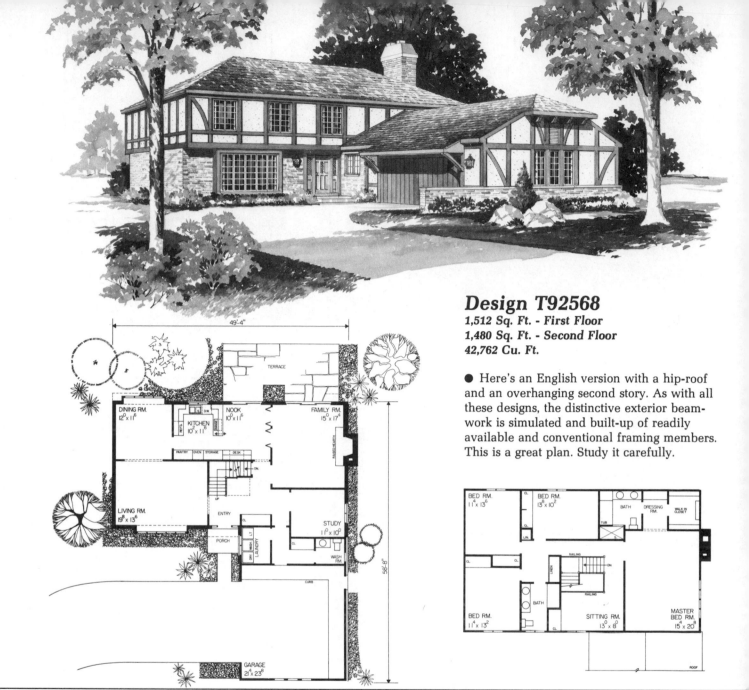

Design T92568

1,512 Sq. Ft. - First Floor
1,480 Sq. Ft. - Second Floor
42,762 Cu. Ft.

● Here's an English version with a hip-roof and an overhanging second story. As with all these designs, the distinctive exterior beamwork is simulated and built-up of readily available and conventional framing members. This is a great plan. Study it carefully.

● A Tudor adaptation with unique appeal and interesting living patterns. The main, two-story section of this house is flanked by two, one-story wings. Balancing the two-car garage is the living wing comprised of the formal living room and the informal family room.

Design T92242

1,327 Sq. Ft. - First Floor; 832 Sq. Ft. - Second Floor
35,315 Cu. Ft.

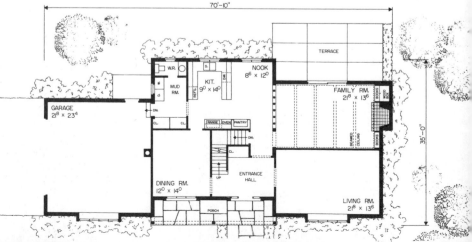

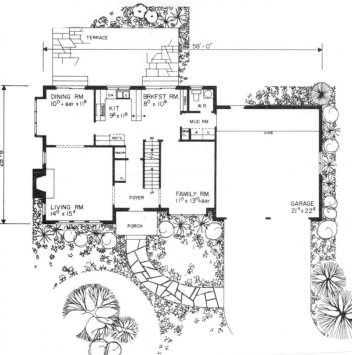

Design T92800 999 Sq. Ft. - First Floor
997 Sq. Ft. - Second Floor; 31,390 Cu. Ft.

● Note the fine features on the first floor of this design. Attractively detailed bay windows are in both the formal dining room and the family room. The beauty and warmth of a fireplace will be enjoyed from the formal living room. U-shaped kitchen, breakfast room, laundry and washroom are also on the first floor. Two bedrooms, bath and master bedroom with adjoining nursery/study are on the second floor.

Design T92829
2,044 Sq. Ft. - First Floor
1,962 Sq. Ft. - Second Floor; 74,360 Cu. Ft.

● The architecture of this design is Post-Modern with a taste of Victorian styling. Detailed with gingerbread woodwork and a handsome double-width chimney, this two-story design is breathtaking. Enter this home to the large, tiled receiving hall and begin to explore this very livable floor plan. Formal areas consist of the front living room and the dining room. Each has features to make it memorable. The living room is spacious, has a fireplace and access to the covered porch; the dining room has a delightful bay window and is convenient to the kitchen for ease in meal serving. The library is tucked between these two formal areas. Now let's go to the informal area. The family room will welcome many an explorer. It will be a great place for many family activities. Note the L-shaped snack bar with cabinets below. Onward to the second floor, where the private area will be found. Start with the two bedrooms that have two full bathrooms joining them together. The older children will marvel at this area's efficiency and privacy. A third family bedroom is nearby. Then, there is the master bedroom suite. Its list of features is long, indeed. Begin with the "his" and "her" baths and see how many features you can list. A guest bedroom and bath are on the first floor.

194

Design T92855 1,372 Sq. Ft. - First Floor
1,245 Sq. Ft. - Second Floor; 44,495 Cu. Ft.

● This elegant Tudor house is perfect for the family who wants to move-up in living area, style and luxury. As you enter this home, you will find a large living room with a fireplace on your right. Adjacent, the formal dining room has easy access to both the living room and the kitchen. The kitchen/breakfast room has an open plan and access to the rear terrace. The sunken family room can be entered by either the breakfast room or the foyer.

Design T92508 1,692 Sq. Ft. - First Floor
1,445 Sq. Ft. - Second Floor; 53,120 Cu. Ft.

● Dramatic, indeed! Both the inside and outside of this design are noteworthy. The two-story Tudor exterior will catch the eye of even the most casual onlooker. Note the impressive chimney. Inside, this plan will meet every family need. Formal and informal areas are separated and each is a good size. The cooking island in the kitchen will be well received. Three bedrooms are on the second floor. A study area is adjacent to the master bedroom. It overlooks the living room and foyer below.

195

● This authentic Spanish Colonial adaptation has its roots in the past. Here is a design whose exterior captures the romance of a by-gone era, while its floor plan offers all the up-to-date conveniences of today's living. Space is obviously the byword. for there are over 3,300 square feet. List your favorite features.

Design T92136
1,688 Sq. Ft. - First Floor
1,688 Sq. Ft. - Second Floor
50,353 Cu. Ft.

Design T92214

3,011 Sq. Ft. - First Floor
2,297 Sq. Ft. - Second Floor
78,585 Cu. Ft.

● A Spanish hacienda with all the appeal and all the comforts one would want in a new home. This is a house that looks big and really is big. Measuring 100 feet across the front with various appendages and roof planes, this design gives the appearance of a cluster of units. And with the long balcony and overhanging roof the size appears even greater. The house represents over 5,000 square feet without the garage. And the available living space is utilized in grand fashion. There are five bedrooms on the second floor plus a sixth and a study on the first. The master bedroom features two full baths and a sleeping porch. The living room is 27 feet long and if you wanted more space you could do away with the plant area. Or, maybe you'd prefer to make this a music area. The 18 foot dining room will seat a houseful. The kitchen is nearby, but a step from the breakfast nook and the family room. Then there is the three car garage with a big bulk storage room. Don't overlook the private front courtyard. Just a great house for the large, active family.

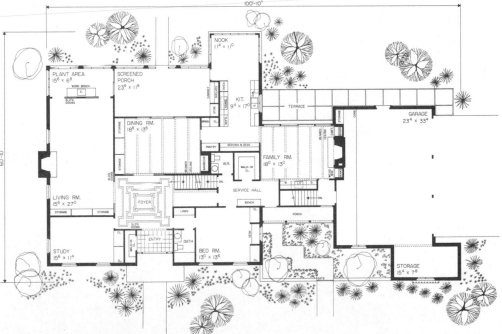

Design T92379

1,525 Sq. Ft. - First Floor
748 Sq. Ft. - Second Floor
26,000 Cu. Ft.

● A house that has "everything" may very well look just like this design. Its exterior is well-proportioned and impressive. Inside the inviting double front doors there are features galore. The living room and family room level is sunken. Separating these two rooms is a dramatic thru fireplace. A built-in bar, planter and beamed ceiling highlight the family room. The fine functioning kitchen has a pass-thru to the snack bar in the breakfast nook. The adjacent dining room overlooks the living room.

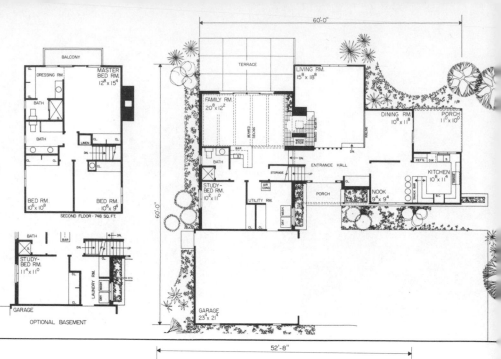

Design T92925

1,128 Sq. Ft. - First Floor
884 Sq. Ft. - Second Floor
35,220 Cu. Ft.

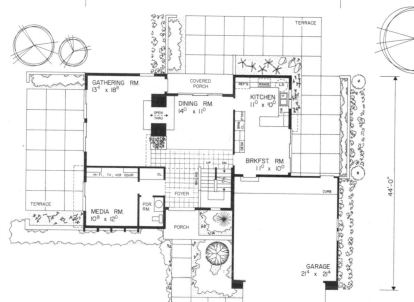

● This attractive two-story home with the vertical, textured look of stone and wood offers plenty of comfort for Contemporary lifestyles. Two bedrooms including master suite with whirlpool are located upstairs, along with an upper gathering room, railed balcony, and upper foyer. Downstairs one finds a front media room, large rear gathering room, convenient kitchen with adjoining breakfast room, and a formal dining room. Note also the foyer and two-car garage with storage behind the curb.

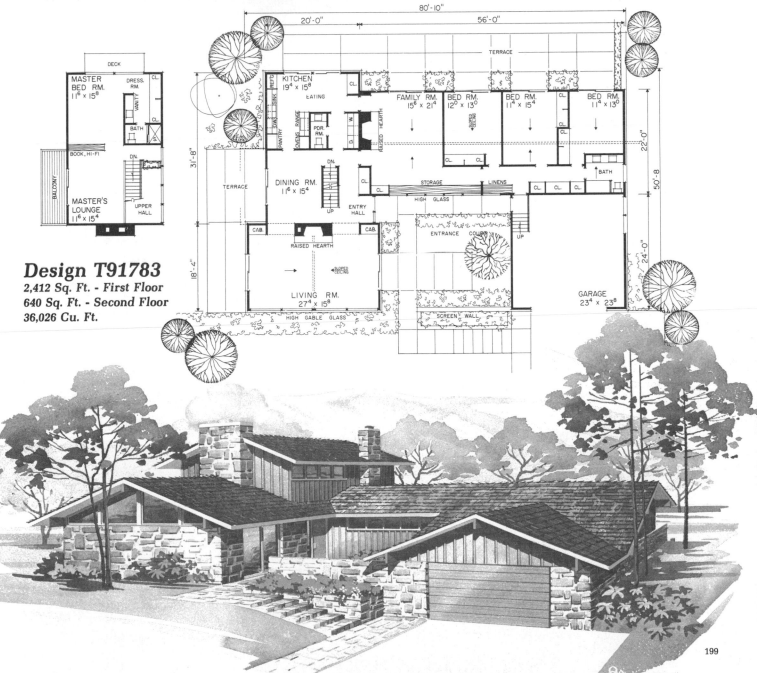

Design T91783

2,412 Sq. Ft. - First Floor
640 Sq. Ft. - Second Floor
36,026 Cu. Ft.

MASTER BED RM.
$11^6 \times 15^8$

DRESS. RM.
CL.
VANITY
BATH
CL.
S.

BOOK, HI-FI

DN.

BALCONY

MASTER'S LOUNGE
$11^6 \times 15^4$

UPPER HALL

DECK

80'-10"
20'-0"
56'-0"

TERRACE

KITCHEN
$19^4 \times 15^8$

EATING

SINK
REFG.
CL.

PANTRY
OVENS
RANGE

PDR. RM.

D.
W.

RAISED HEARTH

FAMILY RM.
$15^6 \times 21^4$

BED RM.
$12^0 \times 13^0$

BED RM.
$11^4 \times 15^4$

BED RM.
$11^4 \times 13^0$

CL.
CL.

CL.

31'-8"

TERRACE

DINING RM.
$11^6 \times 15^4$

DN.
UP

CL.
CL.

ENTRY HALL

STORAGE

LINENS

HIGH GLASS

CL.
CL.
CL.

BATH

22'-0"

50'-8"

18'-4"

CAB.

RAISED HEARTH

CAB.

SLOPED CEILING

LIVING RM.
$27^4 \times 15^8$

ENTRANCE

COURT

UP

24'-0"

GARAGE
$23^4 \times 23^8$

HIGH GABLE GLASS

SCREEN WALL

Design T92123

1,624 Sq. Ft. - First Floor; 1,335 Sq. Ft. - Second Floor
42,728 Cu. Ft.

● Inside there is close to 3,000 square feet of uniquely planned floor area. The spacious, well-lighted entry has, of course, a high sloping ceiling. A second floor balcony looks down from above. This area features two walk-in closets. Between the dining and living rooms is a thru fireplace which may be enjoyed from either room. Between the garage and the family room is the laundry and the compartmented powder room. The second floor ceilings slope and, consequently, add to the feeling of spaciousness.

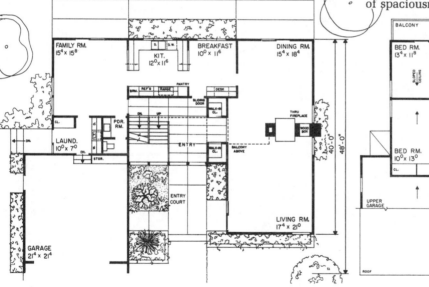

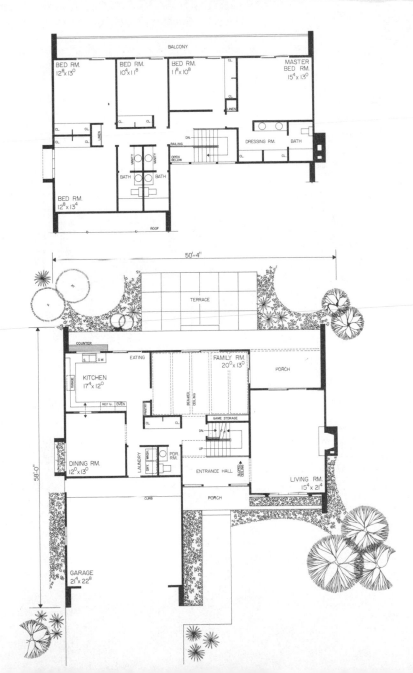

Design T92390
1,368 Sq. Ft. - First Floor
1,428 Sq. Ft. - Second Floor
37,734 Cu. Ft.

● If yours is a large family and you like the architecture of the Far West don't look further. Particularly if you envision building on a modest sized lot. Projecting the garage to the front contributes to the drama of this contemporary two-story. Its stucco exterior is beautifully enhanced by the clay tiles of the varying roof surfaces. Inside the double front doors is just about everything a large, active family would require for pleasurable, convenient living. The focal point, of course, is the five bedroom (count'em), three bath second floor. Four bedrooms have access to the outdoor balcony. The first floor offers two large living areas - the formal living and the informal family rooms - plus, two eating areas. Although there is the basement, the laundry is on the first floor. Don't overlook the covered porch accessible by family and living rooms.

Design T92711 975 Sq. Ft. - First Floor
1,024 Sq. Ft. - Second Floor; 31,380 Cu. Ft.

● Special features! A complete master suite with a private balcony plus two more bedrooms and a bath upstairs. The first floor has a study with a storage closet. A convenient snack bar between kitchen and dining room. The kitchen offers many built-in appliances. Plus a gathering room and dining room that measures 31 feet wide. Note the curb area in the garage and fireplace in gathering room.

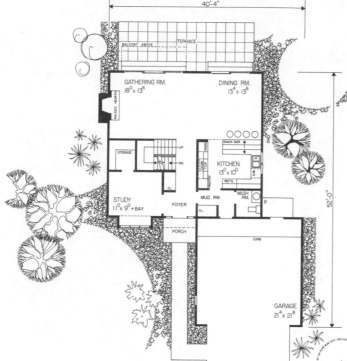

Design T92748
1,232 Sq. Ft. - First Floor
720 Sq. Ft. - Second Floor
27,550 Cu. Ft.

● This four bedroom contemporary will definitely have appeal for the entire family. The U-shaped kitchen-nook area with its built-in desk, adjacent laundry/wash room and service entrance will be very efficient for the busy kitchen activities. The living and family rooms are both sunken one step.

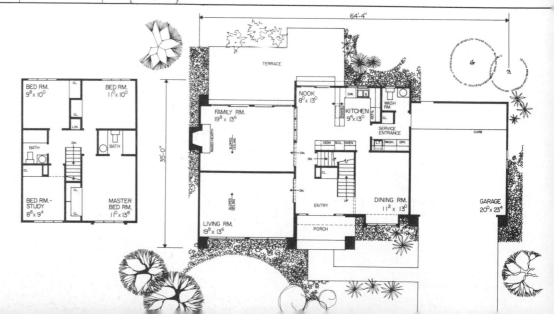

Design T92701 1,909 Sq. Ft. - First Floor
891 Sq. Ft. - Second Floor; 50,830 Cu. Ft.

● A snack bar in the kitchen! Plus a breakfast nook and formal dining room. Whether it's an elegant dinner party or a quick lunch, this home provides the right spot. There's a wet bar in the gathering room. Built-in bookcases in the study. And between these two rooms, a gracious fireplace. Three large bedrooms. Including a luxury master suite. Plus a balcony lounge overlooking gathering room below.

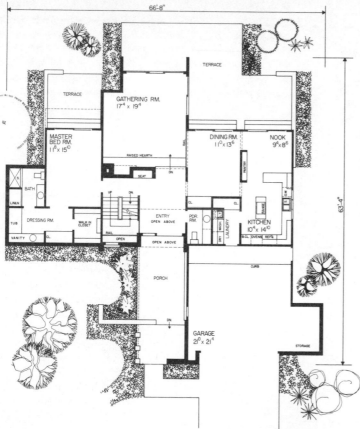

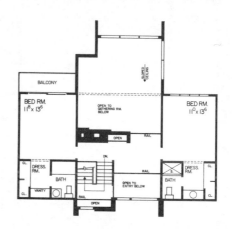

Design T92729
1,590 Sq. Ft. - First Floor
756 Sq. Ft. - Second Floor
39,310 Cu. Ft.

● Entering this home will surely be a pleasure through the sheltered walk-way to the double front doors. And the pleasure and beauty does not stop there. The entry hall and sunken gathering room are open to the upstairs for added dimension.

There's even a built-in seat in the entry area. The kitchen-nook area is very efficient with its many built-ins and the adjacent laundry room. There is a fine indoor-outdoor living relationship in this design. Note the private terrace off the luxurious

master bedroom suite, a living terrace accessible from the gathering room, dining room and nook plus the balcony off the upstairs bedroom. Upstairs there is a total of two bedrooms, each having its own private bath and plenty of closets.

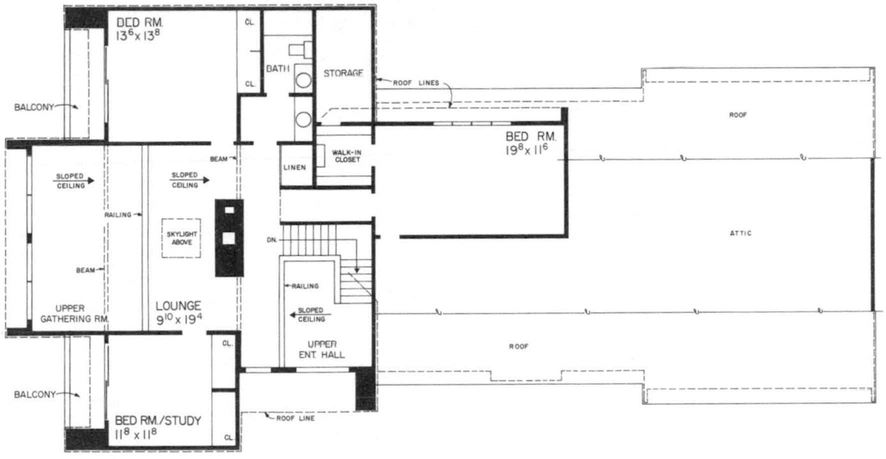

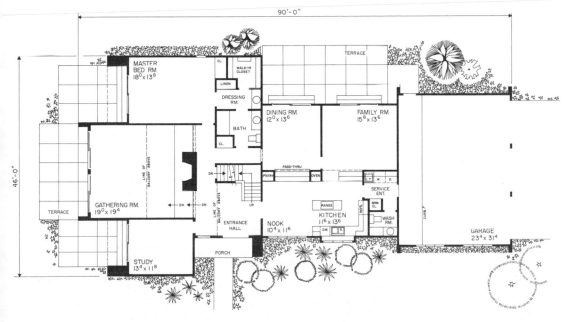

Upper floor plan labels:
BED RM. 13⁶x13⁸
BALCONY
CL.
CL.
BATH
STORAGE
ROOF LINES
SLOPED CEILING
SLOPED CEILING
BEAM
RAILING
SKYLIGHT ABOVE
BEAM
LINEN
WALK-IN CLOSET
BED RM. 19⁸x11⁶
ROOF
ATTIC
UPPER GATHERING RM.
LOUNGE 9¹⁰x19⁴
DN.
RAILING
SLOPED CEILING
UPPER ENT. HALL
BALCONY
BED RM./STUDY 11⁸x11⁸
CL.
ROOF LINE
ROOF
CL.

First floor plan labels:
90'-0"
46'-0"
MASTER BED RM. 18⁰x13⁸
CL.
WALK-IN CLOSET
TERRACE
LINEN
DRESSING RM.
BATH
CL.
DINING RM. 12⁰x13⁶
FAMILY RM. 15⁸x13⁶
TERRACE
LINE OF BALCONY ABOVE
DN.
PASS-THRU
OVEN
PNTRY
SERVICE ENT.
GATHERING RM. 19⁰x19⁴
LINE OF BALCONY ABOVE
DN.
DN.
UP
W. D.
RANGE
BRM. CL.
WASH RM.
TERRACE
ENTRANCE HALL
NOOK 10⁴x11⁶
KITCHEN 11⁶x13⁶
DW.
CURB
GARAGE 23⁴x31⁴
STUDY 13⁴x11⁸
PORCH

Design T92781

2,132 Sq. Ft. - First Floor
1,156 Sq. Ft. - Second Floor
47,365 Cu. Ft.

● This beautifully designed two-story could be con-
sidered a dream house of a
lifetime. The exterior is
sure to catch the eye of
anyone who takes sight of
its unique construction.
The front kitchen features
an island range, adjacent
breakfast nook and pass-
thru to formal dining room.
The master bedroom suite
with its privacy and con-
venience on the first floor
has a spacious walk-in
closet and dressing room.
The side terrace is accessible through sliding glass
doors from the master bedroom, gathering room and
study. The second floor has
three bedrooms and storage
space galore. Also notice
the lounge which has a
sloped ceiling and a sky-
light above. This delightful
area looks down into the
gathering room. The out-
door balconies overlook the
wrap-around terrace. Surely an outstanding trend
house for decades to come.

Design T92905 *1,342 Sq. Ft. - First Floor; 619 Sq. Ft. - Second Floor; 33,655 Cu. Ft.*

● All of the livability in this plan is in the back! Each first floor room, except the kitchen, has access to the rear terrace via sliding glass doors. A great way to capture an excellent view. This plan is also ideal for a narrow lot seeing that its width is less than 50 feet. Two bedrooms and a lounge, overlooking the gathering room, are on the second floor.

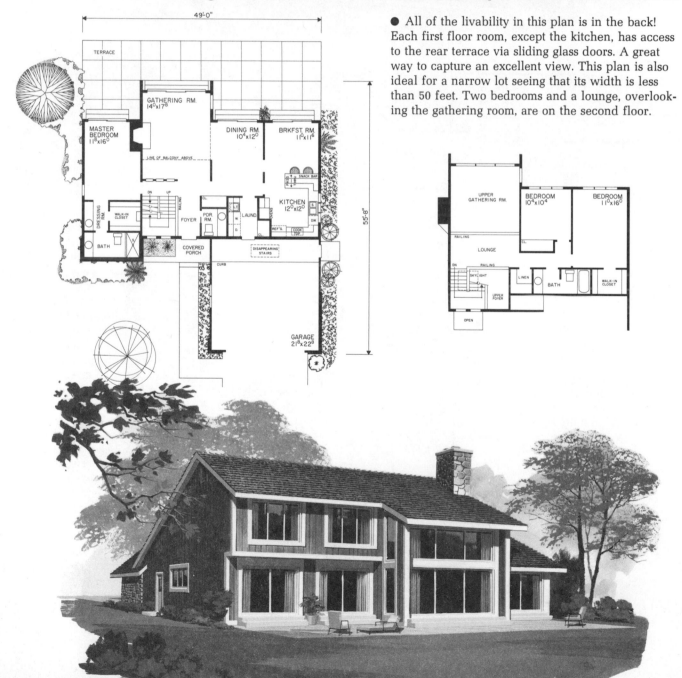

Design T92883
1,919 Sq. Ft. - First Floor
895 Sq. Ft. - Second Floor; 46,489 Cu. Ft.

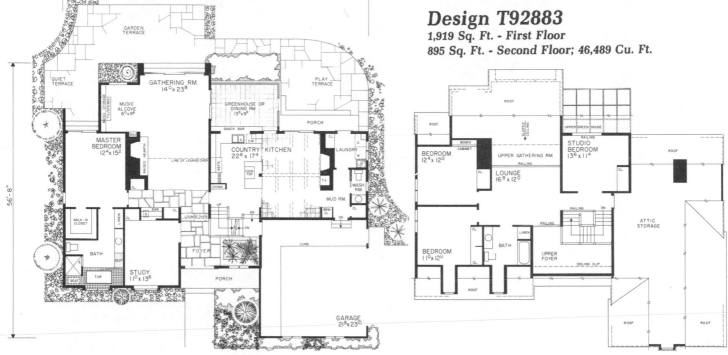

● A country-style home is part of America's fascination with the rural past. This home's emphasis of the traditional home is in its gambrel roof, dormers and fanlight windows. Having a traditional exterior from the street view, this home has window walls and a greenhouse, which opens the house to the outdoors in a thoroughly contemporary manner. The interior meets the requirements of today's active family. Like the country houses of the past, it has a gathering room for family get-togethers or entertaining. The adjacent two-story greenhouse doubles as the dining room. There is a pass-thru snack bar to the country kitchen here. This country kitchen just might be the heart of the house with its two areas - work zone and sitting room. There are four bedrooms on the two floors - the master bedroom suite on the first floor; three more on the second floor. A lounge, overlooking the gathering room and front foyer, is also on the second floor.

Design T92823
1,370 Sq. Ft. - First Floor
927 Sq. Ft. - Second Floor
34,860 Cu. Ft.

● The street view of this contemporary design features a small courtyard entrance as well as a private terrace off the study. Inside the livability will be outstanding. This design features spacious first floor activity areas that flow smoothly into each other. In the gathering room a raised hearth fireplace creates a dramatic focal point. An adjacent covered terrace, featuring a skylight, is ideal for outdoor dining and could be screened in later for an additional room.

Design T92488 1,113 Sq. Ft. - First Floor; 543 Sq. Ft. - Second Floor; 36,055 Cu. Ft.

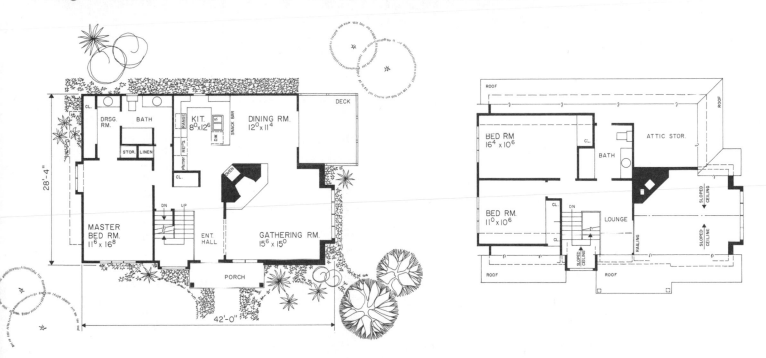

● A cozy cottage for the young at heart! Whether called upon to serve the young active family as a leisure-time retreat at the lake, or the retired couple as a quiet haven in later years, this charming design will perform well. As a year round second home, the up- stairs with its two sizable bedrooms, full bath and lounge area looking down into the gathering room below, will ideally accommodate the younger generation. When called upon to func- tion as a retirement home, the second floor will cater to the visiting family members and friends. Also, it will be available for use as a home office, study, sewing room, music area, the pursuit of hobbies, etc. Of course, as an efficient, economical home for the young, growing family, this design will function well.

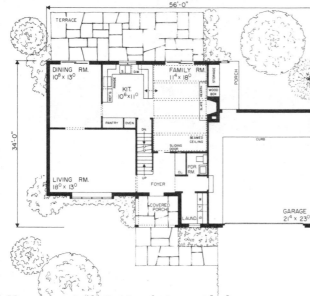

Design T92151

991 Sq. Ft. - First Floor
952 Sq. Ft. - Second Floor
28,964 Cu. Ft.

● Here are two distinctive designs with the same basic floor plan. Whether you order blueprints for the Tudor design T92151 above, or the Farmhouse design T92150 below, you will receive details for both the four and five bedroom versions. Note laundry, powder room, beamed ceiling, separate dining room.

OPTIONAL 4 BEDROOM PLAN

Design T92150

991 Sq. Ft. - First Floor
952 Sq. Ft. - Second Floor
27,850 Cu. Ft.

Design T91305 1,382 Sq. Ft.; 16,584 Cu. Ft.

● Order blueprints for any one of the three exteriors shown on this page and you will receive details for building this outstanding floor plan. You'll find the appeal of these exteriors difficult to beat. As for the plan, in less than 1,400 square feet there are three bedrooms, two full baths, a separate dining room, a formal living room, a fine kitchen overlooking the rear yard and an informal family room. In addition, there is the attached two-car garage. Note the location of the stairs when this plan is built with a basement. Each of the exteriors is predominantly brick - the front of Design T91305 (above) features both stone and vertical boards and battens with brick on the other three sides. Observe the double front doors of the French design, T91382 (below) and the Contemporary design, T91383 (bottom). Study the window treatment.

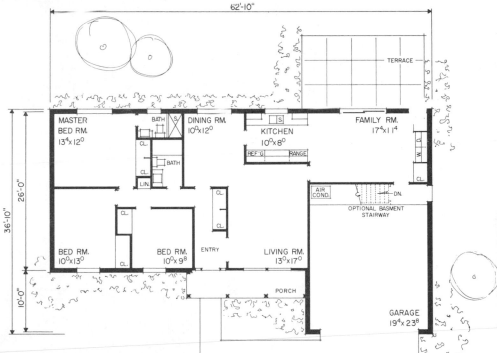

Design T91382
1,382 Sq. Ft.; 17,164 Cu. Ft.

Design T91383
1,382 Sq. Ft.; 15,448 Cu. Ft.

OPTIONAL BASEMENT

Design T91920
1,600 Sq. Ft.; 18,996 Cu. Ft.

● A charming exterior with a truly great floor plan. The front entrance with its covered porch seems to herald all the outstanding features to be found inside. Study the sleeping zone with its three bedrooms and two full baths. Note the efficient kitchen with the family and dining rooms to each side. Observe the laundry and the extra washroom.

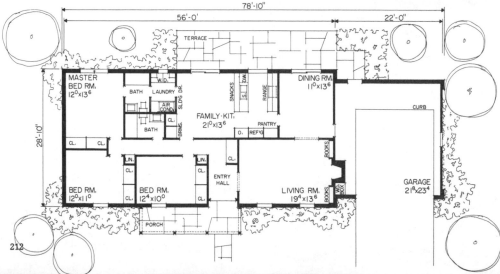

Design T91890
1,628 Sq. Ft.; 20,350 Cu. Ft.

● The pediment gable and columns help set the charm of this modestly sized home. Here is graciousness normally associated with homes twice its size. The pleasant symmetry of the windows and the double front doors complete the picture. Inside, each square foot is wisely planned to assure years of convenient living. There are three bedrooms, each with twin wardrobe closets.

OPTIONAL BASEMENT

Design T92607
1,208 Sq. Ft.; 15,183 Cu. Ft.

● Subtly Tudor! With stylish features. Like a large bay window in the kitchen. It's a perfect spot for the breakfast table . . . sunny and pleasant whatever the season. Adjoining living/dining rooms with a built-in bookcase and china cabinet. A traditionally styled fireplace, too. Two large bedrooms. A bath and a half. Plus a conveniently located laundry room. This is a delightfully appointed home! Perfect for small families who want luxury in a limited space.

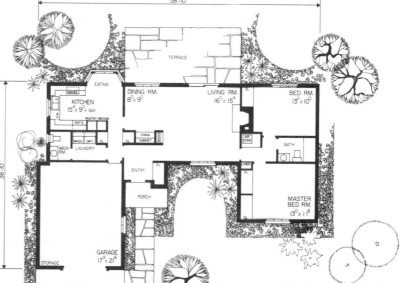

OPTIONAL BASEMENT

Design T92606
1,499 Sq. Ft.; 29,266 Cu. Ft.

● This modest sized house could hardly offer more in the way of exterior charm and interior livability. The orientation of the garage and the front drive court are features which promote an economical use of property. In addition to the formal, separate living and dining rooms, there are the informal kitchen-family room areas. Note the beamed ceiling the fireplace and the sliding glass doors.

Design T92570
1,176 Sq. Ft.; 26,800 Cu. Ft.

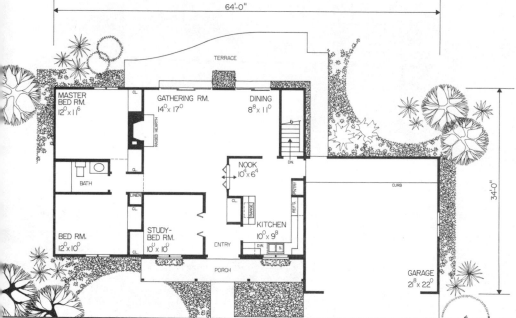

● This attractive Tudor is another economically built design which will cater
admirably to the living patterns of the
retired couple. In addition to the two
bedrooms this plan offers a study which
could double ideally as a guest room,
sewing room or even serve as the TV
room. The living area is a spacious L-
shaped zone for formal living and dining. The efficient kitchen is handy to the
front door and overlooks the front yard.
It features a convenient breakfast nook
for those informal meals. Handy to the
entry from the garage and the yard are
the stairs to the basement. Don't overlook the attractive front porch.

Design T91325
1,942 Sq. Ft.; 35,384 Cu. Ft.

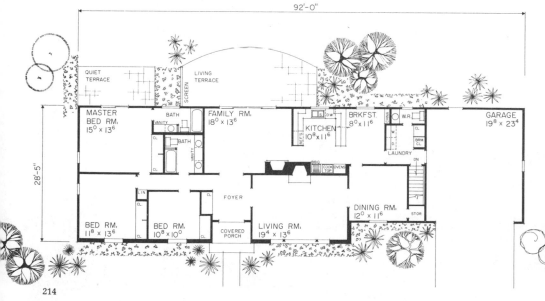

● The large front entry hall permits direct access to the formal living room, the sleeping area and
the informal family room. Both of
the living areas have a fireplace.
When formal dining is the occasion of the evening the separate
dining room is but a step from the
living room. The U-shaped kitchen
is strategically flanked by the family room and the breakfast areas.

214

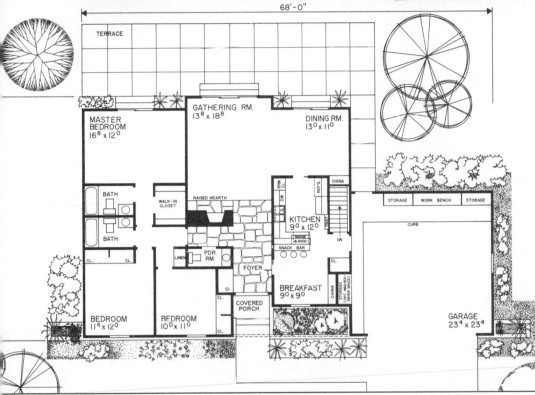

TERRACE

68'-0"

MASTER BEDROOM
16⁸ x 12⁰

GATHERING RM.
13⁸ x 18⁸

DINING RM.
13⁰ x 11⁰

BATH

BATH

WALK-IN CLOSET

RAISED HEARTH

KITCHEN
9⁰ x 12⁰

SNACK BAR

CHINA

REF'G.

STORAGE   WORK BENCH   STORAGE

CURB

LINEN

PDR. RM.

FOYER

CL.

CL.

BEDROOM
11⁴ x 12⁰

BEDROOM
10⁰ x 11⁰

COVERED PORCH

BREAKFAST
9⁰ x 9⁰

CHINA

STORAGE
(OPT. WASHER-DRYER SPACE)

GARAGE
23⁴ x 23⁴

Design T92671
1,589 Sq. Ft.; 36,210 Cu. Ft.

● The rustic exterior of this one-story home features vertical wood siding. The entry foyer is floored with flagstone and leads to the three areas of the plan: sleeping, living and work center. The sleeping area has three bedrooms, the master bedroom has sliding glass doors to the rear terrace. The living area, consisting of gathering and dining rooms, also has access to the terrace. The work center is efficiently planned. It houses the kitchen with snack bar, breakfast room with built-in china cabinet and stairs to the basement. This is a very livable plan.

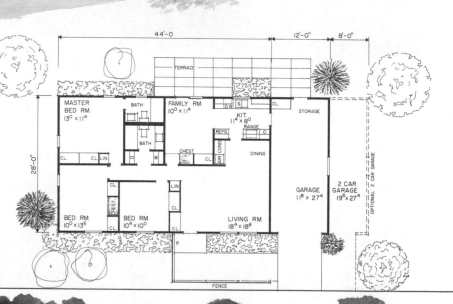

Design T91191
1,232 Sq. Ft.; 15,400 Cu. Ft.

● A careful study of the floor plan for this cozy appearing traditional home reveals a fine combination of features which add tremendously to convenient living. For instance, observe the wardrobe and storage facilities of the bedroom area. Then, notice the economical plumbing of the two back-to-back baths. Further, don't overlook the locations of the washer and dryer which have cupboards above the units themselves. Observe storage facilities.

Design T91939
1,387 Sq. Ft.; 28,000 Cu. Ft.

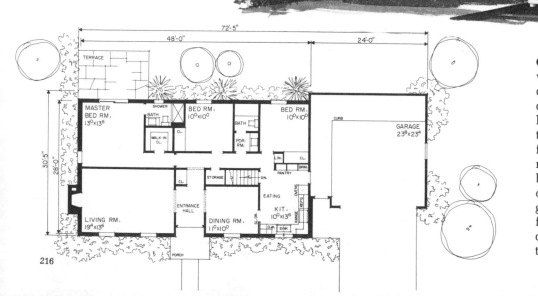

● A delightfully proportioned house with more than its full share of charm. The brick veneer exterior contrasts pleasingly with the narrow horizontal siding of the oversized attached two-car garage. Perhaps the focal point of the exterior is the recessed front entrance with its double Colonial styled doors. The secondary service entrance through the garage to the kitchen area is a handy feature. The pantry units are strategically located as are the stairs to the basement.

● Delightful design and effective, flexible planning come in little packages, too. This fine traditional exterior with its covered front entrance features an alternate basement plan. Note how the non-basement layout provides a family room and mud room, while the basement option shows kitchen eating and dining room.

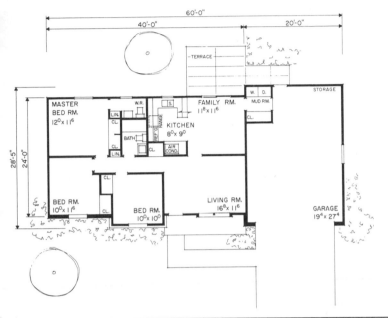

OPTIONAL BASEMENT PLAN

Design T91311
1,050 Sq. Ft.; 11,370 Cu. Ft.

Design T91075
1,232 Sq. Ft.; 24,123 Cu. Ft.

● This picturesque traditional one-story home has much to offer the young family. Because of it rectangular shape and its predominantly frame exterior, construction costs will be economical. Passing through the front entrance, visitors will be surprised to find so much livability in only 1232 square feet. Consider these features: spacious formal living and dining area; two full baths; efficient kitchen; large rear family room. In addition, there is the full basement for further recreational facilities and storage.

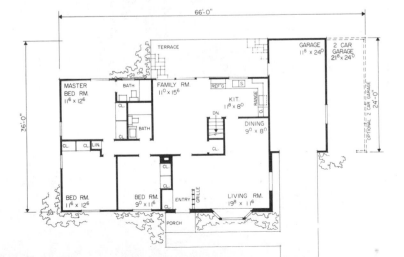

Design T92810
3-Bedroom Plan

Design T92814
4-Bedroom Plan

1,536 Sq. Ft.; 34,560 Cu. Ft.

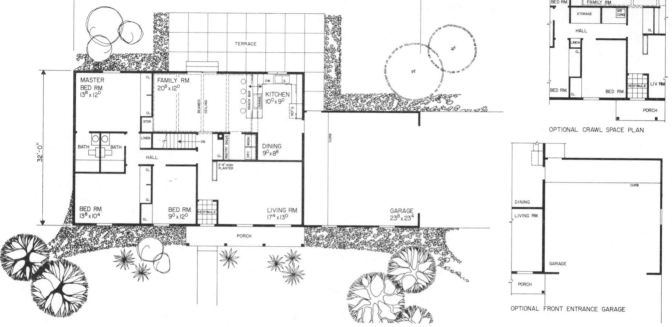

OPTIONAL CRAWL SPACE PLAN

OPTIONAL FRONT ENTRANCE GARAGE

● 2 x 6 stud wall construction front and center! The designs on these two pages are particularly energy-efficient minded. All exterior walls employ the use of the larger size stud (in preference to the traditional 2 x 4 stud) to permit the installation of extra thick insulation. The high cornice design also allows for more ceiling insulation. In addition to the insulation factor, 2 x 6 studs are practical from an economic standpoint. According to many experts, the use of 2 x 6's spaced 24 inches O.C. results in the need for less lumber and saves construction time. However, the energy-efficient features of this series do not end with the basic framing members. Efficiency begins right at the front door where the vestibule acts as an airlock restricting the flow of cold air to the interior. The basic rectangular shape of the house spells efficiency. No complicated and costly construction here. Yet, there has been no sacrifice of delightful exterior appeal. Efficiency and economy are also embodied in such features as back-to-back plumbing, centrally located furnace, minimal window and door openings and, most important of all - size.

Design T92811
3-Bedroom Plan

Design T92815
4-Bedroom Plan

1,581 Sq. Ft.; 36,694 Cu. Ft.

Design T92812
3-Bedroom Plan

Design T92816
4-Bedroom Plan

1,581 Sq. Ft.; 35,040 Cu. Ft.

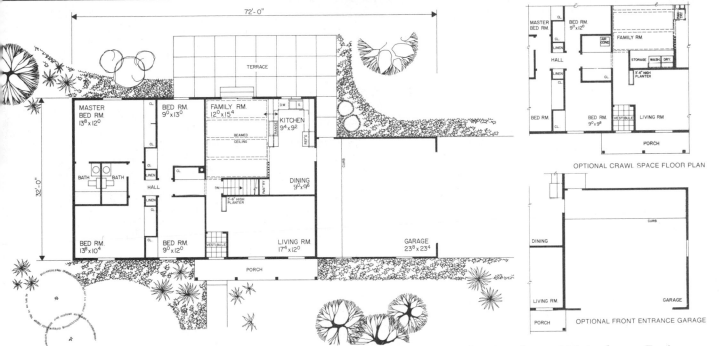

OPTIONAL CRAWL SPACE FLOOR PLAN

OPTIONAL FRONT ENTRANCE GARAGE

● Within 1,536 square feet there is outstanding livability and a huge variety of options from which to choose. For instance, of the four stylish exteriors, which is your favorite? The cozy, front porch Farmhouse adaptation; the pleasing Southern Colonial version, the French creation, or the rugged Western facade? Further, do you prefer a three or a four bedroom floor plan? With or without a basement? Front or side-opening garage? If you wish to order blueprints for the hip-roofed design with three bedrooms, specify Design T92812; for the four bedroom option specify T92816. To order blueprints for the three bedroom Southern Colonial, request Design T92811; for the four bedroom model, ask for Design T92815, etc. All blueprints include the optional non-basement and front opening garage details. Whatever the version you select, you and your family will enjoy the beamed ceiling of the family room, the efficient, U-shaped kitchen, the dining area, the traffic-free living room and the fine storage facilities. Truly, a fine design series created to give each home buyer the maximum amount of choice and flexibility.

Design T92813
3-Bedroom Plan

Design T92817
4-Bedroom Plan

1,536 Sq. Ft.; 33,334 Cu. Ft.

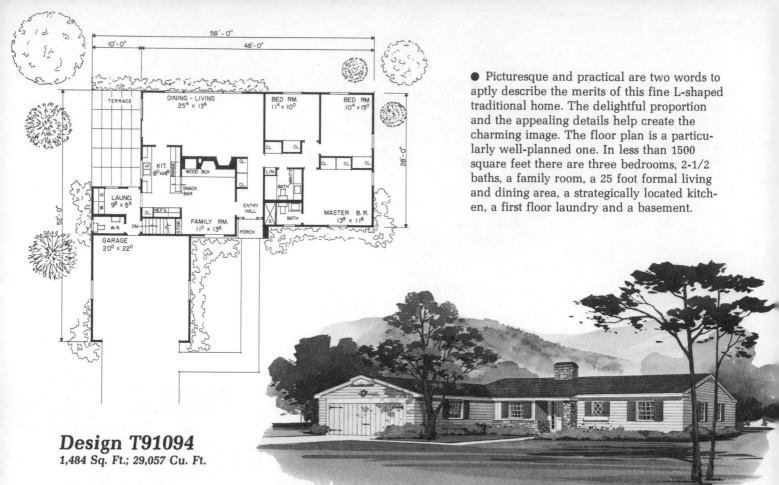

Design T91094
1,484 Sq. Ft.; 29,057 Cu. Ft.

● Picturesque and practical are two words to aptly describe the merits of this fine L-shaped traditional home. The delightful proportion and the appealing details help create the charming image. The floor plan is a particularly well-planned one. In less than 1500 square feet there are three bedrooms, 2-1/2 baths, a family room, a 25 foot formal living and dining area, a strategically located kitchen, a first floor laundry and a basement.

● The extension of the wide overhanging roof of this distinctive home provides shelter for the walkway to the front door. A raised brick planter adds appeal. The living patterns offered by this plan are delightfully different, yet extremely practical. Locating the kitchen in the middle of the plan frees up valuable outside wall space and leads to interesting planning. The front dining room is sunken for dramatic appeal and need not have any crossroom traffic.

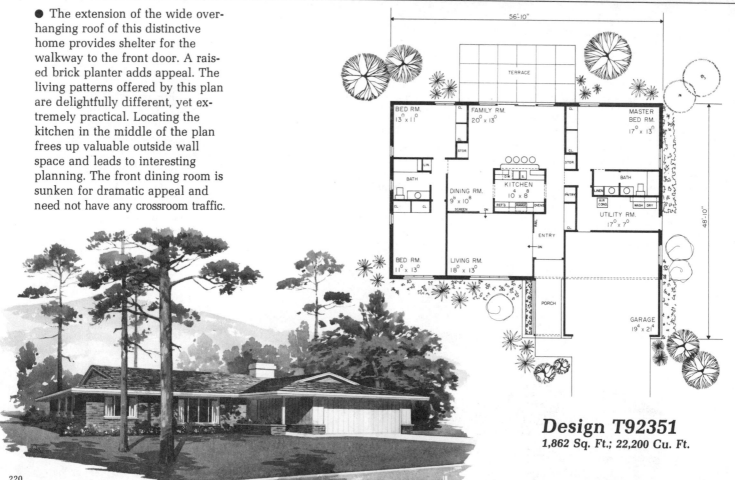

Design T92351
1,862 Sq. Ft.; 22,200 Cu. Ft.

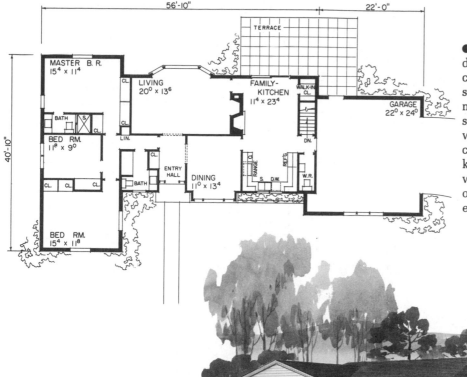

MASTER B.R. 15⁴ x 11⁴

LIVING 20⁰ x 13⁶

TERRACE

FAMILY-KITCHEN 11⁴ x 23⁴

WALK-IN CL.

GARAGE 22⁰ x 24⁰

BED RM. 11⁸ x 9⁰

ENTRY HALL

DINING 11⁰ x 13⁴

BATH

BED RM. 15⁴ x 11⁸

56'-10"   22'-0"

40'-10"

● What could be finer than to live in a delightfully designed home with all the charm of the exterior carried right inside. The interior points of interest are many. However, the focal point will surely be the big family-kitchen. The work center is U-shaped and most efficient. The family activity portion of the kitchen features an attractive fireplace which will contribute to an atmosphere of warmth and fellowship. Note extra washroom.

Design T91091
1,666 Sq. Ft.; 28,853 Cu. Ft.

● This inviting U-shaped western ranch adaptation offers outstanding living potential behind its double front doors and flanking glass panels. In but 1,754 square feet there are three bedrooms, 2½ baths, both formal and informal living areas, an excellently functioning kitchen, an adjacent breakfast nook and good storage facilities. The open stairwell to the lower level basement can be an interesting, interior feature. Note raised hearth fireplace and sloped ceiling.

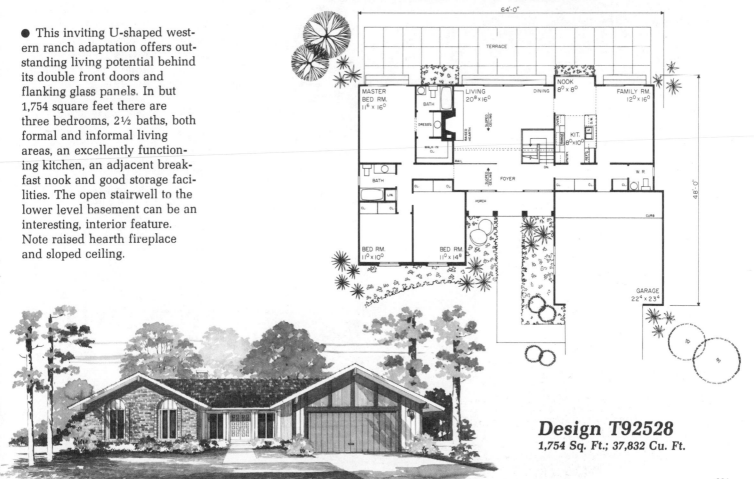

TERRACE

MASTER BED RM. 11⁶ x 16⁰

BATH

LIVING 20⁸ x 16⁰

DINING

NOOK 8⁰ x 8⁰

FAMILY RM. 12⁰ x 16⁰

DRESS'G

WALK-IN CL.

SLOPED CEILING

RAISED HEARTH

KIT. 8⁰ x 10⁰

BATH

SLOPED CEILING

FOYER

W.R.

BED RM. 11⁰ x 10⁰

BED RM. 11⁰ x 14⁸

PORCH

CURB

GARAGE 22⁴ x 23⁴

64'-0"

48'-0"

Design T92528
1,754 Sq. Ft.; 37,832 Cu. Ft.

221

Design T92802
1,729 Sq. Ft.; 42,640 Cu. Ft.

● The three exteriors shown at the left house the same, efficiently planned one-story floor plan shown below. Be sure to notice the design variations in the window placement and roof pitch. The Tudor design to the left is delightful. Half-timbered stucco and brick comprise the facade of this English Tudor variation of the plan. Note authentic bay window in the front bedroom.

Design T92803
1,679 Sq. Ft.; 36,755 Cu. Ft.

● Housed in varying facades, this floor plan is very efficient. The front foyer leads to each of the living areas. The sleeping area of two, or optional three, bedrooms is ready to serve the family. Then there is the gathering room. This room is highlighted by its size, 16 x 20 feet. A contemporary mix of fieldstone and vertical wood siding characterizes this exterior. The absence of columns or posts gives a modern look to the covered porch.

Design T92804
1,674 Sq. Ft.; 35,465 Cu. Ft.

● Stuccoed arches, multi-paned windows and a gracefully sloped roof accent the exterior of this Spanish-inspired design. Like the other two designs, the interior kitchen will efficiently serve the dining room, covered dining porch and breakfast room with great ease. Blueprints for all three designs include details for an optional non-basement plan.

OPTIONAL NON - BASEMENT

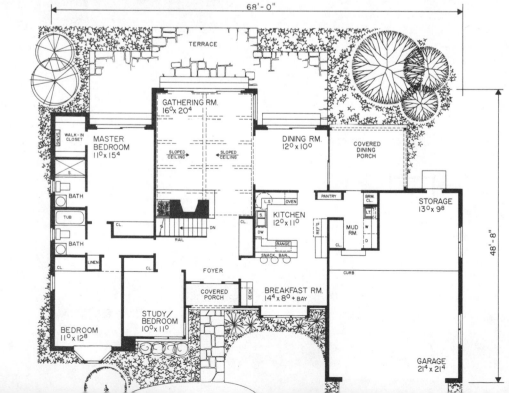

Design T92805
1,547 Sq. Ft.; 40,880 Cu. Ft.

● Three completely different exterior facades
share one compact, practical and economical
floor plan. The major design variations are
roof pitch, window placement and garage
openings. Each design will hold its own when
comparing the three exteriors. The design to
the right is a romantic stone-and-shingle cottage design. This design, along with the other
two designs presented here, is outstanding.

Design T92806
1,584 Sq. Ft.; 41,880 Cu. Ft.

● Even though these exteriors are extremely
different in their styling and also have a few
design variations, their floor plans are identi-
cal. Each will provide the family with a livable plan. In this brick and half-timbered
stucco Tudor version, like the other two, the
living-dining room expands across the rear of
the plan and has direct access to the covered
porch. Notice the built-in planter adjacent to
the open staircase leading to the basement.

Design T92807
1,576 Sq. Ft.; 35,355 Cu. Ft.

● Along with the living-dining areas of the
other two plans, this sleek contemporary
styled home's breakfast room also will have a
view of the covered porch. A desk, snack bar
and mud room housing the laundry facilities
are near the U-shaped kitchen. Clustering
these work areas together is very convenient.
The master bedroom has a private bath.

OPTIONAL NON-BASEMENT

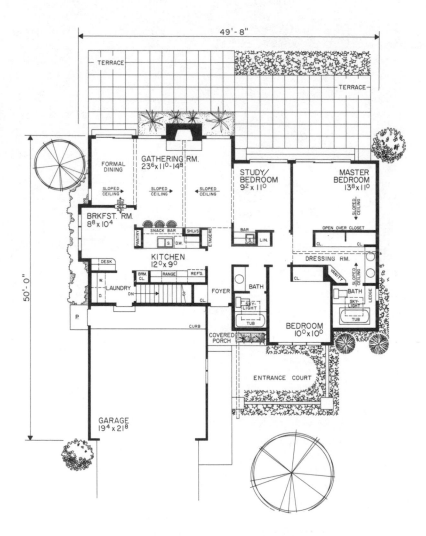

TERRACE

49' - 8"

TERRACE

50' - 0"

FORMAL DINING

GATHERING RM.
23⁶x11⁰-14⁸

STUDY/
BEDROOM
9² x 11⁰

MASTER
BEDROOM
13⁸ x 11⁰

SLOPED CEILING

SLOPED CEILING

SLOPED CEILING

SLOPED CEILING

OPEN OVER CLOSET

BRKFST. RM.
8⁸ x 10⁴

PANTRY

SNACK BAR

SHLVS

BAR

LIN

CL

CL

KITCHEN
12⁰ x 9⁰

DESK

S

D.W.

STAGE RM

DRESSING RM.

BRM. CL.

RANGE

REF'G.

CL

VANITY

SLOPED CEILING

LEDGE

W.

LAUNDRY

DN

FOYER

BATH

SKY-LIGHT

CL

BATH

SKY-LIGHT

D.

CL

TUB

TUB

P.

CURB

BEDROOM
10⁰ x 10⁰

COVERED PORCH

ENTRANCE COURT

GARAGE
19⁴ x 21⁸

Design T92864
1,387 Sq. Ft.; 29,160 Cu. Ft.

● Projecting the garage to the front of a house is very economical in two ways. One, it reduces the required lot size for building (in this case the overall width is under 50 feet). And, two, it will protect the interior from street noise and unfavorable winds. Many other characteristics about this design deserve mention, too. The entrance court and covered porch are a delightful way to enter this home. Upon entering, the foyer will take you to the various areas. The interior kitchen has an adjacent breakfast room and a snack bar on the gathering room side. Here, one will enjoy a sloped ceiling and a fireplace. A study with a wet bar is adjacent. If need be, adjust the plan and make the study the third bedroom. Sliding glass doors in the study and master bedroom open to the terrace.

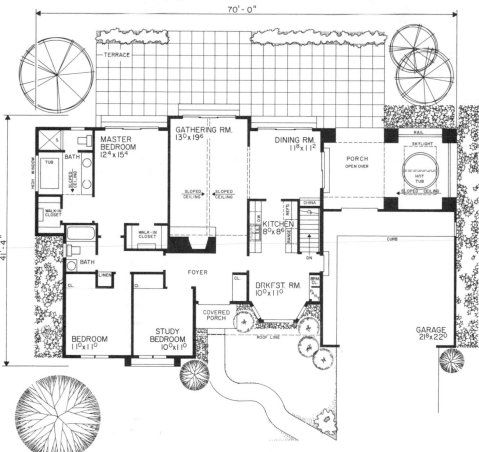

Design T92809
1,551 Sq. Ft.; 42,615 Cu. Ft.

● One-story living can be very rewarding and this contemporary home will be just that. Study the indoor-outdoor living relationships which are offered in the back of the plan. Sliding glass doors are in each of the rear rooms leading to the terrace. The for-mal dining room has a second set of doors to the porch. Many enjoyable hours will be spent here in the hot tub. A sloped ceiling with skylights is above the hot tub area. Back to the interior, there is a large gathering room. It, too, has a sloped ceiling which will add to its spacious appearance. The interior kitchen is conveniently located between the formal and informal dining areas. Two, or optional three, bedrooms are ready to serve the small family. Observe the two walk-in closets of the master bedroom.

Design T91346
1,644 Sq. Ft.; 19,070 Cu. Ft.

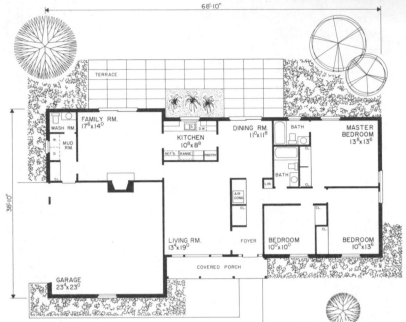

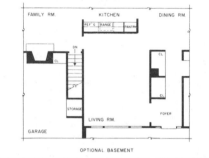

OPTIONAL BASEMENT

● Whether you enter through the service door of the attached garage, or through the centered front entry your appreciation of what this plan has to offer will grow. The mud room area is certainly an outstanding feature. Traffic flows from this area to the informal family room with its fireplace and access to the rear terrace. The efficient, strategically located kitchen looks out upon the yard.

Design T91357
1,258 Sq. Ft.; 13,606 Cu. Ft.

● Here is a relatively low-cost home with a majority of features found in today's high-priced homes. The three bedroom sleeping area highlights two full baths. The living area is a huge room of approximately 25 feet in depth zoned for both formal living and dining. The kitchen is extremely well-planned with even a built-in desk and pantry. The family room has a snack bar and sliding glass doors to the terrace. Blueprints include basement details.

OPTIONAL BASEMENT PLAN

Design T92597
1,515 Sq. Ft.; 32,000 Cu. Ft.

● Whether it be a starter house you are after, or one in which to spend your retirement years, this pleasing frame home will provide a full measure of pride of ownership. The contrast of vertical and horizontal lines, the double front doors and the coach lamp post at the garage create an inviting exterior. The floor plan functions in an orderly and efficient manner. The 26 foot gathering room has a delightful view of the rear yard and will take care of those formal dining occasions. There are two full baths serving the three bedrooms.

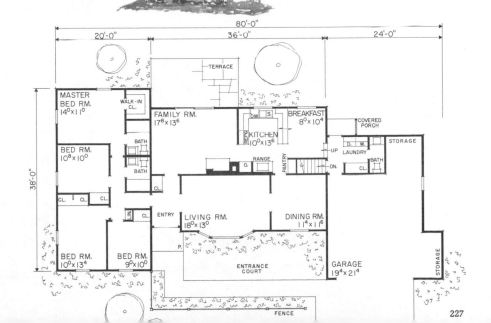

Design T91829
1,800 Sq. Ft.; 32,236 Cu. Ft.

● All the charm of a traditional heritage is wrapped up in this U-shaped home with its narrow, horizontal siding, delightful window treatment, and high pitched roof. The massive center chimney, the bay window, and the double front doors are plus features. Inside, the living potential is outstanding. The sleeping wing is self-contained and has four bedrooms and two baths. The large family and living rooms permit divergent age groups in the family to enjoy themselves to the fullest.

Design T91380
1,399 Sq. Ft.; 28,024 Cu. Ft.

● These two stylish exteriors have the same practical, L-shaped floor plan. Each design has a covered front porch. Inside, there is an abundance of livability. The formal living and dining area is spacious, and the U-shaped kitchen is efficient.

OPTIONAL NON-BASEMENT

There is informal eating space, a separate laundry and a fine family room. Note the sliding glass doors to the terrace. The blueprints include details for building either with or without a basement. Observe the pantry of the non-basement plan. The storage of staples will be handy.

Design T91381
1,399 Sq. Ft.; 28,024 Cu. Ft.

Design T91323 1,344 Sq. Ft.; 17,472 Cu. Ft.

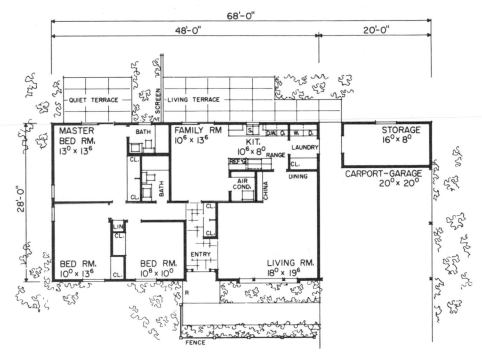

● Incorporated in each set of blueprints for this design are details for building each of the three charming, traditional exteriors. Each of the three alternate exteriors has a distinction all its own. A study of the floor plan reveals fine livability. There are two full baths, a fine family room, an efficient work center, a formal dining area, bulk storage facilities, and sliding glass doors to the quiet living terraces.

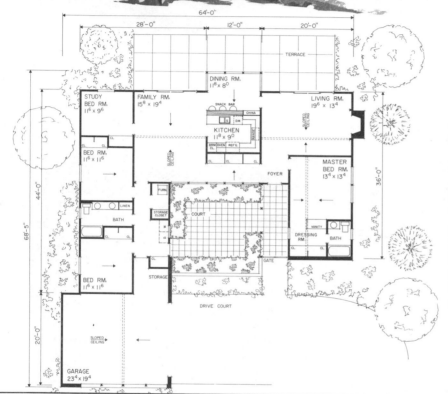

Design T91726
1,910 Sq. Ft.; 19,264 Cu. Ft.

● The U-shaped plan has long been honored for its excellent zoning. As the plan for this fine Spanish adaptation illustrates, it not only provides separation between parents' area and children's wing, but also places a buffer area in the center. This makes the kitchen the "control center" for the home – handy to the family room, living room, dining alcove. Take another look at the dining space. There's a special treat here with floor-to-ceiling windows on the three sides. Can you imagine a more cheerful spot in which to dine?

Design T92386
1,994 Sq. Ft.; 22,160 Cu. Ft.

● This distinctive home may look like the Far West, but don't let that inhibit you from enjoying the great livability it has to offer. Wherever built, you will surely experience a satisfying pride of ownership. Imagine, an entrance court in addition to a large side courtyard! A central core is made up of the living, dining and family rooms, plus the kitchen. Each functions with an outdoor living area. The younger generation has its sleeping zone divorced from the master bedroom. Don't miss the vanity, the utility room with laundry equipment, the snack bar and the raised hearth fireplace. Note three pass-thrus from the kitchen. Observe the beamed and sloping ceilings of the living areas.

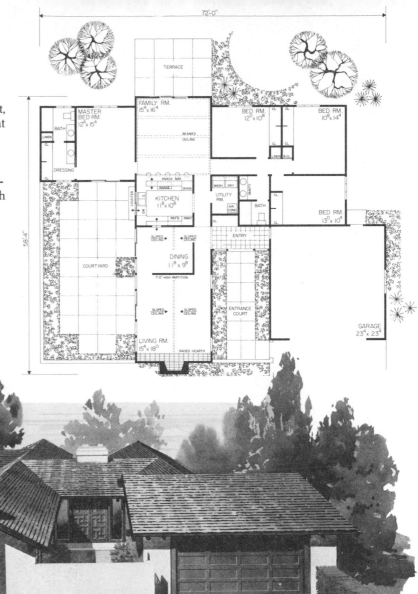

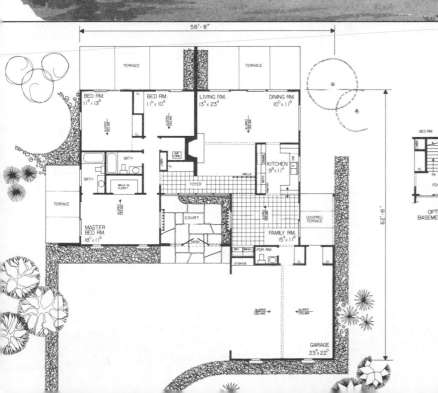

Design T92200
1,695 Sq. Ft.; 18,916 Cu. Ft.

● If you have a penchant for something delightfully different, then this Spanish adaptation may be just what you've been waiting for. This L-shaped ranch home will go well on any site – large or small. A popular feature will be the court. Of great interest are the indoor-outdoor relationships. Observe how the major rooms function through sliding glass doors with the terraces. The interior has a feeling of spaciousness with a number of large glass areas and sloping ceilings. The open planning of the living area will be enjoyable, indeed.

Design T92604
1,956 Sq. Ft.; 28,212 Cu. Ft.

● Here's a liveable floor plan! Notice how all the rooms are accessible from either the foyer or hallway. That prevents unnecessary traffic . . . giving carpet a longer life and keeping work to a minimum. Lots of living space! There's the country kitchen with a beamed ceiling, fireplace and sliding door onto the terrace . . . a great work area, too, including an island counter, built-in range and oven, large pantry. Plus a laundry room just a step away.

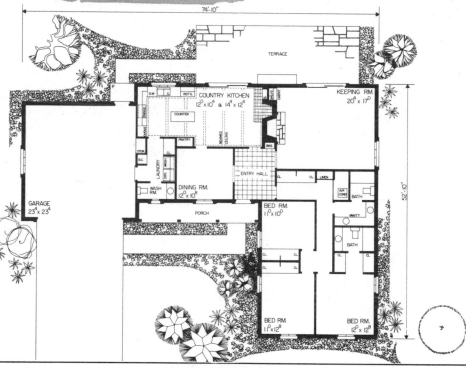

OPTIONAL BASEMENT

Design T91748
1,986 Sq. Ft.; 23,311 Cu. Ft.

● This convenient living design features a sleeping zone comprised of three bedrooms and two full baths; a formal living zone made up of a sunken living room, and a separate dining room; an informal living zone highlighting a family room and a spacious U-shaped kitchen.

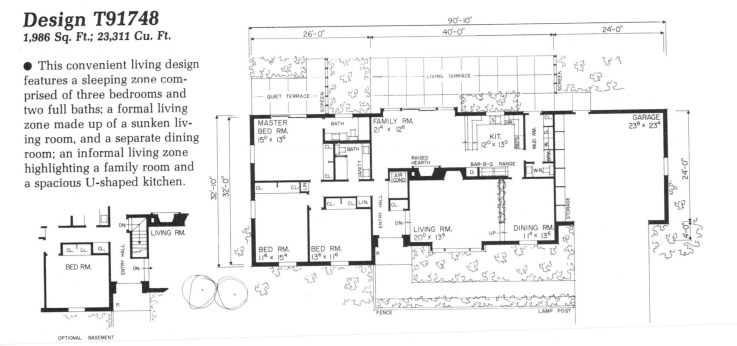

OPTIONAL BASEMENT

Design T92707
1,267 Sq. Ft.; 27,125 Cu. Ft.

● Here is a charming Early American adaptation that will serve as a picturesque and practical retirement home. Also, it will serve admirably those with a small family in search of an efficient, economically built home. The living area, highlighted by the raised hearth fireplace, is spacious. The kitchen features eating space and easy access to the garage and basement. The dining room is adjacent to the kitchen and views the rear yard. Then, there is the basement for recreation and hobby pursuits. The bedroom wing offers three bedrooms and two full baths.

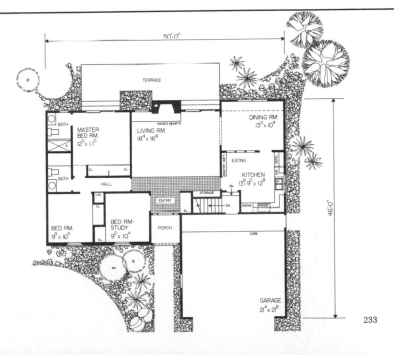

233

Here is a unique series of designs with three charming exterior adaptations – Southern Colonial, Western Ranch, French Provincial – and two distinctive floor plans. Each plan has a different number and is less than 1,600 square feet.

If yours is a preference for the floor plan featuring the 26 foot keeping room, you should order blueprints for Design T92611. Of course, the details for each of the three exteriors will be included. On the other hand, should the plan with the living, dining and family rooms be your favorite, order blueprints for Design T92612 and get details for all three exteriors.

There are many points of similarity in the two designs. Each has a fireplace, 2½ baths, sliding glass doors to the rear terrace, master bedrooms with walk-in closet and private bath with stall shower, and a basement. It is interesting to note that two of the exteriors have covered porches. Don't miss the beamed ceilings, the various storage facilities and the stall showers.

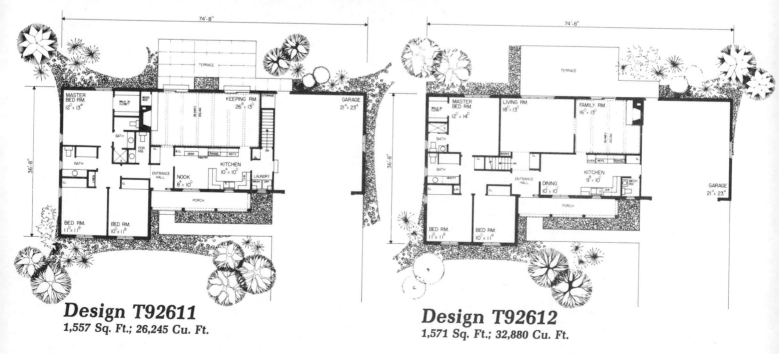

Design T92611
1,557 Sq. Ft.; 26,245 Cu. Ft.

Design T92612
1,571 Sq. Ft.; 32,880 Cu. Ft.

Design T92704
1,746 Sq. Ft.; 38,000 Cu. Ft.

● Three different exteriors! But inside it's all the same livable house. Begin with the impressive entry hall which is more than 19' long and offering double entry to the gathering room. Now the gathering room which is notable for its size and design. Notice how the fireplace is flanked by sliding glass doors leading to the terrace.

Design T92705
1,746 Sq. Ft.; 37,000 Cu. Ft.

● There's a formal dining room, too! The right spot for special birthday dinners as well as supper parties for friends. And an efficient kitchen that makes meal preparation easy whatever the occasion. Look for a built-in range and oven here plus a bright dining nook with sliding glass doors to a second terrace.

Design T92706
1,746 Sq. Ft.; 36,800 Cu. Ft.

● Three large bedrooms! All located to give family members the utmost of privacy. Including a master suite with a dressing room, bath and sliding glass doors opening onto the main terrace. For blueprints of the Colonial adaptation (top) order Design T92704; the hip-roof French version (middle) Design T92705; and the Contemporary, (bottom) order Design T92706.

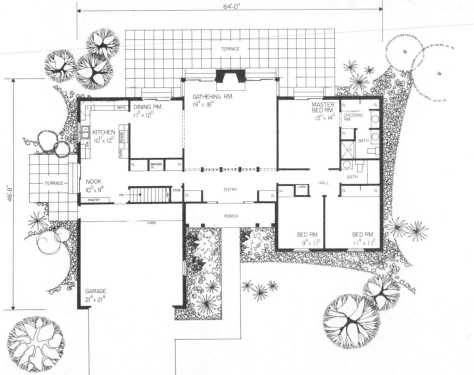

Design T92859
1,599 Sq. Ft.; 37,497 Cu. Ft.

● Here is a popular basic floor plan with an equally popular Tudor style exterior. For the benefit of those who wish to enjoy perhaps the ultimate in winter weather comfort, this home has been designed to incorporate the principles of super-insulation. The typical wall section above details the intricacies of such an installation which are shown in greater detail on the blueprints ordered for this design. Of course, should you wish to build this design without super-insulation, modifications in the construction details can be made after consultation with your local builder. Regardless of how you choose to build this home, you will know it will return outstanding livability for the construction dollar. Don't miss the energy-conscious feature of the vestibule air lock.

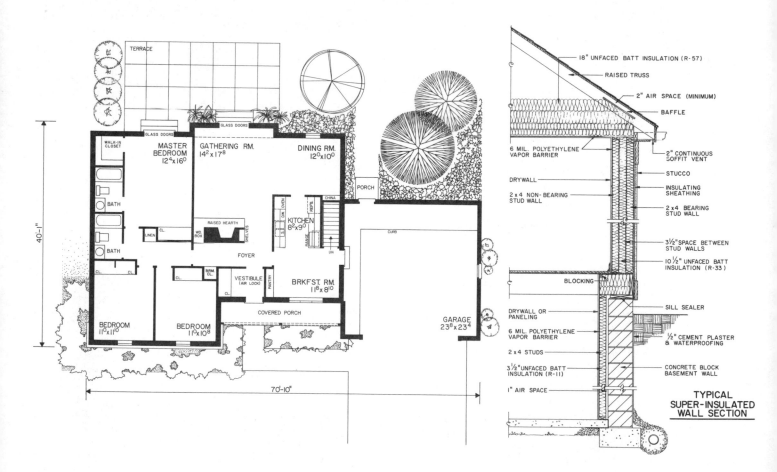

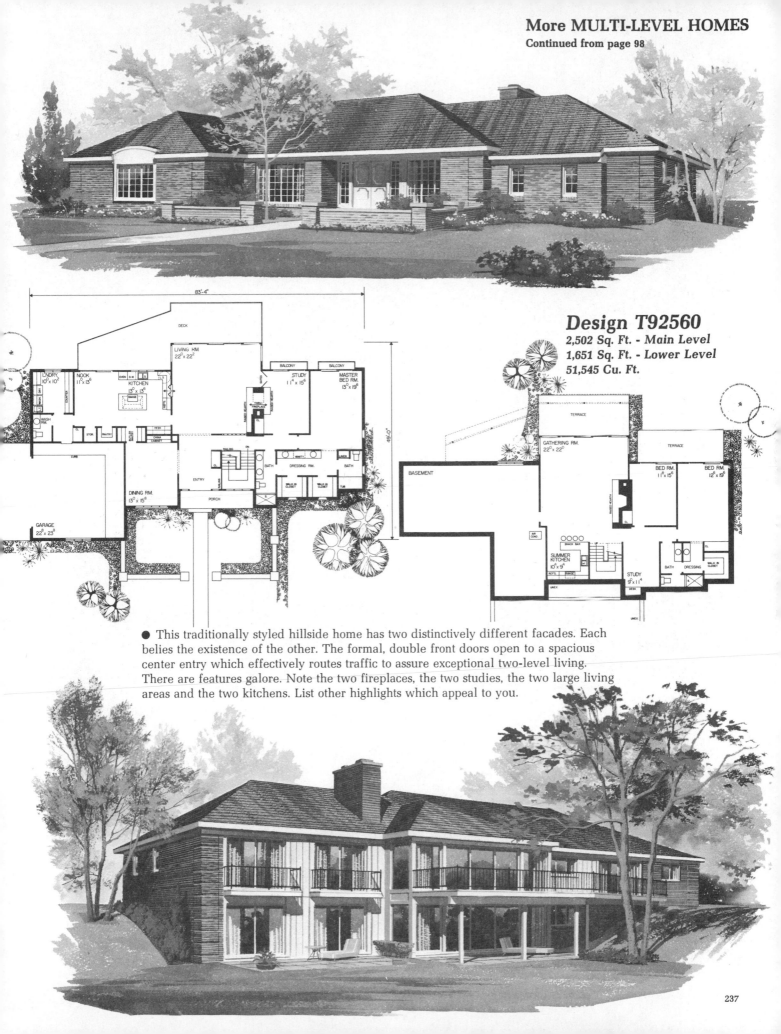

Design T92560
2,502 Sq. Ft. - Main Level
1,651 Sq. Ft. - Lower Level
51,545 Cu. Ft.

● This traditionally styled hillside home has two distinctively different facades. Each belies the existence of the other. The formal, double front doors open to a spacious center entry which effectively routes traffic to assure exceptional two-level living. There are features galore. Note the two fireplaces, the two studies, the two large living areas and the two kitchens. List other highlights which appeal to you.

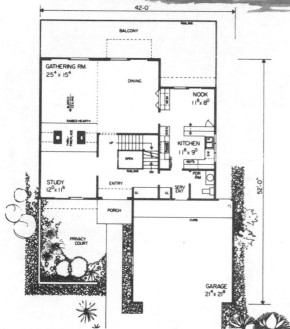

Design T92716 1,013 Sq. Ft. - Main Level
885 Sq. Ft. - Upper Level; 1,074 Sq. Ft. - Lower Level; 32,100 Cu. Ft.

● A genuine master suite! It overlooks the gathering room through shuttered windows and includes a private balcony, a 9'x 9' sitting/dressing room and a full bath. There's more, a two-story gathering room with a raised hearth fireplace, sloped ceiling and sliding glass doors onto the main balcony. Plus, a family room and a study both having a fireplace. A kitchen with lots of built-ins and a separate dining nook.

Design T92769
1,898 Sq. Ft. - Main Level
1,134 Sq. Ft. - Lower Level; 41,910 Cu. Ft.

● This traditional hillside design has fine architectural styling. It possesses all of the qualities that a great design should have to serve its occupants fully.

Main Level Floor Plan (70'-8" × 54'-4"):

- DECK
- LIVING RM. 15¹⁰ x 20⁴
- DINING RM. 11⁶ x 12⁴
- NOOK 10⁰ x 10⁸
- LAUNDRY
- SERV. ENT.
- KITCHEN 13⁰ x 9⁸
- WASH RM.
- RAILING
- ENTRY
- PORCH
- CURB
- GARAGE 23⁴ x 23⁴
- BED RM.-SITTING RM. 11⁶ x 12⁰
- BATH
- VANITY
- WALK IN CLOSET
- BATH
- BED RM. 11⁶ x 14⁰
- MASTER BED RM. 15⁶ x 13⁰

Lower Level Floor Plan:

- TERRACE
- FAMILY RM. 14¹⁰ x 25⁴
- STUDY - BED RM. 11⁶ x 12⁰
- GUEST BED RM. 15⁰ x 11⁶
- RAISED HEARTH
- CABINET BOOKS
- BATH
- STOR.
- LINEN
- UNEX.
- AIR COND.
- BASEMENT

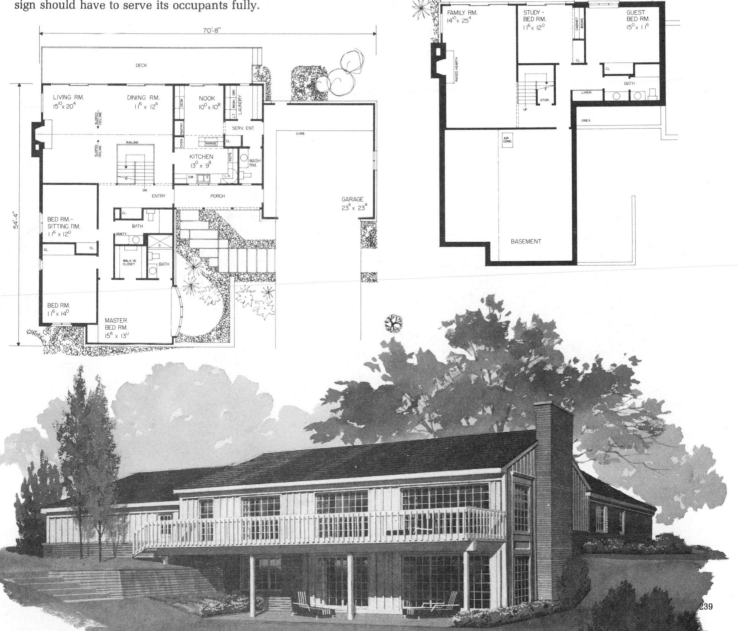

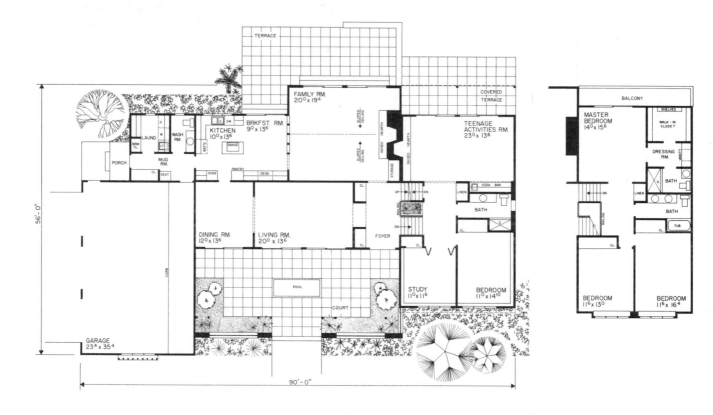

Design T92850
1,530 Sq. Ft. - Main Level; 984 Sq. Ft. - Upper Level; 951 Sq. Ft. - Lower Level; 53,780 Cu. Ft.

● Entering through the entry court of this Spanish design is very impressive. Partially shielded from the street, this court features planting areas and a small pool. Enter into the foyer and this split-level interior will begin to unfold. Down six steps from the foyer is the lower level housing a bedroom and full bath, study and teenage activities room. Adults, along with teenagers, will enjoy the activities room which has a raised hearth fireplace, soda bar and sliding glass doors leading to a covered terrace. Six steps up from the foyer is the upper level bedroom area. The main level has the majority of the living areas. Formal living and dining rooms, informal family room, kitchen with accompanying breakfast room and mud room consisting of laundry and wash room. This home even has a three-car garage. Livability will be achieved with the greatest amount of comfort in this home.

Design T92843
1,861 Sq. Ft. - Upper Level
1,181 Sq. Ft. - Lower Level; 32,485 Cu. Ft.

54'-0"

40'-4"

TERRACE

FAMILY RM.
14⁰ x 21⁶

LOUNGE
11⁴ x 13⁶

STORAGE
10⁴ x 11²

BEDROOM
11⁰ x 11²

CL

CL

RAISED HEARTH

CL

FURN

STOR

UP DN

BATH

FOYER

LAUNDRY/
HOBBIES
14⁰ x 14⁰ BAY

W

D

GARAGE
24⁰ x 19²

PORCH

DECK

LIVING RM.
14⁰ x 21⁶

DINING
12⁰ x 13⁶

BEDROOM
11⁰ x 13⁶

BEDROOM/
STUDY
11⁰ x 13⁶

CL

OPEN
THRU

CL

LIN

BATH

CL

OVEN

CAB'T.

REF'S

KITCHEN
15⁴ x 8⁰

RANGE

BATH

UP DN

CL

DW

SNACK BAR

LINEN

FOYER

PANTRY

DRESSING
RM.

MASTER
BEDROOM
14⁰ x 16⁰

PORCH

BREAKFAST
15⁴ x 9⁶

DECK

● Bi-level living will be enjoyed to its fullest in this
Spanish styled design. There is a lot of room for the
various family activities. Informal living will take place
on the lower level in the family room and lounge. The
formal living and dining rooms, sharing a thru-fireplace, are located on the upper level.

Design T92846
2,341 Sq. Ft. - Main Level; 1,380 Sq. Ft. - Lower Level; 51,290 Cu. Ft.

● The street view of this Spanish design shows a beautifully designed one-story home, but now take a look at the rear elevation. This home has been designed to be built into a hill so the lower level can be opened to the sun. By so doing, the total livability is almost doubled. A unique feature of the lower level is the summer kitchen.

Floor plan labels (upper/lower level):

STUDY 15⁰ x 11⁴ STUDY $15^0 \times 11^4$

Lower level:
- STUDY $15^0 \times 11^4$
- FAMILY/PLAY RM. $15^8 \times 21^6$
- HOBBIES $16^0 \times 13^0$
- TERRACE
- BALCONY ABOVE
- CL. CHEST CL.
- LINEN BATH
- AIR. COND.
- STORAGE
- UNEXCAVATED
- UP
- GARAGE $23^4 \times 22^0$

Upper level:
- 68'-0"
- 57'-4"
- 10'-8"
- 40'-0"
- TERRACE
- BALCONY
- MASTER BED RM. $15^0 \times 15^0$
- SLOPED CEILING
- BATH
- VANITY
- CL. CL. CL. CL.
- CL. CL. CL. CL.
- LINEN LINEN
- CL. CL.
- BED RM. $11^6 \times 15^4$
- SLOPED CEILING
- BED RM. $11^6 \times 11^8$
- SLOPED CEILING
- ROOF
- FAMILY DINING $15^8 \times 21^4$
- KITCHEN $10^0 \times 13^8$
- W.R.
- REF'S.
- D. W.
- LAUND.
- CABINET
- PANTRY CL.
- OVEN RANGE
- RAISED HEARTH
- RAISED HEARTH
- SLOPED CEILING
- LIVING RM. $16^0 \times 21^8$
- LIVING TERRACE
- UP

Design T92248
1,501 Sq. Ft. - Upper Level; 511 Sq. Ft. - Living Room Level
1,095 Sq. Ft. - Lower Level; 30,486 Cu. Ft.

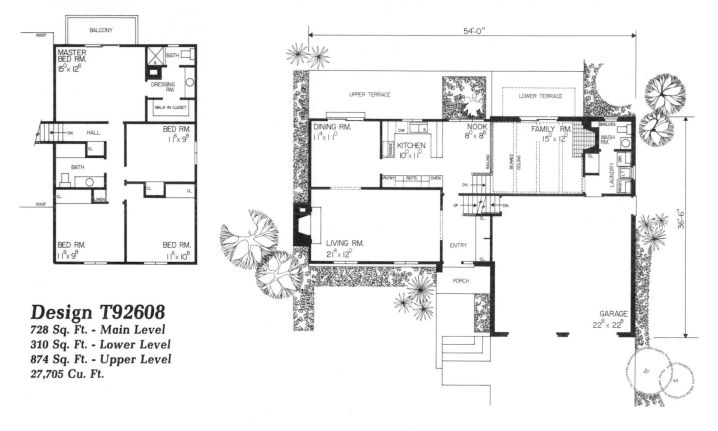

Design T92608

728 Sq. Ft. - *Main Level*
310 Sq. Ft. - *Lower Level*
874 Sq. Ft. - *Upper Level*
27,705 Cu. Ft.

● Tri-level living could hardly ask for more than this design has to offer. Not only can one enjoy the three levels but also there is a fourth basement level for bulk storage and perhaps, a shop area. The interior livability is outstand-ing. The main level has an L-shaped formal living/dining room with a fire-place in the living room and sliding glass door in the dining area to upper terrace, a U-shaped kitchen and nook. Down a few steps to the lower level is the beamed ceilinged family room with another fireplace and sliding doors to the lower terrace, plus a washroom and laundry. The upper level houses all of the sleeping facilities including three bedrooms, bath and master suite.

Design T92628
649 Sq. Ft. - Main Level; 672 Sq. Ft. - Upper Level
624 Sq. Ft. - Lower Level; 25,650 Cu. Ft.

● Impressive! This split-level design is housed in a distinctive Rustic exterior. Its interior has lots of extras, too. Like a wet bar and game storage in the family room. A beamed ceiling, too, and a sliding glass door onto the terrace. In short, a family room designed to make your life easy and enjoyable. There's more. A living room with a traditionally styled fireplace and built-in bookshelves. And a dining room with a sliding glass door that opens to a second terrace. Here's the appropriate setting for those times when you want a touch of elegance. A sunny kitchen, too. It features a built-in oven and range, pantry, broom closet and plenty of space for a breakfast table. A convenient laundry room as well. Four large bedrooms, or three plus a study, if that arrangement suits you better. Also on the upper level is two full back-to-back baths for economical plumbing. This home has style and space to serve any family admirably.

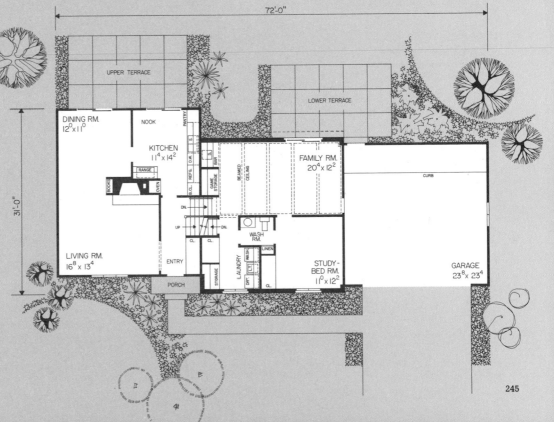

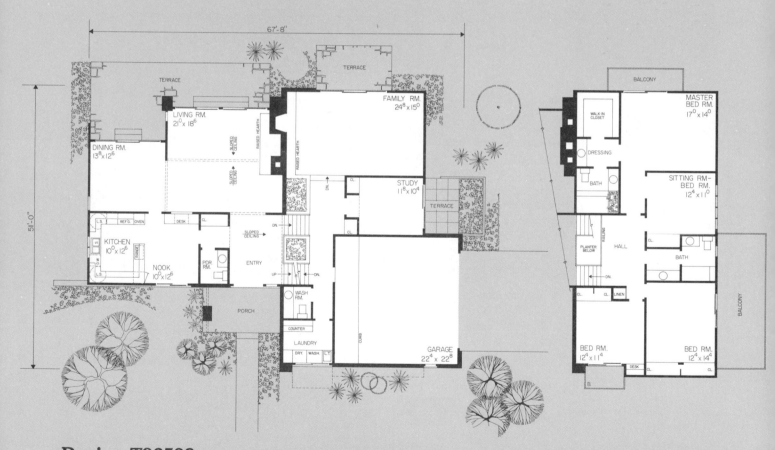

Design T92536 1,077 Sq. Ft. - Main Level; 1,319 Sq. Ft. - Upper Level; 914 Sq. Ft. - Lower Level; 31,266 Cu. Ft.

● Here are three levels of outstanding livability all packed in a delightfully contemporary exterior. The low pitched roof has a wide overhang with exposed rafter tails. The stone masses contrast effectively with the vertical siding and the glass areas. The extension of the sloping roof provides the recessed feature of the front entrance with the patterned double doors. The homemaker's favorite highlight will be the layout of the kitchen. No crossroom traffic here. Only a few steps from the formal and informal eating areas, it is the epitome of efficiency. A sloping beamed ceiling, sliding glass doors and a raised hearth fireplace enhance the appeal of the living room. The upper level offers the option of a fourth bedroom or a sitting room functioning with the master bedroom. Note the three balconies. On the lower level, the big family room, quiet study, laundry and extra washroom are present.

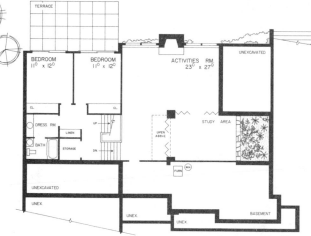

Design T92936

1,357 Sq. Ft. - Main Level; 623 Sq. Ft. Master Bedroom Level
623 Sq. Ft. - Lower Level; 852 Sq. Ft. - Activity Room
56,105 Cu. Ft.

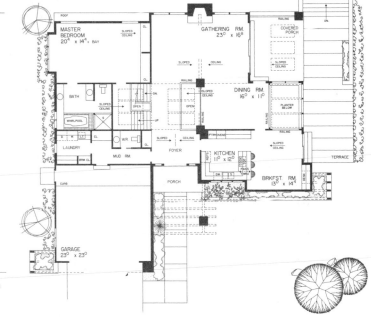

● This dramatic contemporary multi-level will offer the active family exciting new living patterns. The main level is spacious. Sloping ceilings and easy access to the outdoor living areas contribute to that feeling of openness. Imagine the enjoyment to be experienced when passing through the dining area and looking down upon the planting area of the activities level. Observe that the parents and the children each have a separate sleeping level. Don't miss the laundry, covered porch, and basement utility area.

● This luxurious three-bedroom home offers comfort on many levels. Its modern design incorporates a rear garden room and conversation pit off a living room and dining room plus skylights in an adjacent family room with high sloped ceiling. Other features include an entrance court, activities room, modern kitchen, upper lounge, and master bedroom.

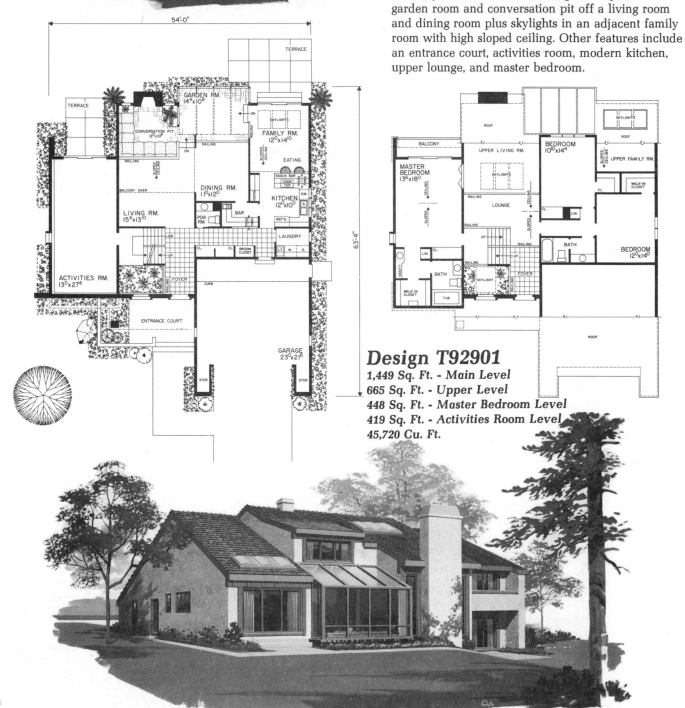

Design T92901

1,449 Sq. Ft. - Main Level
665 Sq. Ft. - Upper Level
448 Sq. Ft. - Master Bedroom Level
419 Sq. Ft. - Activities Room Level
45,720 Cu. Ft.

Design T92932 2,070 Sq. Ft. - Main & Family Room Levels
680 Sq. Ft. - Upper Level; 640 Sq. Ft. - Master Bedroom Level; 55,046 Cu. Ft.

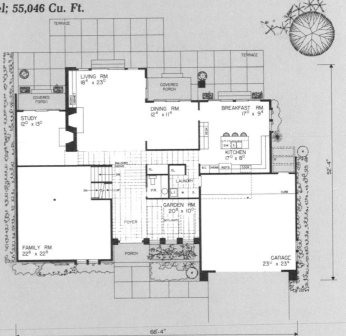

● This attractive split-level comtempo-rary home includes a garden room just off the foyer. Note also the master bed-room with whirlpool bath, large living room, and large family room.

● This attractive, contemporary bi-level will overwhelm you with its features: two balconies, an open staircase with planter below, two lower level bedrooms, six sets of sliding glass doors and an outstanding master suite loaded with features. The occupants of this house will love the large exercise room. After a tough workout, you can relax in the whirlpool or the sauna or simply take a shower!

Design T92856 1,801 Sq. Ft. - Upper Level
2,170 Sq. Ft. - Lower Level; 44,935 Cu. Ft.

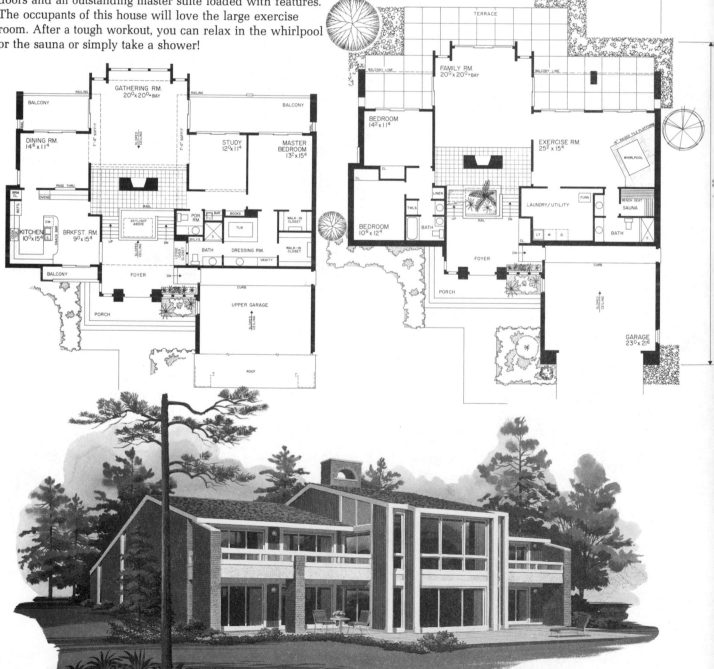

All The "TOOLS" You And Your Builder Need. . .

1. THE PLAN BOOKS

Home Planners' unique Design Category Series makes it easy to look at and study only the types of designs for which you and your family have an interest. Each of six plan books features a specific type of home, namely: Two-Story, 1½ Story, One-Story Over 2000 Sq. Ft., One-Story Under 2000 Sq. Ft., Multi-Levels and Vacation Homes. In addition to the convenient Design Category Series, there is an impressive selection of other current titles. While the home plans featured in these books are also to be found in the Design Category Series, they, too, are edited for those with special tastes and requirements. Your family will spend many enjoyable hours reviewing the delightfully designed exteriors and the practical floor plans. Surely your home or office library should include a selection of these popular plan books. Your complete satisfaction is guaranteed.

2. THE CONSTRUCTION BLUEPRINTS

There are blueprints available for each of the designs published in Home Planners' current plan books. Depending upon the size, the style and the type of home, each set of blueprints consists of from five to ten large sheets. Only by studying the blueprints is it possible to give complete and final consideration to the proper selection of a design for your next home. The blueprints provide the opportunity for all family members to familiarize themselves with the features of all exterior elevations, interior elevations and details, all dimensions, special built-in features and effects. They also provide a full understanding of the materials to be used and/or selected. The low-cost of our blueprints makes it possible and indeed, practical, to study in detail a number of different sets of blueprints before deciding upon which design to build.

3. THE MATERIALS LIST

A separate list of materials, available for a small fee, is an important part of the plan package. It comprises the last sheet of each set of blueprints and serves as a handy reference during the period of construction. Of course, at the pricing and the material ordering stages, it is indispensable.

4. THE SPECIFICATION OUTLINE

Each order for blueprints is accompanied by one Specification Outline. You and your builder will find this a time-saving tool when deciding upon your own individual specifications. An important reference document should you wish to write your own specifications.

5. THE PLUMBING & ELECTRICAL PACKAGE

The construction blueprints you order from Home Planners, Inc. include locations for all plumbing fixtures — sinks, lavatories, tubs, showers, water closets, laundry trays, hot water heaters, etc. The blueprints also show the locations of all electrical switches, plugs, and outlets. These plumbing and electrical details are sufficient to present to your local contractor for discussions about your individual specifications and subsequent installations in conformance with local codes. However, for those who wish to acquaint themselves with many of the intricacies of residential plumbing and electrical details and installations, Home Planners, Inc. has made available this package. We do not recommend that the layman attempt to do his own plumbing and electrical work. It is, nevertheless, advisable that owners be as knowledgeable as possible about each of these disciplines. The entire family will appreciate the educational value of these low-cost, easy-to-understand details.

Frontal
Sheet

Foundation
Plans

Detailed
Floor
Plans

House
Cross-
Sections

Interior
Elevations

Exterior
Elevations

Materials
List

What Our Plans Include

The Blueprints

1. FRONTAL SHEET.
Artist's landscaped sketch of the exterior and ink-line floor plans are on the frontal sheet of each set of blueprints.

2. FOUNDATION PLAN.
¼" Scale basement and foundation plan. All necessary notations and dimensions. Plot plan diagram for locating house on building site.

3. DETAILED FLOOR PLAN.
¼" Scale first and second floor plans with complete dimensions. Cross-section detail keys. Diagrammatic layout of electrical outlets and switches.

4. HOUSE CROSS-SECTIONS.
Large scale sections of foundation, interior and exterior walls, floors and roof details for design and construction control.

5. INTERIOR ELEVATIONS.
Large scale interior details of the complete kitchen cabinet design, bathrooms, powder room, laundry, fireplaces, paneling, beam ceilings, built-in cabinets, etc.

6. EXTERIOR ELEVATIONS.
¼" Scale exterior elevation drawings of front, rear, and both sides of the house. All exterior materials and details are shown to indicate the complete design and proportions of the house.

7. MATERIALS LIST.
For a small additional fee, complete lists of all materials required for the construction of the house as designed are included in each set of blueprints (one charge for any size order).

THIS BLUEPRINT PACKAGE
will help you and your family take a major step forward in the final appraisal and planning of your new home. Only by spending many enjoyable and informative hours studying the numerous details included in the complete package will you feel sure of, and comfortable with, your commitment to build your new home. To assure successful and productive consultation with your builder and/or architect, reference to the various elements of the blueprint package is a must. The blueprints, materials list and specification outline will save much consultation time and expense. Don't be without them.

The Materials List

For a small extra charge, you will receive a materials list with each set of blueprints you order (one fee for any size order). Each list shows you the quantity, type and size of the non-mechanical materials required to build your home. It also tells you where these materials are used. This makes the blueprints easy to understand.

Influencing the mechanical requirements are geographical differences in availability of materials, local codes, methods of installation and individual preferences. Because of these factors, your local heating, plumbing and electrical contractors can supply you with necessary material take-offs for their particular trades.

Materials lists simplify your material ordering and enable you to get quicker price quotations from your builder and material dealer. Because the materials list is an integral part of each set of blueprints, it is not available separately.

Among the materials listed:

• Masonry, Veneer & Fireplace • Framing Lumber • Roofing & Sheet Metal • Windows & Door Frames • Exterior Trim & Insulation • Tile Work, Finish Floors • Interior Trim, Kitchen Cabinets • Rough & Finish Hardware

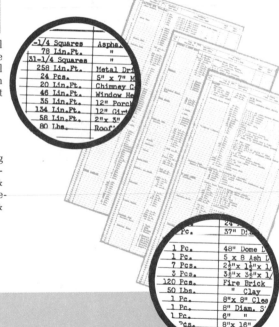

The Specification Outline

This fill-in type specification lists over 150 phases of home construction from excavating to painting and includes wiring, plumbing, heating and air-conditioning. It consists of 16 pages and will prove invaluable for specifying to your builder the exact materials, equipment and methods of construction you want in your new home. One Specification Outline is included free with each order for blueprints. Additional Specification Outlines are available at $5.00 each.

CONTENTS
• General Instructions, Suggestions and Information • Excavating and Grading • Masonry and Concrete Work • Sheet Metal Work • Carpentry, Millwork, Roofing, and Miscellaneous Items • Lath and Plaster or Drywall Wallboard • Schedule for Room Finishes • Painting and Finishing • Tile Work • Electrical Work • Plumbing • Heating and Air-Conditioning

Announcing-

A "MUST" Book for Anyone Involved in the Planning of a New Home

This book features a wealth of information vital to the successful planning of a new home. Discussed in a highly illustrated manner, is a great variety of subjects concerning residential design and planning. Written and edited specifically for use during the early planning and pre-construction stages of the building program, this book may save you many times its cost. In addition to giving a layman's overview of the architectural side of residential design, it helps the reader give due consideration to the innumerable budgetary and livability aspects of the planning process. A CHECKLIST FOR PLAN SELECTION lists over 650 items that will guide and help assure proper decision-making which involve the myriad of subjects influencing proper residential design and planning.
224 pages, soft cover.

A Most Rewarding and Money-Saving Book.

$23.50
Postpaid

HOME PLANNERS' GUIDE TO
RESIDENTIAL D·E·S·I·G·N

CHARLES TALCOTT   DON HEPLER   PAUL WALLACH

Contents

Preface
Illustrated Designs Index

PART ONE

Principles of Residential Design

CHAPTER ONE   Introduction

Reading Architectural Drawings   3
  Pictorial drawings   3
  Multiview drawings   3
  Elevation drawings   4
  Floor plans   5
  Architectural symbols   7
Design Factors   10
  Principles of floor plan design   10
  Area planning   11
  Traffic patterns   11
  Room locations   14
  Effect of levels on room locations   24
  Room sizes   26
  Floor plan sizes   29
  Fundamentals of elevation design   32
  Elements of design   33
  Principles of design   37

CHAPTER TWO   Defining Personal Requirements
  Assessing Lifestyles   41
  Determining Needs and Wants   41
  General Financial Considerations   46
    Site   46
    Building materials   46
    Specifications   46
    Labor costs   47
    Estimating costs   47
    Mortgage planning   47
    Expandable plans   48

CHAPTER THREE   Site Considerations
  Orientation   53
  Solar Planning   55
  Earth Sheltered Housing   60
  Building Code Considerations   63

CHAPTER FOUR   Area Planning
  Living Area   65
  Service Area   65
  Sleeping Area   68
  Types of Plans   69
  Levels   70
    Bi-level   74
    Split-level   80
    Story-and-a-half   83
    Lofts   85
  Basement Plans   85

CHAPTER FIVE   Guidelines for Room Planning
  Room Sizes   89
  Room Functions   89
  Room Locations   96

Room Shapes   100
  Living room shapes   100
  Kitchen shapes   104
  Utility room shapes   107
  Garage shapes   107
  Bedroom and bath shapes   107
Storage   111
  Closets   111
  Built-in storage facilities   111
  Furniture storage   114
Windows and Doors   114
  Windows   114
  Doors   115
Fireplaces   116
Fixtures and Appliances   125
  Kitchen appliances   125
  Laundry appliances   128
  Bath appliances and fixtures   132
Traffic Patterns   136
  External Traffic   136
  Internal Traffic   142
Lighting   148
  Lighting fixtures   148
  Illumination planning   149

CHAPTER SIX   Design Skills

  The Architect's Scale   151
  Dimensioning   155
  Sketching   156

PART TWO

Residential Design Practices

CHAPTER SEVEN   Plan Selection
  Satisfying Basic Needs and Wants   161
  Short-Cutting Process   161
  Financial Considerations   165
    Methods of controlling costs   167
  Checklist for Plan Selection   167

CHAPTER EIGHT   Altering Plans
  Methods of Making Changes   175
  Types of Design Alterations   175
    Altering room sizes   176
    Room location changes   182
    Altering room shapes   182
    Moving doors and windows   182
    Altering traffic space   188
    Expanding living space   191
    Solar adaptations   197

CHAPTER NINE   Adapting Elevation Styles
  Elevation Design   203
    Form and space   203
    Roof styles   205
    Design adjustment guidelines   205
  A Final Word on Styles   214
    European styles   214
    Early American styles   215
    Later American styles   215
    Contemporary styles   215
Index

1250 HOME DESIGNS
ONE OF THEM IS YOURS.

You and your family will enjoy browsing through the hundreds of traditional and contemporary home designs, each featuring detailed exterior illustrations and innovative floor plans.

(1) 315 ONE STORY HOMES UNDER 2,000 Sq. Ft.
Create a fantastic home on a modest budget. Gathering rooms, formal and informal dining, two to four bedrooms, great indoor/outdoor livability. 192 pages. $4.95

(2) 210 ONE STORY HOMES OVER 2,000 Sq. Ft.
Enjoy gracious living in one-story, Spanish, Western, Tudor, French, Contemporary and other styles. Sunken living rooms, master bedroom suites, atriums and courtyards. 192 pages. $4.95

(3) 150 1-1/2 STORY HOMES
Explore Cape Cod, Georgian, Tudor and Contemporary homes in low-budget and country-estate sizes. Formal dining rooms, sloped ceilings, country kitchens, covered porches and terraces. 128 pages. $3.95

(4) 360 TWO STORY HOMES
Experience two-story living at its finest. English and American Tudors, Farmhouses, Georgians, Southern Colonials, French Mansards and more! Fabulous entryways, gathering rooms, libraries and dining rooms. 288 pages. $6.95

(5) 215 MULTI-LEVEL HOMES
Discover new dimensions in family living! Exciting designs for flat and sloping sites. Bi-levels, tri-levels, hillside homes with sloped ceilings, balconies, decks and terraces. 192 pages. $4.95

(6) 223 VACATION HOMES
Recreation or year-round homes. A-Frames, Chalets, Hexagons, Ski Lodges, and Cluster Homes. Dual-purpose spaces, decks, balconies, terraces, lofts and fireplaces. 176 pages, (120 in full color). $4.95

SAVE! Order our complete collection, all 6 books, a $30.70 value, for only $19.95!

**Credit Card Orders Call
Toll-Free 1-800-322-6797**

HOME PLANNERS, INC.   Satisfaction Guaranteed!

Dept. BK, 23761 Research Drive, Farmington Hills, MI 48024   TB9
Please RUSH by return mail (check choice):

☐ (1) 315 ONE STORY HOMES   ☐ (4) 360 TWO STORY HOMES $6.95
   (under 2,000 sq. ft.) $4.95   ☐ (5) 215 MULTI-LEVEL HOMES $4.95
☐ (2) 210 ONE STORY HOMES   ☐ (6) 223 VACATION HOMES $4.95
   (over 2,000 sq. ft) $4.95   ☐ **SEND ALL 6 BOOKS AT $19.95**
☐ (3) 150 1-1/2 STORY HOMES $3.95   **(A $30.70 VALUE!)**

Name _____

Address _____

City _____ State _____ Zip _____

In Canada, add 20% to above prices
and mail in Canadian funds to: Amount Enclosed: $
HOME PLANNERS, INC.   **Add $1.50 for Postage.**
20 Cedar St. N., Kitchener, Ontario N2H2W8   Mich. residents add 4% sales tax.

More Products from Home Planners To Help You Plan Your Home

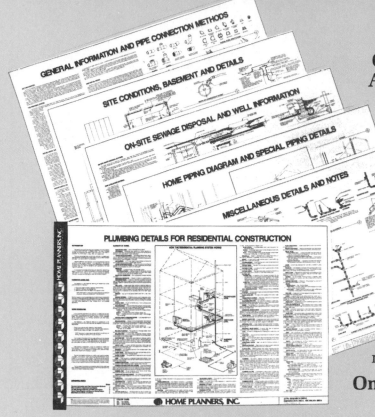

Comprehensive Plumbing Details for All Types of Residential Construction

If you want to find out more about the intricacies of household plumbing, these 24x36-inch drawings– six individual, fact-packed sheets– will prove to be remarkably useful tools. Prepared to meet requirements of the National Plumbing Code, they show pipe schedules, fittings, sump-pump details, water-softener hookups, septic-system details, and many more. Sheets are bound together and color coded for easy reference. Glossary of terms included.

Only $14.95

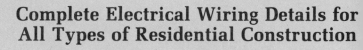

Complete Electrical Wiring Details for All Types of Residential Construction

Designed to take the mystery out of household electrical systems, these comprehensive 24x36-inch drawings come packed with details. Prepared to meet requirements of the National Electrical Code, the six fact-filled sheets cover a variety of topics, including appliance wattage, wire sizing, switch-installation schematics, cable-routing details, doorbell hookups, and many others. Sheets are bound together and color coded for easy reference. Glossary of terms included.

Only $14.95

Plan Your Home with Plan-A-Home™

Plan-A-Home™ is a very useful tool. It's a simple product that will help you design a new home, plan a remodeling project or arrange furniture on an existing plan. Each package contains: more than 700 peel-and-stick *planning symbols* on a self-stick, vinyl sheet, including walls, windows, doors, furniture, kitchen components, bath fixtures, and many more; a reusable, transparent, ¼-inch-scale *planning grid* that can help you create houses up to 140x92 feet; *tracing paper;* and a *felt-tip pen,* with water-soluble ink that wipes away quickly. The transparent planning grid matches the scale of working blueprints, so you can lay it over existing drawings and modify them as necessary.

Only $24.95

Residential Construction Details

Home Planners' blueprint package contains everything an experienced builder needs to construct a particular plan. However, it doesn't show the thousands upon thousands of ways building materials come together to form a house. Prepared to meet requirements of the Uniform Building Code, these drawings–eight large, fact-filled sheets–depict the materials and methods used to build foundations, fireplaces, walls, floors, and roofs. What's more, where appropriate, they show acceptable alternatives. Bound together for easy reference.

Only $14.95

Get any two of Plumbing, Electrical, and Construction Details for just $22.95 (save $6.95). Get all three for only $29.95 (save $14.90).

To order, turn the page . . .

The Blueprint Price Schedule

The blueprint package you order will be an invaluable tool for the complete study of the details relating to the construction of your favorite design, as well as the master plan for building your home. Even the smallest of homes require much construction data and architectural detailing. As the house grows in size, so does the need for more data and details. Frequently, a house of only modest size can require an inordinate amount of data and detailing. This may be the result of its irregular shape and/or the complexity of its architectural features. In the pricing of its blueprints, Home Planners, Inc. has taken into account these factors. Before completing the blueprint order form on the opposite page, be sure to refer to the price schedule below for the appropriate blueprint charges for the design of your choice.

Schedule A: Single Sets, $125.00; Four Set Package, $175.00; Eight Set Package, $225.00. Additional Identical Sets in Same Order, $30.00 each. Sepia, $250.00.

Schedule B: Single Sets, $150.00; Four Set Package, $200.00; Eight Set Package, $250.00. Additional Identical Sets in Same Order, $30.00 each. Sepia, $300.00.

Schedule C: Single Sets, $175.00; Four Set Package, $225.00; Eight Set Package, $275.00. Additional Identical Sets in Same Order, $30.00 each. Sepia, $350.00.

Schedule D: Single Sets, $200.00; Four Set Package, $250.00; Eight Set Package, $300.00. Additional Identical Sets in Same Order, $30.00 each. Sepia, $400.00.

DESIGN NO.	PRICE SCHEDULE	DESIGN NO.	PRICE SCHEDULE	DESIGN NO.	PRICE SCHEDULE	DESIGN NO.	PRICE SCHEDULE	DESIGN NO.	PRICE SCHEDULE
T91054	B	T91929	C	T92281	C	T92612	B	T92798	A
T91060	D	T91933	B	T92283	C	T92615	D	T92800	B
T91075	A	T91935	B	T92294	D	T92617	B	T92802	B
T91091	B	T91939	A	T92309	B	T92618	B	T92803	B
T91094	A	T91956	A	T92317	D	T92619	B	T92804	B
T91142	B	T91957	A	T92318	B	T92622	A	T92805	B
T91191	A	T91974	C	T92320	C	T92624	B	T92806	B
T91208	A	T91986	B	T92330	B	T92626	B	T92807	B
T91220	B	T91987	B	T92335	C	T92628	A	T92809	B
T91223	C	T91988	C	T92343	D	T92637	B	T92810	B
T91228	D	T91989	C	T92351	B	T92650	B	T92811	B
T91241	A	T91991	B	T92354	C	T92655	A	T92812	B
T91269	B	T91993	D	T92356	D	T92657	B	T92813	B
T91285	B	T91996	B	T92374	B	T92661	A	T92814	B
T91300	A	T92107	A	T92377	A	T92662	C	T92815	B
T91301	A	T92123	C	T92378	C	T92668	B	T92816	B
T91305	A	T92124	B	T92379	B	T92670	D	T92817	B
T91308	A	T92127	B	T92386	B	T92671	B	T92818	B
T91310	A	T92128	B	T92390	C	T92678	B	T92820	C
T91311	A	T92129	B	T92391	C	T92680	C	T92821	A
T91323	A	T92131	B	T92392	D	T92682	A	T92822	A
T91325	B	T92132	C	T92393	B	T92683	D	T92823	B
T91345	B	T92133	D	T92395	B	T92686	C	T92824	B
T91346	B	T92134	C	T92488	A	T92687	C	T92826	B
T91354	A	T92135	C	T92500	B	T92688	B	T92829	D
T91357	A	T92136	C	T92502	C	T92693	D	T92832	C
T91358	A	T92137	B	T92504	C	T92694	C	T92842	B
T91361	A	T92140	C	T92505	A	T92701	C	T92843	C
T91365	A	T92141	C	T92508	C	T92704	B	T92846	C
T91372	A	T92142	C	T92510	A	T92705	B	T92847	C
T91380	A	T92143	B	T92511	B	T92706	B	T92848	C
T91381	A	T92145	A	T92520	B	T92707	A	T92850	C
T91382	A	T92146	A	T92524	A	T92708	C	T92851	C
T91383	A	T92148	C	T92527	C	T92711	B	T92854	B
T91387	A	T92150	A	T92528	B	T92713	C	T92855	B
T91388	A	T92151	A	T92534	D	T92716	C	T92856	C
T91389	A	T92162	A	T92536	C	T92718	C	T92857	D
T91394	A	T92170	B	T92538	B	T92728	B	T92858	C
T91701	B	T92171	B	T92539	B	T92729	B	T92859	B
T91711	D	T92174	B	T92540	B	T92731	B	T92864	A
T91715	B	T92176	B	T92543	D	T92733	B	T92867	C
T91718	B	T92181	C	T92544	C	T92737	B	T92877	C
T91719	A	T92183	D	T92549	C	T92740	C	T92883	C
T91726	B	T92189	B	T92552	C	T92741	B	T92886	B
T91748	B	T92192	D	T92557	B	T92746	C	T92887	A
T91754	B	T92200	B	T92558	A	T92748	A	T92888	D
T91761	C	T92206	B	T92559	B	T92756	C	T92889	D
T91767	C	T92209	C	T92560	C	T92758	C	T92890	C
T91770	A	T92211	B	T92563	B	T92761	B	T92892	B
T91778	B	T92212	D	T92565	B	T92765	D	T92901	C
T91783	C	T92214	D	T92568	C	T92766	C	T92902	B
T91787	C	T92218	C	T92569	A	T92767	D	T92905	B
T91788	B	T92220	C	T92570	A	T92768	D	T92906	C
T91791	B	T92221	C	T92571	A	T92769	C	T92908	B
T91793	C	T92223	B	T92573	C	T92771	C	T92909	B
T91827	B	T92224	B	T92583	C	T92772	C	T92915	C
T91829	B	T92230	D	T92585	B	T92774	B	T92918	B
T91835	B	T92236	C	T92586	A	T92776	B	T92920	D
T91850	B	T92242	B	T92587	A	T92778	C	T92921	D
T91856	A	T92243	C	T92596	B	T92779	D	T92925	B
T91858	C	T92245	D	T92597	B	T92780	C	T92927	B
T91868	B	T92248	C	T92599	C	T92781	C	T92929	B
T91882	B	T92251	D	T92603	B	T92782	C	T92932	C
T91887	B	T92254	C	T92604	B	T92784	C	T92934	D
T91890	B	T92256	C	T92606	A	T92785	C	T92936	C
T91892	B	T92272	B	T92607	A	T92786	B	T92937	C
T91911	D	T92276	B	T92608	A	T92787	B	T93126	A
T91920	B	T92277	B	T92610	C	T92788	B	T93189	A
T91927	C	T92278	C	T92611	B	T92789	C	T93221	A
								T93223	A

Before You Order

1. STUDY THE DESIGNS . . . found in Home Planners and Heritage Homes plan books. As you review these delightful custom homes, you should keep in mind the total living requirements of your family — both indoors and outdoors. Although we do not make changes in plans, many minor changes can be made prior to construction. If major changes are involved to satisfy your personal requirements, you should consider ordering one set of sepias and having them modified. Consultation with your architect is strongly advised when contemplating major changes.

2. HOW TO ORDER BLUEPRINTS . . . After you have chosen the design that satisfies your requirements, or if you have selected one that you wish to study in more detail, simply clip the accompanying order blank and mail with your remittance. However, if it is not convenient for you to send a check or money order, you can use your credit card, or merely indicate C.O.D. shipment. Postman will collect all charges, including postage and C.O.D. fee. C.O.D. shipments are not permitted to Canada or foreign countries. Should time be of essence, as it sometimes is with many of our customers, your telephone order usually can be processed and shipped in the next day's mail. Simply call toll free 1-800-521-6797, (Michigan residents call collect 0-313-477-1850).

3. OUR SERVICE . . . Home Planners makes every effort to process and ship each order for blueprints and books within 48 hours. Because of this, we have deemed it unnecessary to acknowledge receipt of our customers orders. See order coupon for the postage and handling charges for surface mail, air mail or foreign mail.

4. MODIFYING OUR PLANS . . . Slight revisions are easy to do before you start building. (We don't alter plans, by the way.) If you're thinking about major changes, consider ordering a set of sepias. After changes have been made on the sepia, additional sets of plans may be reproduced from the sepia master. Should you decide to revise the plan significantly, we strongly suggest that you consult an experienced architect or designer.

5. A NOTE REGARDING REVERSE BLUE-PRINTS . . . As a special service to those wishing to build in reverse of the plan as shown, we do include an extra set of reversed blueprints for only $30.00 additional with each order. Even though the lettering and dimensions appear backward on reversed blueprints, they make a handy reference because they show the house just as it's being built in reverse from the standard blueprints — thereby helping you visualize the home better.

6. OUR EXCHANGE POLICY . . . Since blueprints are printed in response to your order, we cannot honor requests for refunds. However, we will exchange your entire first order for an equal number of blueprints at a price of $20.00 for the first set and $10.00 for each additional set. All sets from the previous order must be returned before the exchange can take place. Please add $3.00 for postage and handling via surface mail; $4.00 via air mail.

How Many Blueprints Do You Need?

Because additional sets of the same design in each order are only $30.00 each, you save considerably by ordering your total requirements now. To help you determine the exact number of sets, please refer to the handy checklist below.

Blueprint Checklist

___ **OWNER'S SET(S)**

___ **BUILDER** (Usually requires at least three sets: one as legal document; one for inspection; and at least one for tradesmen — usually more.)

___ **BUILDING PERMIT** (Sometimes two sets are required.)

___ **MORTGAGE SOURCE** (Usually one set for a conventional mortgage; three sets for F.H.A. or V.A. type mortgages.)

___ **SUBDIVISION COMMITTEE** (If any.)

___ **TOTAL NUMBER SETS REQUIRED**

BLUEPRINT HOTLINE

PHONE TOLL FREE: 1-800-521-6797. Orders received by 3 p.m. (Eastern time) will be processed the same day and shipped to you the following day. Use of this line is restricted to blueprint and book ordering only. Michigan residents simply call collect 0-313-477-1850.

KINDLY NOTE: When ordering by phone, please state Order Form Key Number located in box at lower left corner of the blueprint order form.

IN CANADA: Add 20% to prices listed on this order form and mail in Canadian funds to:
HOME PLANNERS, INC.
20 Cedar St. North
Kitchener, Ontario N2H 2W8
Phone: (519) 743-4169

TO: **HOME PLANNERS, INC., 23761 RESEARCH DRIVE FARMINGTON HILLS, MICHIGAN 48024**

Please rush me the following:

___ SET(S) BLUEPRINTS FOR DESIGN NO(S). .... $_____
Kindly refer to Blueprint Price Schedule on opposite page.

___ SEPIA FOR DESIGN NO(S). .... $_____

___ MATERIALS LIST just $25.00 for Entire Order (1 List per Set) .... $_____

___ ADDITIONAL SPECIFICATION OUTLINES @ $5.00 each .... $_____

___ DETAIL SETS @ $14.95 ea.; any two for $22.95; all three for $29.95 .... $_____
☐ PLUMBING ☐ ELECTRICAL ☐ CONSTRUCTION

___ PLAN-A-HOME™ Design Kit @ $24.95 ea. (plus $3.00 postage) .... $_____

Michigan Residents add 4% sales tax $_____

FOR POSTAGE AND HANDLING PLEASE CHECK ✔ & REMIT	☐ $3.00 Added to Order for Surface Mail (UPS) – Any Mdse.
	☐ $5.00 Added for Priority Mail of One-Three Sets of Blueprints.
	☐ $8.00 Added for Priority Mail of Four or more Sets of Blueprints.
	☐ For Canadian orders add $2.00 to above applicable rates.

$_____

☐ C.O.D. PAY POSTMAN (U.S. ONLY)

TOTAL in U.S. funds $_____

PLEASE PRINT
Name _____
Street _____
City _____ State _____ Zip _____

CREDIT CARD ORDERS ONLY: Fill in the boxes below   Prices subject to change without notice

Credit Card No. [ ][ ][ ][ ][ ][ ][ ][ ][ ][ ][ ][ ][ ][ ][ ][ ]   Expiration Date Month/Year [ ][ ][ ][ ]

CHECK ONE: ☐ VISA ☐ MasterCard
Order Form Key TB9
Your Signature _____

BLUEPRINT ORDERS SHIPPED WITHIN 48 HOURS OF RECEIPT!

TO: **HOME PLANNERS, INC., 23761 RESEARCH DRIVE FARMINGTON HILLS, MICHIGAN 48024**

Please rush me the following:

___ SET(S) BLUEPRINTS FOR DESIGN NO(S). .... $_____
Kindly refer to Blueprint Price Schedule on opposite page.

___ SEPIA FOR DESIGN NO(S). .... $_____

___ MATERIALS LIST just $25.00 for Entire Order (1 List per Set) .... $_____

___ ADDITIONAL SPECIFICATION OUTLINES @ $5.00 each .... $_____

___ DETAIL SETS @ $14.95 ea.; any two for $22.95; all three for $29.95 .... $_____
☐ PLUMBING ☐ ELECTRICAL ☐ CONSTRUCTION

___ PLAN-A-HOME™ Design Kit @ $24.95 ea. (plus $3.00 postage) .... $_____

Michigan Residents add 4% sales tax $_____

FOR POSTAGE AND HANDLING PLEASE CHECK ✔ & REMIT	☐ $3.00 Added to Order for Surface Mail (UPS) – Any Mdse.
	☐ $5.00 Added for Priority Mail of One-Three Sets of Blueprints.
	☐ $8.00 Added for Priority Mail of Four or more Sets of Blueprints
	☐ For Canadian orders add $2.00 to above applicable rates.

$_____

☐ C.O.D. PAY POSTMAN (U.S. ONLY)

TOTAL in U.S. funds $_____

PLEASE PRINT
Name _____
Street _____
City _____ State _____ Zip _____

CREDIT CARD ORDERS ONLY: Fill in the boxes below   Prices subject to change without notice

Credit Card No. [ ][ ][ ][ ][ ][ ][ ][ ][ ][ ][ ][ ][ ][ ][ ][ ]   Expiration Date Month/Year [ ][ ][ ][ ]

CHECK ONE: ☐ VISA ☐ MasterCard
Order Form Key TB9
Your Signature _____

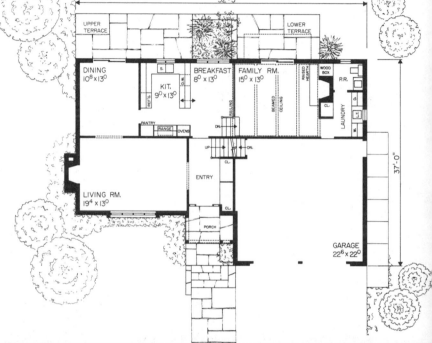

Design T92171

795 Sq. Ft. - Main Level
912 Sq. Ft. - Upper Level
335 Sq. Ft. - Lower Level
33,243 Cu. Ft.

● This English Tudor split-level adaptation has much in common with its counterpart on the opposing page. While some 400 square feet smaller it offers a number of distinguishing features. Observe the living room and family room fireplaces along with other fine features.

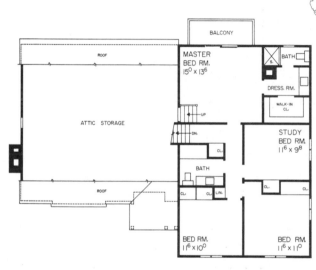

Upper Level

BALCONY
ROOF
MASTER BED RM. 15⁰ x 13⁶
BATH
DRESS. RM.
WALK-IN CL.
UP
DN.
ATTIC STORAGE
STUDY BED RM. 11⁶ x 9⁸
CL.
BATH
CL. CL. LIN.
CL.
CL.
ROOF
BED RM. 11⁶ x 10⁰
BED RM. 11⁶ x 11⁰

Main Level

52'-5"
UPPER TERRACE
LOWER TERRACE
DINING 10⁸ x 13⁰
KIT. 9⁰ x 13⁰
BREAKFAST 8⁰ x 13⁰
FAMILY RM. 15⁰ x 13⁰
WOOD BOX
RAISED HEARTH
R.R.
REF'G.
D.W.
BEAMED CEILING
CL.
LAUNDRY
W. D.
PANTRY
RANGE OVENS
DN.
RAILING
LIVING RM. 19⁴ x 13⁰
UP
CL.
DN.
ENTRY
PORCH
37'-0"
GARAGE 22⁶ x 22⁰

● Here is a fine marriage of a Tudor exterior with a split-level plan. The result is delightful to look at and a joy to live in. The features are almost endless. Try listing them.

Design T92137

987 Sq. Ft. - Main Level
1,043 Sq. Ft. - Upper Level
463 Sq. Ft. - Lower Level
29,382 Cu. Ft.

● Tudor design adapts to split-level living. The result is an unique charm for all to remember. As for the livability, the happy occupants of this tri-level home will experience wonderful living patterns. A covered porch protects, and adds charm to front entry.

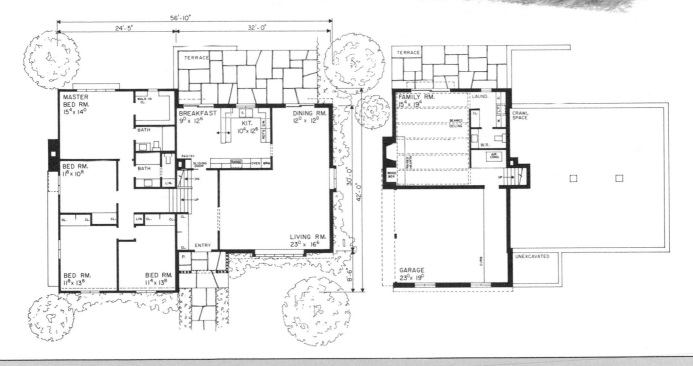

Design T92243

1,274 Sq. Ft. - Main Level; 960 Sq. Ft. - Upper Level; 936 Sq. Ft. - Lower Level
42,478 Cu. Ft

Design T92393
392 Sq. Ft. - Entry Level; 841 Sq. Ft. - Upper Level
848 Sq. Ft. - Lower Level; 24,980 Cu. Ft.

● This design is for those with a flair for something refreshingly contemporary both inside and out. Modest sized, this multi-level has a unique exterior and an equally interesting interior. The low-pitched, wide-overhanging roof protects the double front doors and the large picture window. Inside, the living patterns will be delightful! The angular, open stairwell to the upper level is dramatic, indeed.

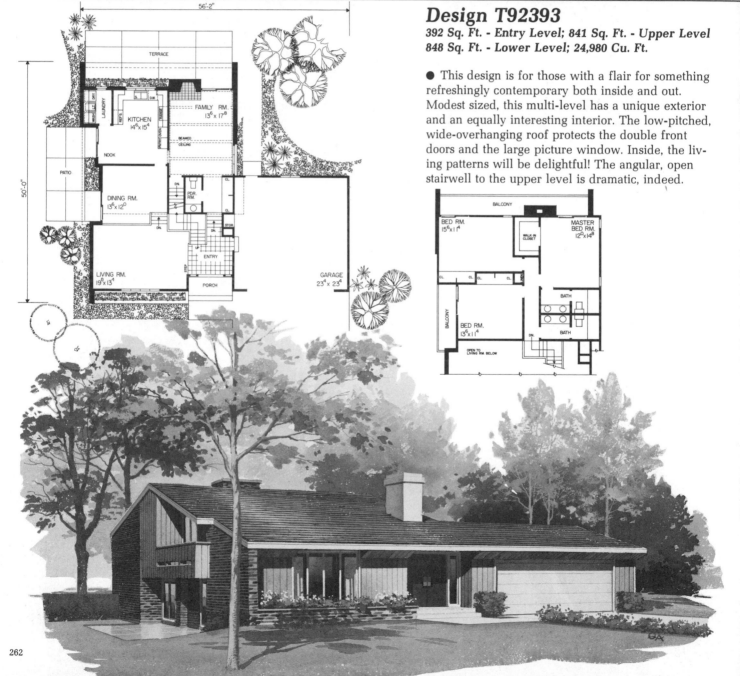

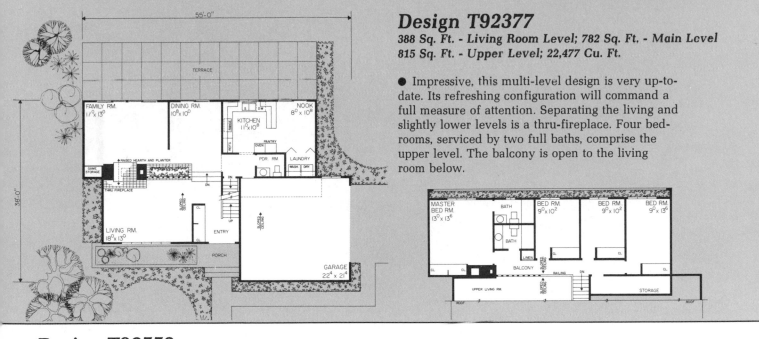

Design T92377
388 Sq. Ft. - Living Room Level; 782 Sq. Ft. - Main Level
815 Sq. Ft. - Upper Level; 22,477 Cu. Ft.

● Impressive, this multi-level design is very up-to-date. Its refreshing configuration will command a full measure of attention. Separating the living and slightly lower levels is a thru-fireplace. Four bedrooms, serviced by two full baths, comprise the upper level. The balcony is open to the living room below.

Design T92552 1,437 Sq. Ft. - Main Level; 1,158 Sq. Ft. - Upper Level; 1,056 Sq. Ft. - Lower Level; 43,000 Cu. Ft.

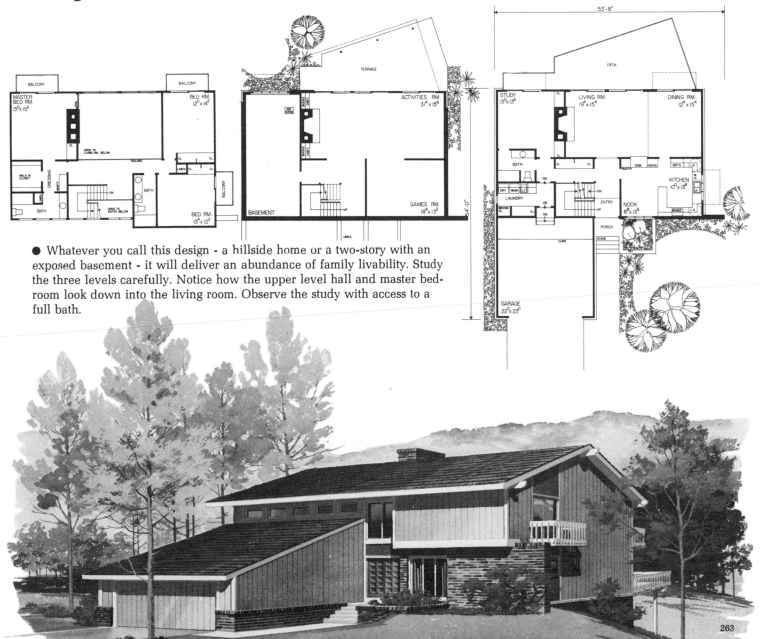

● Whatever you call this design - a hillside home or a two-story with an exposed basement - it will deliver an abundance of family livability. Study the three levels carefully. Notice how the upper level hall and master bedroom look down into the living room. Observe the study with access to a full bath.

Design T91927
1,272 Sq. Ft. - Main Level
960 Sq. Ft. - Upper Level; 936 Sq. Ft. - Lower Level; 36,815 Cu. Ft.

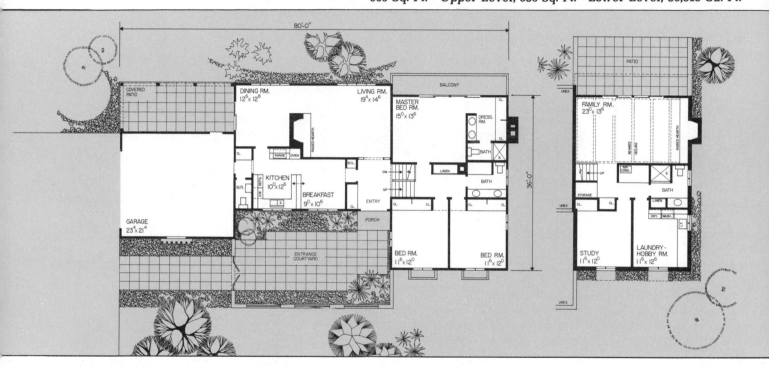

Design T91935
904 Sq. Ft. - Main Level
864 Sq. Ft. - Upper Level; 840 Sq. Ft. - Lower Level; 26,745 Cu. Ft.

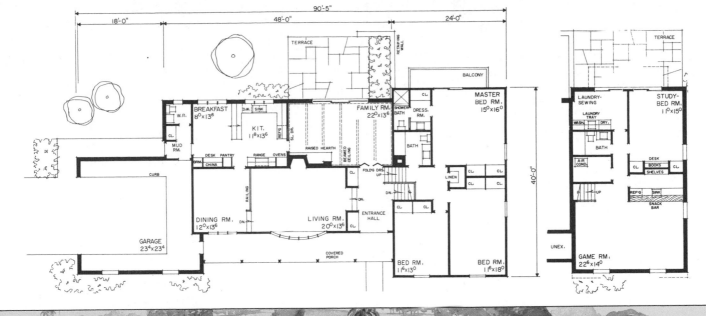

Design T92143

832 Sq. Ft. - Main Level; 864 Sq. Ft. - Upper Level
864 Sq. Ft. - Lower Level; 27,473 Cu. Ft.

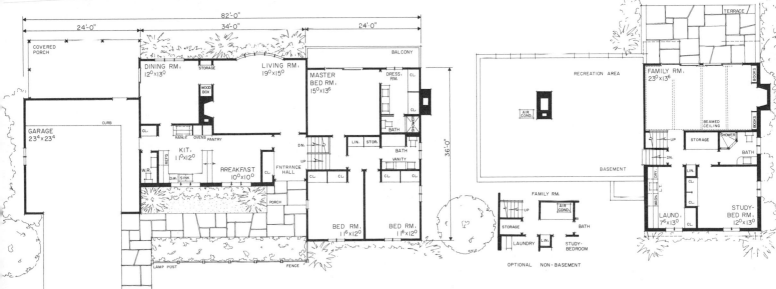

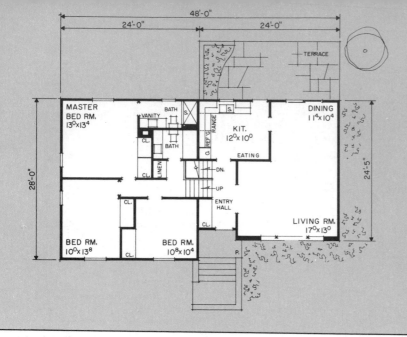

● Here are three charming split-levels designed for the modest budget. They will not require a large, expensive piece of property. Nevertheless, each is long on livability and offers all the features necessary to guarantee years of convenient living.

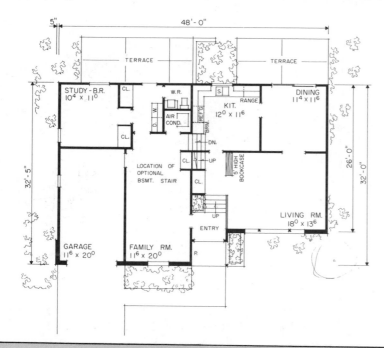

● Charming? It certainly is. And with good reason, too. This delightfully proportioned split level is highlighted by fine window treatment, interesting roof lines, an attractive use of materials and an inviting front entrance with double doors.

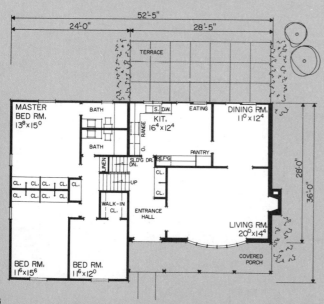

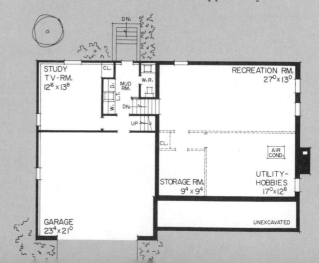

● Four level livability. And what livability it will be! This home will be most economical to build. As the house begins to take form you'll appreciate even more all the livable space you and your family will enjoy. List features that appeal to you.

Design T91358 576 Sq. Ft. - Main Level; 672 Sq. Ft. - Upper Level: 328 Sq. Ft. - Lower Level; 20,784 Cu. Ft.

Design T91770 636 Sq. Ft. - Main Level; 672 Sq. Ft. - Upper Level; 528 Sq. Ft. - Lower Level; 19,980 Cu. Ft.

Design T91882 800 Sq. Ft. - Main Level; 864 Sq. Ft. - Upper Level; 344 Sq. Ft. - Lower Level; 28,600 Cu. Ft.

Design T91778
1,344 Sq. Ft. - Upper Level
768 Sq. Ft. - Lower Level
22,266 Cu. Ft.

● Interesting? You bet it is. The low-pitched, wide overhanging roof, the vertical siding, and the dramatic glass areas give the facade of this contemporary bi-level house an appearance all its own. This type of house provides an outstanding return on your construction dollar.

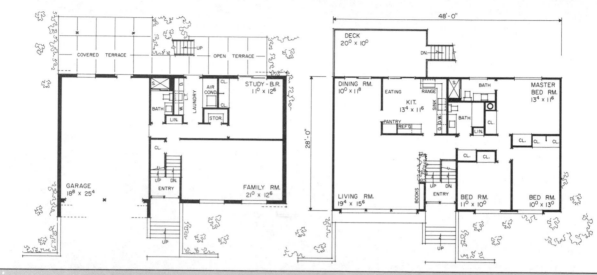

Design T91220
1,456 Sq. Ft. - Upper Level
862 Sq. Ft. - Lower Level
22,563 Cu. Ft.

● This fresh, contemporary exterior sets the stage for exceptional livability. Measuring only 52 feet across the front, this bi-level home offers the large family outstanding features. Whether called upon to function as a four or five bedroom home, there is plenty of space in which to move around. Note both balconies.

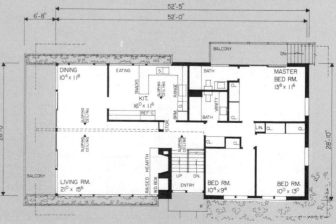

Design T91310

1,040 Sq. Ft. - Upper Level
694 Sq. Ft. - Lower Level
17,755 Cu. Ft.

● An interesting version of the ever-popular two-story. If you want something new in low-cost living patterns, this two-level home may be just the right one for you. This economically built 40' x 26' basic rectangle incorporates the oversized garage and the huge family room on the first level.

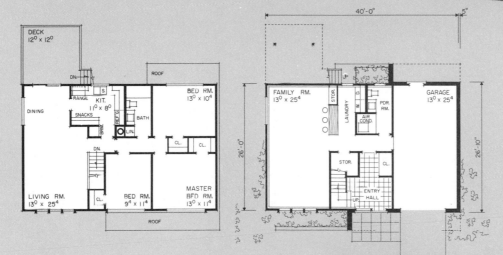

Design T91850

1,456 Sq. Ft. - Upper Level
728 Sq. Ft. - Lower Level
23,850 Cu. Ft.

● This attractive, traditional bi-level house will surely prove to be an outstanding investment. While it is a perfect rectangle - which leads to economical construction - it has a full measure of eye-appeal. Setting the character of the exterior is the effective window treatment, plus the unique design of the recessed front entrance.

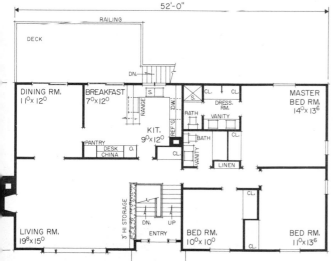

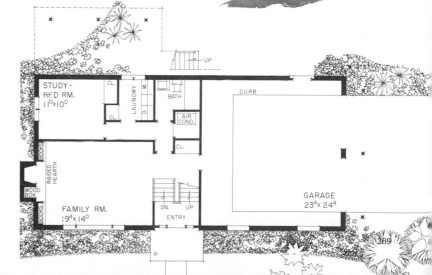

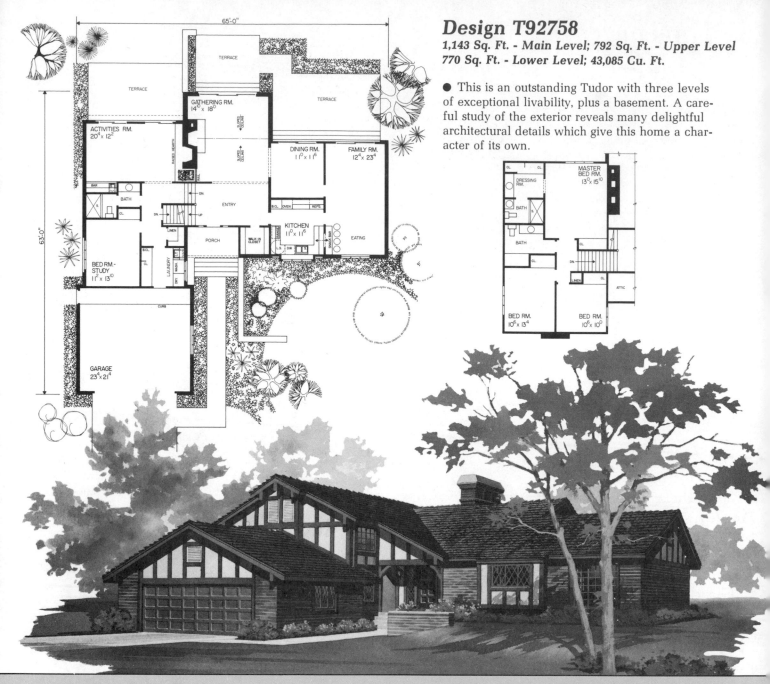

Design T92758
1,143 Sq. Ft. - Main Level; 792 Sq. Ft. - Upper Level
770 Sq. Ft. - Lower Level; 43,085 Cu. Ft.

● This is an outstanding Tudor with three levels of exceptional livability, plus a basement. A careful study of the exterior reveals many delightful architectural details which give this home a character of its own.

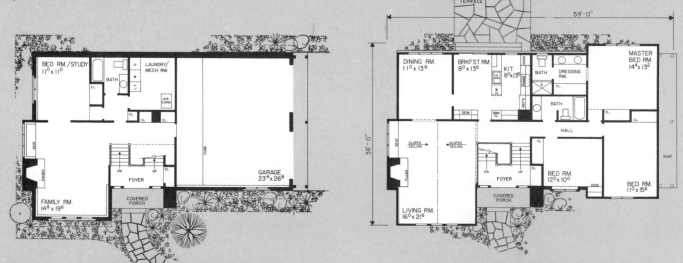

Design T92788
1,795 Sq. Ft. - Upper Level
866 Sq. Ft. - Lower Level
34,230 Cu. Ft.

● Exquisitely styled, this Tudor bi-level has a warm and pleasing appearance. The split-foyer type floor plan will be very efficient for the active family. Both formal and informal activities will have their place in this home, and even on different levels.

Design T92624
904 Sq. Ft. - Main Level; 1,120 Sq. Ft. - Upper Level
404 Sq. Ft. - Lower Level; 39,885 Cu. Ft.

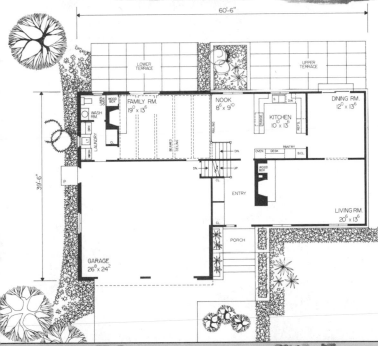

● This is tri-level living at its best. The exterior is that of the most popular Tudor styling. A facade which will hold its own for many a year to come. Inside, the livability will be appreciated. The family room is more than 19' x 13' and has a beamed ceiling and fireplace with wood box. Its formal companion, the living room, is similar in size and also will have the added warmth of a fireplace.

Design T91308
496 Sq. Ft. - Main Level; 572 Sq. Ft. - Upper Level
537 Sq. Ft. - Lower Level; 16,024 Cu. Ft.

● Projecting over the lower level in Garrison Colonial style is the upper level containing three bedrooms a compartmented bath with twin lavatories and two handy linen closets. The main level consists of an L-shaped kitchen with convenient eating space, a formal dining room with sliding glass doors to the terrace and a sizable living room. The lower level is accessible to the outdoors through the study, has a spacious family room and a laundry-wash room area.

STUDY - B.R.
11⁰ x 11⁶

FAMILY RM.
21⁴ x 11⁶

MASTER BED RM.
13⁴ x 11⁶

BED RM.
11⁰ x 11⁰

BED RM.
10⁰ x 10⁰

KIT.
9⁸ x 11⁶

DINING
10⁰ x 11⁶

LIVING
20⁰ x 11⁶

ONE CAR GARAGE
11⁴ x 23⁴

TWO CAR GARAGE
19⁴ x 23⁴

Design T92354
936 Sq. Ft. - Main Level
971 Sq. Ft. - Upper Level; 971 Sq. Ft. - Lower Level; 34,561 Cu. Ft.

● This English flavored tri-level design may be built on a flat site. Its configuration permits a flexible orientation on the site with either the garage doors or the front door facing the street. The interior offers a unique and practical floor plan layout.

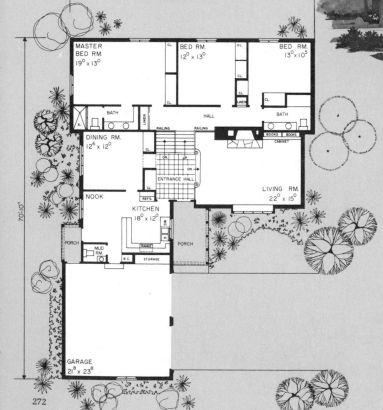

MASTER BED RM.
19⁰ x 13⁰

BED RM.
12⁰ x 13⁰

BED RM.
13⁰ x 10⁵

DINING RM.
12⁶ x 12⁰

NOOK

KITCHEN
18⁰ x 12⁰

LIVING RM.
22⁰ x 15⁰

ENTRANCE HALL

GARAGE
21⁸ x 23⁸

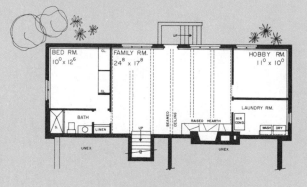

BED RM.
10⁰ x 12⁶

FAMILY RM.
24⁸ x 17⁸

HOBBY RM.
11⁰ x 10⁰

LAUNDRY RM.